Jacques Dupuis Faces the Inquisition

Jacques Dupuis Faces the Inquisition:

Two Essays by Jacques Dupuis on Dominus Iesus
and the Roman Investigation of His Work

Introduced and edited by

WILLIAM R. BURROWS

☙PICKWICK *Publications* · Eugene, Oregon

JACQUES DUPUIS FACES THE INQUISITION
Two Essays by Jacques Dupuis on *Dominus Iesus* and the Roman Investigation of His Work

Pickwick Publications
An Imprint of Wipf and Stock Publishers
199 W. 8th Ave., Suite 3
Eugene, OR 97401

www.wipfandstock.com

ISBN 13: 978-1-62032-335-9

Cataloging-in-Publication data:

Dupuis, Jacques, 1923–2004.

   Jacques Dupuis faces the inquisition : two essays by Jacques Dupuis on Dominus Iesus and the Roman investigation of his work / introduced and edited by William R. Burrows.

   xxviii + 198 p. ; 23 cm. — Includes bibliographical references and indexes.

   ISBN 13: 978-1-62032-335-9

   1. Dupuis, Jacques, 1923– 2. Catholic Church. Congregatio pro Doctrina Fidei. Dominus Iesus. I. Burrows, William R. II. Title.

BT83.85 .D87 2012

Manufactured in the U.S.A.

All proceeds from the sale of this book will be given to the Divine Word Missionaries, Techny, Illinois (www.svdmissions.org), to aid the work of Brother Damien Lunders SVD, and Father Philip Gibbs SVD, who have toiled for many years in Thailand and Papua New Guinea—Philip to aid the development of local theology and leadership, as well as to enhance the church's understanding of and response to social problems; Damien to assist persons suffering from HIV and AIDS.

JACQUES DUPUIS, SJ

5 December 1923 – 28 December 2004

For Linda

My wife, my friend,

Who also loved Jacques Dupuis

Contents

Preface

THIS BOOK IS DESIGNED to give Father Jacques Dupuis, SJ, a posthumous chance to answer his critics in a way that he was denied during his lifetime. It also gives me, who worked with him as an editor and friend for twenty-three years, a chance to amplify Father Dupuis's voice by giving background to the two central chapters, which were written by him.

ON THE NATURE OF THE BOOK

A few words may be helpful to explain what this book is about.

1. Chapters two and three are Father Dupuis's perspectives on: (a) *Dominus Iesus*[1] and positions taken by Congregation for the Doctrine of the Faith[2] that criticized his work; and (b) the process that led to CDF releasing a "Notification" critical of his work, including a detailed response to each of CDF's points.

2. The front matter and chapters one and four are my perspectives on the work of Jacques Dupuis and the events surrounding the canonical process and "Notification" he received from the CDF.

3. Calling Dupuis a "conservative revisionist" is my way of conveying the judgment that Dupuis is both theologically "conservative" and what David Tracy calls a "revisionist," that is to say that he is a theologian who has been convinced that neither

> secularism nor supernaturalism can adequately reflect or appropriately ensure our commitment to the final worthwhileness of the struggle for truth and honesty in our inquiry, and for justice and

---

1. *Dominus Iesus* ("The Lord Jesus"), a CDF Declaration, is printed as Appendix 1 in this volume.

2. The Congregation for the Doctrine of the Faith (hereafter "CDF") was founded in 1542 by Pope Paul II as the "Sacred Congregation of the Universal Inquisition" with the duty of defending the church from heresy. It is the oldest of the Roman Curia's nine congregations. For more information, see its website profile: www.vatican.va/roman_curia/congregations/cfaith/documents/ rc_con_cfaith_pro_14071997_en.html.

even agapic love in our individual and social practice . . . precisely because he believes that such understanding negates the fundamental faith of his life as that faith is appropriately expressed in the true faith of Christianity itself. . . .

This, in brief outline, is the situation of the modern Christian theologian. He finds himself disenchanted with the mystifications promulgated by too many church officials and the mystifications proclaimed with equal certitude by the secularist self-understanding of the age. . . . He also realizes that his understanding of Christianity must take a revisionist form which takes proper account of the cognitive, ethical, and existential crises of much traditional Christian self-understanding.[3]

As a "conservative," Dupuis believed that the church's teaching office is guided by the Spirit and that its doctrinal tradition is a faithful explication of the self-revelation of the Trinitarian God: Father, Son, Spirit. As a "revisionist," Dupuis sought to retain the doctrinal core of tradition while carrying forward and developing that Trinitarian and soteriological ensemble in the light of the contemporary experience of the wisdom and richness of these traditions—moving beyond past understandings of that core to propose ways in which God is active in them. As a revisionist, he saw himself in the mold of a John Henry Newman, not an Alfred Loisy: *he sought to carry doctrinal development forward, not to rewrite tradition to conform to contemporary historicist canons of evidence concerning what is "revealed" in the Christ.*

Concretely, Dupuis sought to do this in relationship to the Christian theological appraisal of the "other" religious traditions that are followed by two-thirds of the world's peoples. In his work as a whole, the position corresponding to secularism's rejection of Christian self-understanding (in the Tracy quote above) is occupied by the more radical of the so-called "pluralist theologians." Their proposals for revision, Dupuis believed, surrendered the core of Scripture and tradition to the dogmas of comparative religionists and others who rejected the vital center of the Christian and Catholic tradition. In his *oeuvre* as a whole Dupuis argued that both pluralist reductionism and narrow, "orthodox" Christian portrayal of other religions as paths to perdition (based in an elevated sense of Christianity's total "supernaturality" and superiority over them) are inadequate. His "revision" (a term he never used himself) attempted to keep in dialectic

---

3. Tracy, *Blessed Rage*, 9–10.

tension Scripture and tradition, on the one hand, and the valid insights of both the pluralists and "secular" historians and philosophers of religion, on the other hand.

In the book you hold in your hands, Dupuis's principal adversary, nevertheless, was neither the relativists nor rigidly biblicist exclusivists and fundamentalists. Instead it was the Congregation for the Doctrine of the Faith, whose agents, he believed, did not recognize the nuance of his own "inclusive pluralist" and Christocentric Trinitarian position. They had carelessly put him with pluralist relativists following the line of Professor John Hick. The Roman guardians of faith, he believed, were clinging to the strictest wording of old formulae and stretching their meaning beyond what Scripture and tradition justified. Fear of religious pluralism and relativism were leading them to circle wagons and, as I heard Dupuis himself say on many occasions, "Fear makes a poor counselor." In this regard his particular *bête noire*, as the reader shall soon see, were sections of the CDF Declaration *Dominus Iesus* that Dupuis believed:

1. ignored the Christocentric Trinitarianism of the New Testament and erected a mistaken "Christomonism" in its place;

2. raised the status and role of the church to something that made it virtually as necessary as God in the universal, cosmic economy of salvation, which he viewed as a universal reconciliation larger than the church;

3. neglected implications of the fact that *God* was active throughout our billions of years-old-and-still-expanding universe, a universe that God was bringing to fulfillment in God's eschatological reign and wholeness; and

4. needlessly offended members of churches not in communion with the Roman Catholic Church, obscuring the teaching of Vatican Council II and Pope John Paul II about their status and that of "other" religious Ways. For Dupuis ecumenism meant Christians were part of *one Christic-Ecclesial whole in imperfect communion with itself and Christ*. In similar fashion, Christians and followers of other religious ways were part of one cosmic whole whose future would be revealed to have played a part in Christ's paschal mystery in ways known to God. In the present age, dialogue was how persons of good will discerned God's plan in their various traditions.

The two middle chapters were composed by Dupuis as epilogues to his last book, *Christianity and the Religions: From Confrontation to Dialogue* (Italian original published by Queriniana of Brescia in 2001, the English translation by Orbis in 2002). Interestingly, this book bears the *imprimi potest* ("permission to publish") of Francesco J. Egaña, SJ, vice-rector of the Gregorian University, dated 3 June 2001, four months and fifteen days after the signing of the Notification of the Congregation for the Doctrine of the Faith on 19 January 2001 (and released on 26 February 2001). That Notification stated that his previous book (*Toward a Christian Theology of Religious Pluralism*):

> contained notable ambiguities and difficulties on important doctrinal points, which could lead a reader to erroneous or harmful opinions. These points concerned the interpretation of the sole and universal salvific mediation of Christ, the unicity and completeness of Christ's revelation, the universal salvific action of the Holy Spirit, the orientation of all people to the Church, and the value and significance of the salvific function of other religions.[4]

It is hard to imagine a man as prudent as Father Egaña giving his *imprimi potest* without seeking the advice of responsible authorities within the Jesuit Generalate. And Dupuis himself said he took a certain *dilectatio morosa* ("perverse delight") in the fact that his inquisitors at CDF did not seem to know the new book was nearing publication just as their process of finding fault with the old one was nearing its completion. Yet *Christianity and the Religions* is largely a reiteration of the arguments of the book that CDF was criticizing, albeit shorter, more practical, and more popularly written. In the permission to publish, I suspect we are dealing with a subtle signal of solidarity with a confrere who stood high in the esteem of both the previous (Pedro Arrupe) and incumbent (Peter Hans Kolvenbach) Jesuit superiors general.

Dupuis was happy with this affirmation, but his reaction to the accusations of CDF was always straightforward, often stated in the way he put it a telephone conversation with me about CDF's objections: "If I had said, meant, or believed what they say, I would indeed be a heretic. But I don't."

Could one extrapolate the doctrines condemned by CDF from Dupuis's work? In my opinion, the answer is that this is possible only by taking what he writes out of context or by ignoring words that clarify why

---

4. The text of this Notification is printed as Appendix 2 in this book.

he does not hold the opinions condemned. Yet he ran into severe criticism as he neared the end of a distinguished career, through the whole of which he was considered a conservative upholder of the conciliar and papal magisterium. At an age when most theologians settle into senior status, he was besieged by controversies that did not end till he died at the age of eighty-one—deeply depressed by what he thought was the disrespect of CDF and critics from within his own order who anonymously brought about the CDF proceedings. Those critics may have been well-intentioned but, at least from what I can see, they never fully grasped what he was about in its entirety. More about that below.

MY PERSONAL RECOLLECTIONS

In the twenty-two years that intervened between our first meeting in Rome October 1991 till the last time we parted company in New York City in mid-February 2004, we exchanged hundreds of letters, faxes, and emails, and dozens of phone calls. These contacts were mostly about his books, of course, but the phone calls in later years often moved into the area of the personal. In the entire process I came to know both the meticulous theological craftsman and the warm, human side of a faithful, ascetic priest. The one was an expression of the other. Two of my friends—the superior general of the Society of the Divine Word, Fr Antonio Pernia, and Fr Philip Gibbs—did their doctorates under him, and both reported the same thing. His aloofness dissolved when you began to converse with him. But from several members of the Gregorian Jesuit community I have learned that Dupuis could seem thin-skinned, emotionally remote, and aloof.

Dupuis was also a man who was faithful to his daily spiritual exercises, and his writings and *oeuvre* as a whole are simply not understandable without reference to the *Exercises* of St Ignatius, which, he told me had inculcated a lifelong sense of the importance of intimacy with Jesus and meditation on his person, teaching, and work. When he visited the United States, I came several times to retrieve him from his room to take him to scheduled events, only to find him walking back and forth, praying the Office of the Hours lest the press of appointments and talks find that *officium* unfulfilled at day's end. "Oh, Bill," he would say apologetically, "can you wait till I finish my office?" When he was invited by the Interfaith Center of New York to give a lecture and he learned he was go-

ing to be staying in a Manhattan hotel on Lexington Avenue near Grand
Central Station, his first question to me was, "Is there a church nearby? I'd
like to go to Mass in the morning." There was and he did—every morning. We once walked around Graymoor (the home base of the Franciscan
Friars of the Atonement, known internationally for their work in ecumenism) one chilly late winter day and went into their "Orthodox" chapel
on the summit of the mountain on which the friars' motherhouse is built.
Jacques walked up to one of the icons, bowed his head, stepped back and
prayed, recollected and drawn into silent contemplation. We stayed there
so long that I began to worry we would miss meeting my wife for dinner
at a nearby restaurant.

A word about my recollection of his words in this book. My chapters
often use quotation marks around his or my words. A word on how to
take those quotes is necessary. I took notes of our conversations after
we talked, and I have consulted those notes as I wrote. Where there are
quotation marks in what follows, however, I cannot guarantee I have
always reproduced the *ipsissima verba magistri* ("the very words of the
master," in the Latin my generation of students is still fond of), but they
do faithfully reproduce his thought and ideas. I hope they echo his voice,
although they cannot possibly mime the soft French accent with which
he spoke perfect English. Theologians talk of the importance of narrative,
and narrating his story with the words he used in private is the best way I
know to do justice to this marvelous man. The stories are important. We
became friends and I am a partisan on his behalf.

Many of the issues that we talked about and things that I urged him
to articulate in his writing would, in my opinion, have obviated some
critiques that have been leveled against him. Five such themes are:

- the nature of the "sin" and the severity of the problems from which
  humanity requires forgiveness and liberation,

- ideas on mission in our new context,

- the importance of seeing the gospel as God's promise to
  humankind,

- the internal role of the Holy Spirit leading persons to the *knowledge*
  of God in Christ that becomes the foundation for *trusting faith* in
  him, and

- the probability that the sort of convergence of religions he spoke of (rooted in Teilhard de Chardin's vision) was going to be an *eschatological* and not an *historical* event.

In each case, he expressed ideas in conversation on grace and theological anthropology, mission, the process of coming to faith, and the need of Christianity to express itself in terms that do justice to the emergence of life on earth in a sort of cosmic stew and its Christic destiny of finding eternal life by undergoing death. But these themes are not all fully articulated in his writings. I hope to bring several of these issues into relief below. They add context and breadth to what can sometimes seem concern for theological fine points that predominate in the epilogues and his writings in general. Dupuis usually agreed with or refined my formulations of ideas that I proposed as consistent with and implicit in his writing. He considered himself to be a Christologist and a theologian of religions. It was necessary, he said, for missiologists, ecclesiologists, eschatologists, and theological anthropologists to write on the implications of the new theology of religions for their areas. "I can scarcely keep up with the literature in Christology and theology of religions," he once exclaimed. Yet he was amazingly well-informed on developments in theology, history, exegesis, and philosophy, and it should not be forgotten that he edited both *Vidyajyoti* and *Gregorianum*[5] for many years. This necessitated his reading carefully in areas outside his own interests, including commissioning and editing extensive book reviews that spanned every area of Christian and general religious studies.

One day, in urging him to write on the process of coming to faith, I said, "Jacques, I can see your deep Christocentrism stems from a lifetime of following the *Exercises* of Ignatius, yet you never talk about the *process* of coming to faith in Christ, nor about the Spirit's role in that process, giving one the knowledge of God in Christ that one gains only from prayer and following him in everyday life."

"Everyone knows that!" he said with a certain impatience.

I replied, "*Everyone* doesn't know it," and I added that sometimes both his and the CDF's formulations seemed abstract and reified, not dealing with the inner drama of crossing *limina* from non-belief to faith-

---

5. *Vidyajyoti* is the theological and pastoral journal of the Jesuits in India; *Gregorianum* is the flagship journal of the Gregorian University. Both are among the most important Catholic theological journals in the world.

trust with the help of the Spirit. Nor did they reflect the reality that, in recognizing the authenticity of the "other" in the dialogic encounter, one is talking about crossing boundaries and existentially participating in the Holy in ways concepts cannot render. Over time, I have come to believe that doctrinal formulae—as important as they are as conceptual markers—miss the existential nature of faith-knowledge and the surrender of "fiducial" faith. He listened with interest to me as I replayed the words of Juan Alfaro, SJ (1914–93) on faith-knowledge in Scripture, the Fathers and Thomas.[6] Dupuis agreed that Alfaro, who taught a course entitled *Fides, Spes, Caritas* ("Faith, Hope, Charity") for many years, which I took during my first year at the Gregorian University, was one of the Society's greatest theologians. In contrast to Alfaro's embrace of both the subjective and the objective dimensions of on-going "revelation," I said, "Too much contemporary theology seems focused on specious creativity and a mania for 'critique,' too little about recognition of mystery. A book on the process of coming to inner faith knowledge and commitment to Christ by someone like you, Jacques, might remedy that and bring Alfaro's thought on faith inserting us into the drama of salvation in our own day and extending that issue to issues of religious plurality."

But Dupuis had little interest in writing on the relationship of the inner life, the sort of commitment one makes inwardly to Christ, and the issue of pluralism. Nevertheless, he spoke quite clearly several times of the importance of his friendship with Henri LeSaux (also known as Abhishiktananda), the Benedictine monk, who during his many years in India had gone into the depths of *advaita* both as a philosophical system and as an existential participant in *advaitic* contemplation of the mystery of existence lived between reality and illusion. Based on what LeSaux and Bede Griffiths went through in their depths, Dupuis once said that he despaired of people who made "double-belonging" a matter of taking a bit of Native American Spirituality, mixing it with a bit of Buddhism, Sufism or

---

6. It is worth noting that the present Jesuit Superior General, Fr Adolfo Nicolás, SJ, who spent more than forty years in Japan, chose Juan Alfaro for his doctoral advisor in 1968, when Nicolás began his S.T.D. at the Gregorian. One could not work with Juan Alfaro without being brought deeply into the idea that salvation is an interpersonal drama, not a thing. The homily of Fr Nicolás at the Gesù shortly after his election, drives that home in these words: "What is the color, tone and shape of salvation today for all those many human nations—not geographic ones—that are still longing for salvation? To open ourselves to this reality is perhaps the challenge and call of this moment" (Robert Mickens, *The Tablet*, 26 January 2008).

Hinduism, while praying the Rosary and attending Mass. LeSaux, Dupuis said, suffered to gain his knowledge. I repeated the old adage, *theologus fit non legendo sed moriendo* (a "theologian is made not by reading but by dying"), and he agreed that it was both true of LeSaux and a reminder that no one grows in the spiritual life without undergoing spiritual death and real suffering. Echoing Bonhoeffer's words on the bad results of the doctrine of "cheap grace" on those who misunderstood Luther, Dupuis did not cotton to consumerist approaches to double-belonging.[7]

I hope this little book reveals something of the humanity of Jacques Dupuis as it clarifies his body of work in relationship to *Dominus Iesus* and the tragi-comedy of the multiple Notifications—each weaker than the one before it—with which CDF presented him. The full picture can only be revealed when the several hundred pages of his responses to CDF "interrogatories" are published and the persons involved are relieved of their promises of secrecy about the process. Jacques told me several times that he wanted to give me the interrogatories and his responses, but was forbidden to do so. In the months before his death, we talked by telephone several times about whether he could reveal everything to a journalist who was interviewing him or whether this would break his promise of maintaining secrecy on the process. Those interviews have not been published, and I don't know how he decided that question. In addition, I was asked not to reveal the journalist's name. For my own part, I cannot escape the judgment that there is something deeply flawed in a canonical process in which the accused cannot reveal what transpires.

After Jacques' death, I made discrete inquiries whether I could be given copies of the CDF interrogatories and Dupuis's answers, but I was turned back, the last time when an intermediary said that someone at the Generalate who was very much on the side of Dupuis could not find a way to justify leaking them. "Oh," I replied, "would that we were back in the eighteenth century when Jesuit casuists would have had no trouble in rationalizing the breaking of the promise!" Copies of those documents lie in at least two places: the archives of CDF and at the Jesuit Generalate. The present climate of what Italians call *disagio* (imperfectly but best trans- lated as "uneasiness") between the Holy See and religious orders such as the Jesuits makes it inopportune for the Society of Jesus to leak a copy.

---

7. Dupuis's article on double-belonging in Catherine Cornille, ed., *Many Mansions*, is one of the most penetrating I have ever read. In his analysis double-belonging needs to be taken seriously, and such an identity not purchased cheaply if it is authentic.

A PLAUSIBLE EXPLANATION OF THE BUNGLED
CASE AGAINST DUPUIS?

In his epilogues Dupuis tells the tale of ever-changing CDF Notifications as he and his theological defender rebutted the accusations leveled against him in the previous version. Each of the versions presented to him to sign (and thereby to stipulate that CDF had found errors that he agreed *were errors*) had been vetted by Cardinal Ratzinger and presented to Pope John Paul II for his signature *before* being presented to Dupuis. They represented the CDF's equivalent of an indictment in criminal law. How is it, then, that each of them was taken back and revised, the subsequent versions becoming less serious than their predecessor in what was alleged? The first answer to that question has to be that they were poorly prepared and that Jacques Dupuis punched holes in them. When the final version was presented and he was advised by Peter Hans Kolvenbach to sign it, he did so out of exhaustion and because it had become the politic thing to do. CDF had invested so much in a condemnation of him that it could not back down without losing face. But this book will make it clear that Dupuis's signature was not an admission that Kolvenbach, O'Collins, or Dupuis agreed with the Notification.

From the side of the CDF, a plausible case can be made that when Cardinal Ratzinger himself became involved in the process, after his secretaries and *consiglieri* had prepared documents, he realized that Dupuis could not be demonstrated to be heterodox. On the other hand, the accusations Dupuis had received were from the start an integral aspect of a web of CDF concerns (which Dupuis shared!) that contemporary theology was departing from its biblical and conciliar-creedal roots in essential elements of the Trinitarianism of both Scripture and tradition. In addition, many in Rome believed that the attack on him was a way of warning Fathers Michael Amalodoss, SJ, Aloysius Pieris, SJ, and perhaps Indian Divine Word Missionary theologians and missiologists such as Jacob Kavunkal and Augustine Kanjamala, who were associated with their society's missiological centers. The manner in which news of Dupuis's being under investigation spread like wild fire led to his becoming very ill and dropping his Christology course in the final year of his professoriate. Moreover, the language of *Dominus Iesus* (about which more below) made it clear his theological works were under scrutiny. To drop the case against him in late 2000 and early 2001 would have made it seem CDF was bowing to the widespread protests against *Dominus Iesus*.

The *segretario* and *sotto-segretario* ("secretary" and "sub-secretary) of CDF, under whom both *Dominus Iesus* and the Dupuis Notification were prepared, were both members of the Salesian order (founded by St John Bosco), men who would achieve still higher office under Pope Benedict XVI, Tarcisio Bertone and Angelo Amato. In my judgment Bertone and Amato served Ratzinger poorly in the drafting of both documents. But in approving their texts, Ratzinger was demonstrating a tendency that has perdured into his papacy. He appoints subordinates around whom he is comfortable and leaves them to their work. And he is not comfortable with subordinates who will question his writings and speeches. When the work of aides (whose main attribute sometimes seems to be their *simpatia* with Ratzinger) is substandard, however,—as is the case with both *Dominus Iesus* and the Dupuis Notification—Ratzinger is forced to do what many higher authorities have to do. That is to say, he must put the best face he can on work that he would have done much better, had he done it himself. Loyalty up and loyalty down are important traits if an ecclesiastical bureaucracy or military organization is to survive the follies of its less competent agents. A clear example of this loyalty to less than competent *consiglieri* occurred when a personal friend, whose name I do not have permission to divulge, was being pressured to leave an important teaching post in Rome. When my friend's superior general succeeded in getting Cardinal Ratzinger to talk with my friend personally, two Germans sat down face-to-face. After an hour's conversation in German, Ratzinger apologized: "Father, I can see I have been badly informed, but you know I cannot read everything that goes through this office. I have to rely on my secretaries and *consiglieri*, but they seem not to have understood your work. This is the last you will hear about this matter. I will call the rector immediately and recommend your contract be renewed."

In his only face-to-face session with Ratzinger, Dupuis came away with the impression that the cardinal had still not gotten into the nuances of his work; indeed, he realized that the cardinal had not studied carefully (certainly that he had not *mastered*) his responses to CDF's interrogatories. Although the book in question had been out for three years in French, English, and Italian, neither did it seem that the cardinal had read it carefully. To be loyal to Bertone and Amato, as well as to avoid appearing to walk away from *Dominus Iesus*, the text of the Notification was sanitized and its allegations weakened. Further evidence of this pattern can be found in the continuing pattern of mistakes and blunders made by Cardinal Bertone as Pope Benedict XVI's Secretary of State, as well as papal gaffes that should have been caught *before* they were uttered. In both cases, though, statements have to be endlessly explained to demonstrate that Bertone or the Pope did not mean what their words plainly say. The entire Dupuis Notification episode, I suggest, can be taken as Exhibit A in an appraisal of Ratzinger' *modus operandi*. And the one who writes these words is a profound admirer of Ratzinger's own constructive theological work and homilies.

The arrival of Cardinal William Levada as prefect of CDF in August of 2005 and the concern of him and associates such as J. Augustine DiNoia, OP (now an archbishop and secretary of the Vatican's Congregation for Divine Worship),[8] led to a more professional handling of difficult cases since that of Dupuis, but a reversal of *Dominus Iesus*, elements of which Dupuis so painstakingly pokes holes in, seems improbable. That declaration has been so universally criticized that CDF and Pope Benedict XVI seem determined not to lose face by reversing themselves. Like the *Syllabus Errorum* of Pope Pius IX (1864), *Dominus Iesus* can be explained as an attempt to provide reliable teaching on a number of theological tendencies, but its lack of nuance and ill-timing conspire to make it an embarrassment.

But I am getting ahead of myself. This is the case that the book will unfold. I hope it does, but most of all, I hope it brings the achievements of my friend Jacques Dupuis into relief.

William R. Burrows
Cortlandt Manor, New York
Pentecost 2012

---

8. DiNoia is also the author of *The Diversity of Religions: A Christian Perspective*, a book that Dupuis admired and that I think is one of the best theological treatments of issues involved in religious pluralism and the challenge to Christian theology and identity.

Acknowledgments

IN FIRST PLACE, I wish to acknowledge the authors of the over three hundred books I helped publish and of the many hundreds more manuscripts that I had the privilege of reading during twenty years at Orbis Books. I learned as much from the authors whose work we decided not to publish as from those we did. I have never consciously used any author's work or insights without attribution and, where appropriate, permission. But it is important to acknowledge that their authors have given me an education that has become my mental furniture. I owe them more than words can say.

For forty years now, since we first met in the dining room of Divine Word College in Duxbury, Massachusetts, on 5 September 1962, Stephen Bevans, SVD, has been my conversation partner and best friend. Our conversations have ranged from fiction to history to philosophy to theology to spirituality to mission. We spent three wonderful years together as students in Rome. No one has influenced me more than he, and I stand in awe of his many superbly researched books. He read this manuscript and offered corrections. More importantly, he gave me confidence both that I had something to say and that I was honoring the memory of Jacques Dupuis in what I wrote about him and in getting the two central chapters of this book—which are by Jacques—before the reading public.

Since I first met Paul Knitter in Rome during the Christmas season of 1969, his blend of friendship, geniality, and penetrating intellect have been a precious gift. For twenty years we collaborated in publishing forty-some books in the Faith Meets Faith Series at Orbis, a series that has received international acclaim for its depths and breadth. It was Paul's wide contacts and catholicity that brought those books to the series, and while working with him to select the forty we published from among the hundreds we considered, I found myself in a twenty-year-long seminar. Paul has read these pages and offered dozens of important corrections and suggestions. More importantly, his friendship and that of his wife Cathy Cornell are one of the cornerstones of Linda's and my life.

The third person I want to thank specially is Jack Boberg—like Paul and me—a former member of the Society of the Divine Word, one of the finest communities of priests and brothers in the Catholic Church in our day. Jack is a superb editor, a man whose day is never complete without finding a dubious transition or an improper subject-verb agreement. Much more than that—he holds a doctorate in missiology—he has an eye for substantive issues. He exhibited both the *cura minimorum* ("concern for the little things") that the SVD engrained in us all (and with which I still have difficulties), and a wider concern for clarity in style and accuracy in substance. Most of all, he embodies friendship.

Father Jim Gardiner of the Graymoor Friars has also read, corrected, and made suggestions. Jim was Linda's and my pastor as we attended weekly Mass and the many programs he organized at the Graymoor Spiritual Life Center. As a pastor he epitomized what it means to be a priest. As a Graymoor friar, he is a model for how that community has engaged in ecumenism for over a hundred years. And as a friend to us both, he has been an enrichment in our lives.

My *Doktorvater* at the University of Chicago was the late Langdon Gilkey. As the years go by, I hear the cadences of his voice as I consult his work. It is the voice of a superb theologian, a man who knew the Christian tradition and had drunk deeply at the wells of American philosophy. He embodied the non-reductive naturalism of that philosophy at its best, and used it to bring out deeper dimensions in the Christian tradition. A second Chicago professor has been equally important, David Tracy. He is the deepest and widest-based thinker and theologian I know, at home in the classics of Christianity, in the wider Western tradition of philosophy, history, and literature, and in recent years in the world of religious plurality and its challenge. Renewing our friendship at occasional lunches and dinners has also been a reminder of how much I owe him and my professors at the Divinity School of the University of Chicago. Ongoing contact with my teachers—Brian Gerrish, Anne Carr, Martin Marty, Wendy Doniger, and Bernard McGinn—has only deepened my appreciation for them both as scholars and human beings.

At Father Dupuis's eightieth-birthday observances in Rome on 3 December 2003, I caught sight of John Navone, SJ, making his way across the *aula magna* toward me. When I was a student at the Gregorian University, John was my model as an engaged priest–religious-scholar. John was at home both in the Italian arts scene and developing his own signature body of work on the theology of story and beauty. In the years since we once again met, his friendship and counsel have been precious, and in the context of this book, have given me a sense of the human dimensions of the Gregorian University's Jesuit community.

A second Gregorian Jesuit—Gerald O'Collins, like John Navone, now retired—was, with Herbie Alphonso, SJ, a bulwark of support during the dark months of an inquisition-like examination of Jacques' work. Gerry and I first met in the early 1970s when he stayed in the Holy Spirit Seminary faculty residence in Bomana while visiting his sister Maeve, who was working in Papua New Guinea. Ever since then I've been amazed at both his theological productivity and creative fidelity. Gerry is a man in whose very person is to be found the definition of both a Jesuit and a truly ecclesial theologian, someone who has never stopped being, most of all, a disciple of Jesus. Gerry corrected numerous factual errors in this work, while observing the confidentiality that was enjoined on participants in Fr Dupuis's *processo*.

Finally, I am grateful to my friends Jim Tedrick, Jim Stock, and Charlie Collier at Wipf & Stock / Pickwick Publications in Eugene, Oregon. I have watched their vision expand for ten or more years, as they've made Wipf & Stock one of the nimblest, most important, cutting-edge publishers of theological books—both by keeping classics in print and offering a venue for quality works by new authors, especially of specialized books that are a valuable resource for Christian scholars. They have published scores of important works that would never see the light of day if they had not had the courage of their vision. The urban monastic community that many at Wipf & Stock belong to is a living testament to the way faithful disciples bring both old things out of the warehouse of tradition and new things out of the encounter with the Holy Spirit to embody gospel living in ordinary life—the *nova et vetera* of Matthew 13:52.

To all, my thanks.
Any errors that remain, are mine.

A Note on Inclusive Language and Its Absence

I HAVE ENDEAVORED TO use inclusive language in what I have contributed to this book, including in references to God. Writing in his own voice, Fr Dupuis does so as well, but he does *not* change pronouns to work around the word "man" (when used as a generic term for human beings) in quotations of official documents nor in references to God as "he" in Scripture. I have elected not to edit him to suit my own preferences.

Since I view the pedantic "[*sic*]" that is often used to signal transgressions against inclusive language as worse than the transgressions themselves, I do not use "[*sic*]" when I find the third person masculine pronoun used for God or humanity in quotations. In their official documents Roman Church authorities, however, continue to use "man" for humanity and "he" for God. They know the discomfort it causes to many and yet persist in using it. I have not sanitized official church documents in what follows to diminish the criticism they deservedly receive for refusing to change their language.

Abbreviations

THE ABBREVIATIONS BELOW ARE used in parenthetical references within this volume to refer to the documents and organizations listed below. The numbers following the abbreviation refer to the section number in the respective document.

AG *Ad Gentes*, 1965. Vatican Council II, "Decree on the Church's Missionary Activity."

CDF Congregation for the Doctrine of the Faith, founded in 1542 by Pope Paul III as the Congregation of the Universal Inquisition to defend against heresy; renamed Congregation of the Holy Office by Pope Pius X in 1908; received its present name from Pope Paul VI in 1965; its mission is to promote and safeguard the doctrine of the faith and morals in the Catholic world.

CEP Congregation for the Evangelization of Peoples, founded in 1622 by Pope Gregory XV as Congregation for the Propagation of the Faith (*Propaganda Fide*), given its present name in 1982 by Pope John Paul II.

DM *The Attitude of the Church Towards the Followers of Other Religions: Reflections and Orientations on Dialogue and Mission*, 1984. Vatican Secretariat for Non-Christians.

DP "Dialogue and Proclamation," 1991. Pontifical Council for Interreligious Dialogue.

DI *Dominus Iesus*, 2000. Congregation for the Doctrine of the Faith, "The Lord Jesus: Declaration on the Unicity and Universality of Jesus Christ and the Church."

DS Denzinger-Schönmetzer, *Enchiridion Symbolorum: Definitionum et Declarationum de Rebus Fidei et Morum* (Freiburg: Herder)

DV *Dei Verbum*, 1965. Vatican Council II, "Dogmatic Constitution on Divine Revelation."

FR *Fides et Ratio*, 1998. Encyclical letter of Pope John Paul II, "On the Relationship between Faith and Reason."

GS   *Gaudium et Spes*, 1965. Vatican Council II, "Pastoral Constitution on the Church's Missionary Activity."

ITC   International Theological Commission, founded by Pope Paul VI in 1965 to help the Holy See and the Congregation for the Doctrine of the Faith examine doctrinal questions of major importance.

LG   *Lumen Gentium*, 1964. Vatican Council II, "Dogmatic Constitution on the Church."

NA   *Nostra Aetate*, 1965. Vatican Council II, "Declaration on the Relations of the Church to Non-Christian Religions."

PCID   Pontifical Council for Interreligious Dialogue, established in 1964 by Pope Paul VI as the Secretariat for Non-Christians, given its present name in 1988 by Pope John Paul II.

RH   *Redemptor Hominis,* 1979. Encyclical letter of Pope John Paul II, "The Redeemer of Man."

RM   *Redemptoris Missio*, 1990. Encyclical letter of Pope John Paul II, "On the Permanent Validity of the Church's Missionary Vocation."

1

The Man, the Message, the Controversy

WILLIAM R. BURROWS

MEETING THE MAN

THIS INTRODUCTION IS WRITTEN to bring into relief the life and work of the late Jacques Dupuis (1923–2004), a diminutive Belgian Jesuit who wore thick glasses, possessed an enormous intellect that he dedicated entirely to the service of Christ and his church, and who served that church as a member of the Society of Jesus for fifty-three years, of which thirty-six were spent in India.[1]

He once wrote of those years in India:

> I have said many times, and continue to think today in the light of what I have seen and lived thereafter, that my exposure to the Indian reality has been the greatest grace I received from God as far as my vocation as a theologian and a professor is concerned. One cannot live thirty-six years in India without being deeply affected by the experience. This is already true at the level of sheer human reality. By sheer numbers it is no longer possible to think that the future of the world lies on "this" side; it belongs, whether we like it or not, to the so-called Third World, and especially to the Asian continent.[2]

Father Dupuis was a man of deep faith and had a face that slipped frequently into an ironic, pained smile as uninvited and unwelcome controversies swirled about him in the last years of his life. I felt honored to

1. The most complete account of Jacques Dupuis and his life is to be found in the chapter by Gerald O'Collins in Kendall and O'Collins, *In Many and Diverse Ways*, 18–29.

2. Dupuis, "My Pilgrimage," 169.

1

stand beside him during that time and hope this book will play at least a small part in helping us understand the man and his work and find ways for the Catholic Church to deal better with theologians working on its theological neuralgic points. .

I first met Jacques Dupuis in October 1991. On the recommendation of a Maryknoll missionary who had finished his doctorate in missiology in Rome, Orbis had published his *Jesus Christ at the Encounter of World Religions* that year. We met to discuss whether he would revise the text he had used for many years to teach his signature Christology course. My wife Linda and I had coffee with him in the Gregorian University coffee bar and were delighted when he suggested afterwards that we take the elevator to the roof to enjoy its spectacular views of Rome. There was a ceremony going on in the Palazzo Quirinale—the official residence of the President of Italy—immediately to the east, further up the Quirinale Hill behind the Gregorian. We heard the national anthem being played and had a bird's eye view of both a military band and row upon row of black-plumed *Bersaglieri* (an army unit with a distinguished history) and *Carabinieri* (members of the national police force) standing at attention. The only discordant note that perfect Roman afternoon was Fr Dupuis's ominous word that he feared critics were reporting what they considered "problems in my writings to our 'neighbors' at Piazza del Sant'Uffizio." He was, of course, referring to the Congregation for the Doctrine of the Faith, whose offices are a short distance from the Jesuits' international headquarters, whose doors open on Borgo Santo Spirito several hundred meters east of St Peter's basilica.

In the autumn of 1998, shortly before a new academic year began, came confirmation that Jacques' fears were not those of a paranoiac. On the Gregorian University bulletin board appeared a short notice saying that Fr Dupuis would not be teaching Christology that semester because he needed to devote himself to responding to questions raised about his work. Since he was seventy-four and would reach the mandatory retirement age of 75 on 5 December 1998, this had been planned to be the last time he would teach that Christology course, the one that had been his mainstay for forty years. News quickly trickled out that the Gregorian's administration had been told to take this action because of an investigation into the orthodoxy of his writings in the area of theology of religions by CDF. In effect, the punishment was administered before a verdict was rendered. More shocking to Dupuis than the announcement itself was his being barred—in the last semester of his career—from teaching his signature course, one that he had taught for nearly forty years in India and Rome. The entire episode was, in the opinion of most, a calculated, degrading insult. Were his friends right or wrong in so reacting?

That is the central issue in the book you hold in your hands, at the heart of which are two epilogues that Fr Dupuis was prohibited from publishing in *Il cristianesimo e le religioni: dallo scontro all'incontro* (literally, "Christianity and the Religions: From Confrontation to Encounter").

Two years after that hammer fell, I was in Rome to attend a conference held at the Urbaniana University from 17 to 20 October 2000 to celebrate the tenth anniversary of Pope John Paul II's encyclical on mission, *Redemptoris Missio*. Jacques and I had been in touch by phone often during the intervening two years, and he said he was happy I would be in Rome. To cap off the visit, I planned a dinner on the 21st to celebrate the progress being made in the translation of Fr Dupuis's most recent book, which was to be published by Orbis Books (under the title *Christianity and the Religions: From Confrontation to Dialogue*), the publishing house in which I had worked since 1989. Attending our dinner would be Jacques, my oldest friend, the theologian Stephen Bevans, SVD (with whom I had walked the 3.5 kilometers from the Collegio del Verbo Divino to and from the Gregorian every school day from 1969 to 1972), my wife Linda, and myself. Two months before we arrived, CDF published *Dominus Iesus* ("The Lord Jesus"), its "Declaration on the Unicity and Salvific Universality of Jesus Christ and the Church." Almost universally, much of it was taken to be a condemnation of Dupuis. It exploded like a bombshell, dismaying leaders of non-Catholic churches, other religious traditions, and many theologians.

At our dinner, Jacques told us that he had been at the CDF the day before *Dominus Iesus* was released and that he had refused to sign the *Notificazione* ("Notification") that CDF presented him then, in part because it highlighted the misuse of Scripture and misrepresented his thought.

Jacques asked me that evening what I thought of the Italian manuscript of *Cristianesimo e le Religioni*, the book that Phillip Berryman was then translating and the manuscript of which Jacques was carefully checking. I laughed and said, "Rosino[3] will be disappointed. He wanted

3. Rosino Gibellini was the long-time editorial director at the pre-eminent Italian Catholic book publisher Queriniana in Brescia, a man universally respected as one of the

something for the lay reader, but I think it's more a book for theologians and the theologically well-informed." I added, "What you are doing in it is re-stating very carefully and with new insights what you wrote in *Toward a Christian Theology of Religious Pluralism*. You've not changed your position but you are giving those with eyes to see and ears to hear a chance to understand better what you're about. It's really your best book on the subject. The final chapters on dialogue are the best I've read anywhere."

He was pleased that I liked the book, but nothing that Steve, Linda, or I could say that evening lifted what appeared to be the dark depression into which he was sinking. In later conversations with Gerald O'Collins, SJ, Dupuis's chief defender and theological counselor through the ordeal, I learned that all Jacques' friends were concerned about his health. Gerry and I had first met in the early 1970s when I was teaching theology in Papua New Guinea and he stayed in the seminary staff quarters while he visited his sister who was working in PNG. Over the years I came to regard Gerry as one of the soundest theologians and warmest human beings I knew. The support for Dupuis from Gerry, fellow faculty member Herbie Alfonso, SJ, and Jesuit Superior General Peter Hans Kolvenbach during this ordeal was unwavering, but it was clear to us all that the CDF process had caused a deep wound in the soul of Jacques, and no one's words were able to extract the arrow that caused it.

During the course of the evening, as Jacques told us more about his encounters with CDF, he said that he would send me an epilogue that he wanted to publish in *Christianity and the Religions*. I got it shortly after I returned home. Several months later, after the 26 February publication of the final version of a much-softened Notification, Jacques said there would be a second epilogue to comment on the Notification and the canonical process.[4] These epilogues, which he was not allowed to publish, are chapters two and three of this book.

A MAN IN THE MIDDLE

The central figure in this book is Jacques Dupuis, SJ, born on 5 December 1923 in Huppaye in the province of Brabant in Belgium. He died on 28

---

most discerning theological editors in the world. I came to know him well in the years Orbis Books published the American edition of the international journal *Concilium*.

4. The Notification was shown to Pope John Paul II on 19 January 2001 and dated 24 January 2001 by CDF, but was not actually published until 26 February 2001.

December 2004 in Rome. He was one of three boys and a girl born into an educated professional family. Much later he would say that his father was an engineer and factory manager in a metallurgical field that demanded exactness. His mother, from a family of notaries, he wrote, was "nothing short of a saint. Her meekness, attention to all, and boundless generosity made her an ideal mother."[5]

Growing up in the industrial city of Charleroi, he began twelve years of primary and secondary education under the Jesuits in 1929. In 1941, when Belgium was under German occupation, he entered the Jesuit novitiate and did seven more years of schooling in Europe. Living through the experience of witnessing enormous armies clash without regard for anything but victory had a lasting impact on the young Jesuit. He had no illusions about power and its exercise, nor about the existence of evil.

When he finished his Jesuit philosophical studies, he asked to join their Calcutta mission. His application approved, Dupuis went to India in 1948, at a time when leaving home for a foreign mission meant one would probably never return home again. Arriving in India in 1948, he encountered the turmoil of the split between India and Pakistan at the end of British rule and the headiness of independent India. And in all this he learned not a little about self-deception and the uses of ideology in an India whose people and culture he came to love. But a temperament that had a tendency toward melancholy and exacerbated his disdain of enthusiasms of all sorts kept Dupuis from believing that all India's problems would be solved when British imperialists were gone. As a normal part of Jesuit pre-ordination formation between philosophical and theological studies, Dupuis taught high school subjects to Indian students—in English, a language he barely knew when he began. In an autobiographical essay written after his retirement, he remembers barely keeping one step ahead of his students, discovering in the process their rich human gifts and the "depth of cultural and religious endowments that they carried in themselves and that they had learned from their family education and the religious tradition to which they belonged." After this period as a scholastic-teacher he began his theological studies in India, was ordained there, and in 1955 obtained his licentiate (S.T.L.) in theology. In 1957 he went to the Gregorian University in Rome for further studies, where he wrote his doctoral (S.T.D.) thesis on the religious anthropology of Origen.

---

5. Dupuis, "My Pilgrimage," 168. Details on Dupuis's life in following paragraphs are taken from this autobiographical essay.

In conversation one day, when I learned of his dissertation topic, I mentioned to Dupuis that the historian Andrew Walls often said that Origen was perhaps the church's first and greatest missiologist. "What you are about," I added, "is the equivalent of clearing theological space for Indian philosophy and religion to be used in the incarnation of Christ in India, much the same way Justin Martyr and Origen did with their thought on the *Logos tou Theou* ("Word of God") in the second and third centuries." I don't think I ever said anything that made him happier. I would later write in a *Festschrift* for Jacques (edited by Dan Kendall, SJ, and Gerry O'Collins) that I thought Jacques' greatest achievement had been offering a rationale for dialogue with other religions as an intrinsic element in Christian theology and self-understanding.[6] That still seems a sound judgment.

In India during the Council, Dupuis followed developments avidly, teaching at Kurseong (near Darjeeling) until 1971, when the faculty shifted to New Delhi, where it is now known as the Vidyajyoti Institute of Religious Studies. As a native French-speaker, Dupuis was particularly well equipped to understand what was happening in the Council because he was deeply grounded in the work of such scholars as Jean Danielou, Yves Congar, and Henri de Lubac. Their historical-theological work, which revealed the depths and many-sidedness of the Scriptures in intertestamental period, of patristic literature in the first six centuries, and then of the medieval tradition, was the foundation for Conciliar renewal. They also helped Dupuis's and my own generation realize that the rigid scholasticism that had ruled official Catholic teaching since the dawn of the modern era was not really Thomist in its dynamic, as it was purported to be, but reactionary and that—although it was understandable from an historical point of view—it was inadequate to guide Christians in their new context. In his autobiographical essay, he wrote about the work he was doing in India, where "Growing attention came to be given in teaching and in pastoral and liturgical practice to the religious traditions of India . . . [which] were integrated on the theoretical level into the various subjects . . . and on the practical level into common worship." Rooted in this French theological *ressourcement* ("return to the sources"), Dupuis's theological approach always kept close to Catholic tradition as interpreted in its formal conciliar and papal magisterium.

6. Burrows in Kendall and O'Collins.

In 1984 his superiors decided that he should come to Rome. He wrote later, "I obeyed as I had learned to do as a religious and a Jesuit," although he never wished to leave India, "where I had come to live, to work, and to die." With reluctance, Dupuis told me in conversation that it had become very painful when some of those promoting the Indianization of theology (including his own students), judged him too conservative and insistent on retaining the tradition of the early ecumenical councils and later magisterium. The Jesuit superior general, Pedro Arrupe (1907–1991, a Spaniard who had worked in Japan from 1940 to 1965), however, had great respect for Dupuis and engineered the transfer to Rome, both because he believed that the Gregorian University needed professors with deep experience of life in the church outside the West and to offer Dupuis an environment where his gifts would be better appreciated. In the end, however, the man who was too cautious for Indian Jesuit seminarians and theologians was too radical for the Roman stage.

Returning to Europe after thirty-six years in India, Dupuis took on the work of a Roman professor with quiet competence, not suspecting that when his writings appeared on the international stage in English and in Rome in Italian, a train of events would be set in motion that would lead to the publication of a CDF Notification about "ambiguities" in his work.

THE CONTEXT: "WORLD CHRISTIANITY," AND THE "INTERRELIGIOUS PROBLEM"

At the beginning of the Third Millennium, it is common to talk of the emergence of "world Christianity"[7] or—as it's more commonly called in Roman Catholic circles—the "world church."[8] Those phrases point to the fact that in the years since the close of World War II, Christianity has ceased to be a Western religion and has become the paradigmatic "world religion." Or, as Lamin Sanneh would say in welcoming members of the

---

7. The term "World Christianity" is attributed to many people, but the honor of being its intellectual author is perhaps most deservedly given Andrew F. Walls (b. 1928), founder of the Center for the Study of Christianity in the Non-Western World at the University of Aberdeen in 1982. The Center was moved to the University of Edinburgh in 1987. Walls is today professor in the Center for the Study of African and Asian Christianity at Liverpool Hope University.

8. The latter term was introduced by Karl Rahner, SJ (1904–1984); see his "Basic Theological Interpretation of the Second Vatican Council."

advisory board to his Oxford University Press "World Christianity Series" on 5 May 2011 in New Haven, Connecticut,

> With unflagging momentum, Christianity has become, or is fast becoming, the principal religion of the peoples of the world. Primal societies that once stood well outside the main orbit of the faith have become major centers of Christian impact, while Europe and North America, once considered the religion's heartlands, are in noticeable recession. We seem to be in the middle of massive cultural shifts and realignments whose implications are only now beginning to become clear.

The first and most evident of these is its geographic spread and demographic change. From being an almost exclusively Western, Euro-American faith in 1900,[9] since the late 1960's—precisely when the numbers of foreign missionaries working outside Europe and North America went into a radical decline—Christian growth took off exponentially in the Global South, especially in Africa and China.[10] Since the 1970s, this growth in Africa, Asia, and Latin America, particularly among so-called "independent" Evangelical and Pentecostal Protestants, has largely been the result of indigenous evangelizers. For those seeking to go deeper into the significance of the emergence of world Christianity, I recommend the works of Lamin Sanneh and Andrew Walls in the bibliography of this book. A more recent book by Douglas Jacobsen is magisterial in giving both historical facts and figures and wise interpretations of what is happening in the emergence of world Christianity.[11]

Dupuis makes it clear in the autobiographical essay quoted above that the man who came back to Rome in 1984 was keenly aware of both the demographic shift in Christianity and its theological importance. The

9. With the notable exception of Latin America, where a hierarchy and clergy that was largely European in its outlook had still not succeeded in becoming self-ministering and self-financing three centuries after evangelization, guiding a laity with a deeply hybrid identity.

10. Many point to the large number of so-called "Evangelical" and "Pentecostal" missionaries coming from North America and spreading out across Africa, Oceania, Asia, and Latin America as the source of this growth. And I concede that their role has been significant, but a large percentage of that growth has come from what the church growth movement calls "transfer growth." That is to say, their converts are more likely to be from members of Catholic and historical Protestant churches than from fresh, first-contact evangelization, this despite the attempt to evangelize so-called "unreached peoples."

11. See Jacobsen, *World's Christians*.

idealistic, Eurocentric young Belgian who went to India was nothing if not a traditional Catholic missionary. The mature theologian-missionary who returned had been changed by Asia. Ever the conservative, cautious scholar, he was surprised, even bemused, when his courses and writings on the theology of religion and Christology caught the attention of students at the Gregorian and were thought to be ground-breaking. His lecture courses and seminars at the Gregorian, both in the basic and upper level S.T.L. ("licentiate in sacred theology," roughly equivalent to a master of arts degree) cycles, were filled to overflowing. In addition, Dupuis's doctoral seminars were commonly oversubscribed, and scores of students sought him out to be their doctoral advisor. Meanwhile, he was increasingly invited to speak around Italy, as that nation became more aware of other religious ways and sought to understand better the large number of their adherents who were becoming their neighbors.

Reflecting after his retirement on what was happening during his active years, Dupuis would write:

> Whether in India or in Rome, I have always tried to share with my students what I have personally experienced of the faith, and especially of the person and the mystery of Jesus Christ. Throughout my teaching career, I taught the course on Christology, which I considered a great privilege. I can say sincerely that over my forty years of teaching, trying to deepen my understanding of the mystery of Christ has been a continuous passion. It also helped to enrich my own personal relation with the Lord. If, as I hope, I have been able to convey to the students my passion for Jesus Christ and helped them to increase their own love for the Lord, I will consider myself fully rewarded for my labor. The course on the theology of religions was of course closely related to Christology. I have always been convinced that the mystery of Jesus Christ is of necessity at the center of a Christian theology of religions. I always combined both very closely, as my publications amply show. Over the years I discovered that, far from endangering faith in Jesus Christ, a positive approach to the other religions helps to discover new depths in the mystery. This correlation is also something I hope to have been able to convey to my students.[12]

In Rome, Dupuis encountered a student body that was a microcosm of the entire world, one that mirrored the changing demographics of Catholicism. It was far different from the one in which he had studied

12. Dupuis, "My Pilgrimage," 170.

himself. In the 1950s and 1960s, the Gregorian University (founded by St Ignatius of Loyola in 1551 as the "Roman College" and renamed after its great patron Pope Gregory XIII, pope from 1572 to 1585), it was viewed as one of the premier schools in the Catholic world, a place to which religious orders and dioceses sent promising candidates to receive a solid education at the hand of a professorial corps that numbered many consultors on Vatican commissions. By the late 1980s, however, the Gregorian's professorial corps was less international than it had been in its best days. Without wanting to impugn their abilities or sincerity, I have heard several observers of the Gregorian say that many of the faculty were unable to grasp what Dupuis was about, in part because few had worked or lived outside Europe. Thus they could not understand the immensity of the changes set in motion by globalization, especially since the end of the colonial era, nor could they realize that Western cultural hegemony had been de-throned. By default, they—like Giuseppe DeRosa, SJ, at the journal *Civiltà Cattolica*—read him in the light of the two-century European Catholic battle with reductive, Post-Kantian aspects of the Enlightenment, on the one hand, and French, Spanish, and Italian conflicts with *laïcité,* on the other. This was not an adequate hermeneutic to grasp the theological issues implicated in world Christianity's engagement with the religious and cultural "other."

When I visited Dupuis for the first time in the fall of 1991, seven years after his *hegira* to the administrative center of Catholicism, Jacques was aware that in some circles, there was opposition to his teaching. Most significantly, Pope John Paul II's encyclical on mission, *Redemptoris Missio* (published on 7 December 1990), he told me, was rushed into print before *Dialogue and Proclamation* (published on 19 May 1991) could appear. The latter document bore the stamp of Dupuis's and Missionary of Africa Bishop Michael Fitzgerald's careful analysis of the nature and interrelationship of dialogue and the theology of both mission and religion. *Dialogue and Proclamation* was issued by the Pontifical Council for Interreligious Dialogue, where Dupuis was both a member of PCID's advisory body and a major drafter and supplier of insights in the process that prepared it. "Why," I asked, "would the people at Piazza di Spagna [seat of the Congregation for the Evangelization of Peoples[13]] want to

13. Commonly abbreviated as CEP, the Congregation was founded in 1622 to direct Catholic missions; it was known as the Sacred Congregation for the Propagation of Faith or *Congregatio de Propaganda Fide*; it was commonly referred to as "Propaganda" until 1982, when it received its present name.

get a jump on *Dialogue and Proclamation?*" Because, Dupuis answered, *Dialogue and Proclamation* appeared too radical in its nuanced identification of several types of dialogue—including its approbation of dialogue that did not have conversion as its guiding purpose—each essential to the Catholic concept of its mission in the world (cf. DP 9, 42, 77–86).

I remember saying, "But Jacques, most missionaries think *Dialogue and Proclamation* is a great document. Its theory catches up with the practice of the best missionaries of all times, as they came to appreciate the riches of other cultures and their religious traditions."

He replied, "That is the problem. Propaganda [i.e., the CEP] thinks that an overly positive attitude toward other religious traditions in that document erodes motivation for mission, which they define primarily as the effort to convert." When I realized that in the two documents we had a case of the right and left hands of Rome in disagreement with one another, I decided that Orbis ought to do a book in which both documents would be printed with authoritative commentaries by their principal drafters. When both Dupuis and Marcello Zago[14] agreed to write commentaries, we started work. The book was published in 1993.[15] In the process of putting it together, the opportunity to meet and become a friend of Zago, who later became an archbishop and *segretario* ("secretary," the number two position) at CEP, was a great personal enrichment. Like Dupuis, Marcello Zago had begun his career as a missionary in Asia (he worked in Laos from 1959 to 1966), after which he took a doctorate in missiology at the Gregorian and was elected to the Oblates' general administration. He was deeply affected by his contact with ordinary Buddhists in Laos and by entering deeply into the life of Buddhist monks, where he had the opportunity to teach and learn in a Buddhist monastery.

It was clear that Dupuis and Zago did not agree on every point. And as the Vatican's criticism of his work deepened, Dupuis several times expressed disappointment to me that the now Archbishop Zago had not intervened on his behalf with his (i.e., Zago's) superior, Cardinal Josef Tomko. (Tomko, besides being prefect of CEP, was also a member of CDF and would have been in a position to urge CDF to approach Dupuis's case more sympathetically.) Zago, however, several times told me that he felt

---

14. Marcello Zago (1932–2001) who was then the superior general of the Missionary Oblates of Mary Immaculate, was a major figure in the creation of *Redemptoris Missio*.

15. See Burrows, *Redemption and Dialogue*.

Dupuis had been treated disrespectfully, that he had defended him, and that he found their estrangement painful.

The die had been cast when Dupuis brought with him to Rome what he termed the need to correlate Christology with a positive approach to religions. Over time, Dupuis wrote, he had developed a "concept of theology as hermeneutics (interpretation), which could no longer proceed along a priori dogmatic lines . . . but would first be inductive, starting from the experience of lived reality." He recognized that there were dangers, but "it seemed the only way of doing theology that would really meet the concrete reality of the world in which we were living."[16]

THE BEGINNINGS OF OFFICIAL CRITICISM

The initial Roman shot across Dupuis's bow came in a 1992 review by Giuseppe De Rosa, SJ (1921–2011), of the Italian edition of *Jesus Christ at the Encounter of World Religions*, the first book Dupuis published with Orbis.[17] De Rosa, one of the chief writers of *Civiltà Cattolica*, a journal with semi-official status that enjoyed the reputation of being used by Vatican authorities, in particular by the Secretariat of State and CDF, to communicate their judgments and warnings of unacceptable tendencies, found the book wanting. Looked at with hindsight, it seems probable that the success of that book in both the 1988 French edition and the 1989 Italian edition, followed up by its publication in English in 1991, brought it into prominence. Then came his book on Christology in 1994, which, on top of his role in the drafting of the text of *Dialogue and Proclamation*, made De Rosa realize that Dupuis was becoming influential. This is the background of De Rosa's review of the now four-year-old book. The first two pages of his article begin irenically, albeit with mention of Dupuis treating Christ and his relationship to Hinduism without linking Christ and the church. De Rosa quickly turns to the question, Can one be a "Hindu-Christian"? In that context, he brings into relief Dupuis's singling out the Benedictine mystic, Henri LeSaux, OSB (1910–1973)—also known as Swami Abhishiktananda—as "a prophetic figure." This reservation and those that follow foreshadow virtually every major criticism CDF would eventually make of Dupuis and, later still, those that the Committee on Doctrine of the United States Conference of Catholic Bishops would

16. Dupuis, "My Pilgrimage, 170.
17. De Rosa, "Review."

make of Peter Phan's *Being Religious Interreligiously*.[18] Still later, the willingness of Elizabeth Johnson to gain light on the mystery of God from Asian wisdom would be one of the Doctrine Committee's complaints in 2011 about her 2007 book, *Quest for the Living God*.[19] Which makes it clear that: (1) these issues are not going away; and (2) the accusations against Dupuis are still viewed as relevant.

As we have seen, the Dupuis who became a success in Rome a few years after moving from India was not the traditional Roman professor. He was, for instance, more "Indian" in some ways than his colleague, the Indian historian of religions Mariasusai Dhavamony, SJ, an Indian who taught at the Gregorian. Dhavamony, who can write with great insight into Indian religious texts and traditions in their own right, did so, apparently without incurring censure.[20] Dupuis, however, wrote in ways that advocated the theological ascription of a positive, salvific, divinely willed purpose and role for these texts and traditions. De Rosa finds fault precisely where Dupuis was led to suggest that God had been and still was active in Indian religions and elsewhere. Perhaps more importantly for De Rosa, for decades a defender of the church against relativism and secularism, Dupuis does this without scant reference to the church's agency in making Christ known and mediating salvation. Furthermore, in criticizing Dupuis's ascription of prophetic status to Le Saux, De Rosa seems to realize what Jacques told me several times in reference to both Le Saux and the English Benedictine, Bede Griffiths—namely, that through his friendship with these contemplatives, Dupuis had participated vicariously in the spiritual journey of two of the most significant religious pioneers of our time. In the process of accompanying them, Dupuis became

---

18. USCCB Statement on Phan.

19. USCCB Statement on Johnson, 15–16

20. See Dhavamony, *Jesus Christ*, for an example of a book that was published by the Gregorian University Press after the Dupuis Notification (and thus presumably went through a careful vetting) for a work that lays out a detailed analysis of Jesus vis-à-vis Asian interpretations of him and his significance within lines drawn by *Dominus Iesus*. In my reading of Dhavamony, he never examines the possibility, as many have wondered, of whether the Sanskrit tradition might function in a way analogous to the Hebrew Scriptures in relation to Indian Christianity. The issue is controversial, to be sure, but none the less important because it has immense implications not only for the Sanskrit traditions but also for the Christian identity of former followers of traditions such as those of Sub-Saharan Africa, the Pacific Islands, and Melanesia.

convinced that Le Saux's experience was both genuine and prophetic.[21] While Dupuis never claimed, at least in my hearing, that he himself was the receiver of mystical gifts and insights, he knew the significance of such gifts *as charisms given for the benefit of the entire church.* The receivers of such charisms are saints who experience at a deep, transformative level the concurrence of the invisible transcendent world and the everyday world in which most human beings live with only occasional glimpses of the Holy. Such experiences engendered the writings of such figures as Bernard of Clairvaux and Teresa of Avila and caused them to be named doctors of the church, and the principle that some members of the church received such mystical knowledge *for the benefit of the entire church* has long been accepted.

This entire question is brought to a particularly American perspective in Paul Knitter's 2009 book *Without Buddha I Could Not Be a Christian.* Knitter's spiritual path is being followed by what appears to be an increasing number of American Christians, who take the path of passing over into Buddhism and back again to Christianity, embracing aspects of both. To the gate-keepers of orthodoxy, of course, this sort of passing over is simple nonsense. But among Buddhists in the United States today, in sharp contrast to Islam and Hinduism, three of four Buddhists are converts (73 percent) and twenty-two percent of Buddhists were formerly Catholics.[22] I do not know how many have followed Knitter, but the numbers have to be enormous. In a study of religious practices among Americans, for instance, the Pew Charitable Trusts learned that twenty-five percent of Catholics express acceptance of the beliefs of Eastern Religions.[23] This percentage is roughly the same as the proportion of American people as a whole who express such approval. Knitter asks whether, in his passing back and forth, he ends up "contrary to my intention and awareness, as a form of *cheating*?"[24] He then answers that question in the pages that follow in part by postulating the idea that, "Our religious self, like our cultural or social self, is at its core and in its conduct a *hybrid*." He then defends that statement in a section entitled, "We're all hybrids." At one

---

21. A recent Gregorian dissertation attempts to sort out the significance and soundness of using Le Saux as a model for contextualization of Christianity in India. See Cheruvally, *Quest.*

22. Pew Charitable Trusts, *U.S. Religious Landscape Survey,* 9, 27, 29.

23. Pew Charitable Trusts, "Many Americans Mix Multiple Faiths," 7.

24. Knitter, *Without the Buddha,* 214.

level, Knitter is raising an issue that missionary anthropologists have been dealing with for generations, and that good historians realize is part and parcel of Western Christian history.[25] At another level, though, he raises the question whether his (i.e., Knitter's own) construction of the Christianity he passes over from and back to is adequate. Dupuis's view of Knitter's book *No Other Name?* was that his Christology was not adequate, but also that his subsequent book *Jesus and the Other Names* showed him to be someone who knew quite well the radicality of Christian discipleship and embraced it. Paul and I have carried on a discussion about the adequacy of the Niceo-Chalcedonian creeds for thirty or so years now, especially on the question of how "realistically" or "metaphorically" they are to be interpreted. The issue for the current chapter on Dupuis's views and problems with the CDF is, however, somewhat different. It is important to realize that in our conversations Dupuis clearly recognized that Knitter was bringing two issues into focus. The first is the importance of Christians joining hands with persons of other faiths to alleviate suffering and deep dialogue. The second was the fact that this dialogue was going to have profound impact on Christian self-understanding and practice. What we have in Knitter's writings are the lucid insights of a Christian who has entered into the space between what Panikkar calls the third and fourth phases of dialogue. Talk of superiority and absolutism are largely gone on both sides (in the third phase), at least among academics, but the fourth, according to Panikkar, "challenges the fixed identity of both parties."[26] And here Knitter helps us understand the modern temper in its impatience with the recitation of formulae that seem to obfuscate and occlude rather than illuminate. From the side of the magisterium, as Dupuis would state the issue, however, lies the question whether modern approaches (Panikkar's stage three) explicate the "Truth" of Tradition in our new context or explain it away.

25. See James Russell, *Germanization of Early Medieval Christianity* and Fletcher, *Barbarian Conversion*. These books are masterful summaries of the complex process whereby Mediterranean, Latin Catholicism became the religion of the Frankish peoples of northern Europe. Russell's book is especially interesting because he shows the degree to which what we call "Roman" Catholicism was Germanized as the influence of Merovingian and Carolingian kings, bishops, priests, monks, and theologians crossed back over the Alps. Dupuis knew this history as an example of the complex development of Catholicism, and it made him impatient with Europeans who tried to force the Western form of Catholicism on Asians and Africans.

26. Panikkar, *Intra-Religious Dialogue*, 144.

The deeper issue Dupuis raises in his books is perhaps best put when one asks whether the experiences of contemporary mystics and their writings within Christianity *and* Indian traditions—as well as on the *limina* between them—can function the way Platonic ideas functioned in medieval and early modern Catholicism. It is clear that neo-Platonic anthropology and cosmology undergirded the explications of the great medieval and early modern doctors of the soul's experience of union with God. Can the anthropology and cosmology of *advaita* become the basis for an analogous explication of Le Saux's experiences and broaden the Christian understanding of mystery? Is Knitter's example of passing over into Buddhism and returning with a deeper appreciation for his Christian faith another such example? Dupuis himself, at least to my knowledge, does not ask the question in this way. Still—even if one has doubts about the Christological adequacy of the position of a Knitter—it seems to me that an answer in the affirmative is necessary if one is to move down the road Dupuis points.

WHAT IS AT STAKE

If I am correct, what is being proposed by Dupuis and rejected by CEP and CDF are theological proposals and practices in Asia, Oceania, and Africa that—at least in the eyes of the two leading Vatican congregations—seem "too" conciliatory to other religious traditions or that promote attitudes that give insufficient attention to the nature and mission of the church and are relativistic in regard to divinely revealed truth. The sort of thing that Dupuis was saying *seemed* to echo what Roman authorities judge to be contributing to the erosion of Catholic identity in the West and leading to the church's decline there: *a weakening of Catholic Christian identity.* They are seeing in his work the same spirit they felt was active in theologians such as Edward Schillebeeckx, and they react similarly to the way they reacted to his work—recognizing that if it takes hold, their conception of the church will be breached. That, I believe, is also the Curia officials' basic mistake. As in the case of Schillebeeckx, the challenge of the theological work of Dupuis goes far deeper and requires something more profound than an attack on contemporary exegesis, Western theological critiques of church order, or the pervasive atmosphere of religious and philosophical relativism. Indeed, by holding on to classic dogmas of Christocentric Trinitarianism, yet condemning Dupuis's ascription of the work of the *Logos* and *Pneuma* outside the visible church within other religious traditions, CDF is really attempting to maintain a position of privilege for a hierarchy that has lost the ability to speak effectively to the practical agnosticism and relativistic mindset of secularizing societies. Dupuis's openness to the idea that glimpses of a transcendent order are also revealed in other traditions puts him on the side of those who are suspicious both of Western secularism and the way in which the classic Western theology of religion denigrate their cultures and religious visions.[27]

One only understands the depths of the tragedy in the CDF struggles with Dupuis only if one realizes that Dupuis remained both fully orthodox and traditional, but also that he had been transformed by his years in India and was the heir of 450 years of Jesuit experience in Asia. Like the wise householder of Matthew 13:52, Dupuis knew that the church needed to face the Asian reality with new ways of interpreting old doctrines. "Tragedy," in my opinion, is not too strong a word to characterize what happened between Roman authorities and Jacques Dupuis. Like those who failed to understand the paradoxes of the Kingdom in the Gospel of Matthew, Dupuis's adversaries seemed unable to imagine that today's interreligious situation confronts us with the opportunity and the need to do what Jews and Christians have been forced to do in moments of crisis for four thousand years—to grasp once again what Isaiah said in the "Gospel of the Servant of the Lord" (Isaiah chapters 49–57). Two verses seem particularly apropos for all of us who are tempted to employ mere logical consistency with dogmatic formulae in dealing with religious pluralism:

> For my thoughts are not your thoughts,
> > nor are your ways my ways, says the LORD.
> For as the heavens are higher than the earth,
> > so are my ways higher than your ways
> > and my thoughts than your thoughts. (Isa 55:8–9)

God surprised Israel. Jesus surprised his disciples. And there may be surprises in store for all of us, including those who, like Dupuis and me (with much less depth of learning) believe the creedal formulae are bind-

27. For solid historical treatments of the older theology, see the works of Louis Capéran and Prudencio Damboriena in the bibliography.

ing but do not—at least not in the hermeneutic of *Dominus Iesus*—say the last word on religious plurality.

Having experienced the power of Indian religions to create deep, holy, sincere, richly endowed human beings, Dupuis applied what David Tracy calls "a hermeneutic of trust" toward both individuals and the traditions, scriptures, and practices that produced them.[28] His adversaries could concede that there are valid elements in other traditions but not imagine that their riches, to borrow the words of Peter Phan, require us to learn to live "interreligiously"[29]—that is to say, that their riches might enrich us.

GENESIS OF THIS BOOK

In December 2003, I attended observances of Jacques' 80th birthday in the *aula magna* of the Gregorian, my own alma mater (where I had earned an S.T.L. in 1972). After the public event, I was one of a dozen relatives from Belgium and friends—including Gerry O'Collins, and Peter Phan—invited by the dean of the Gregorian University's theology faculty, the late John O'Donnell, SJ, to continue the celebration at a nearby restaurant. On the way back to the Gregorian, Jacques asked me if I still had the two epilogues he had been refused permission to publish. I said that I did. He repeated what he had said earlier on the phone, "It may be opportune for you to publish them some day." I joked that I would play Jeanne Mortier to his Teilhard de Chardin by keeping them safe and publishing them when the time seemed right.[30] In the light of notifications from Rome on the work of Father Jon Sobrino, SJ, and from the United States Conference of Catholic Bishops on the work of Father Peter C. Phan and Sister Elizabeth Johnson, C.S.J.—on grounds analogous to those used against Dupuis—I judge the moment to be opportune.

When you read Dupuis's two epilogues (chapters two and three of this book), you will find that he judges his central problem with CDF to

---

28. Tracy, *Plurality*, 112–13.

29. Phan, *Being Religious Interreligiously*.

30. Jeanne Mortier was a friend of Pierre Teilhard de Chardin (1881–1955), the imminent Jesuit philosopher and paleontologist. She kept copies of manuscripts that Jesuit superiors would not let him publish, lest they resurrect controversies from the 1930s and 1940s that his theories of evolution and of the relation of spirit and matter amounted to denying original sin. In 1962 the Congregation of the Holy Office, predecessor of today's Congregation for the Doctrine of the Faith, questioned aspects of Teilhard's work.

lie in his finding the work of the Holy Spirit within "other" religions when they produce deep, holy, sincere, richly endowed human beings. Is there not also ambiguity in these traditions? Was he not aware of it? Certainly, but a Christian tradition that for nearly nineteen hundred years failed to recognize the perniciousness of anti-Semitism and in its twentieth century could produce both a Stalin and a Hitler also needs to concede there is ambiguity in Christianity as well. More than once he said, "We need to stop comparing the best of Christianity with the worst in a religion like Hinduism; instead, we need to compare the best in one tradition with the best in the other and the worst in one with the worst in the other." He knew, for example, that in India those who advocated utilizing the Vedic tradition as a sort of "Indian Old Testament" were in danger of building their Christology on a system that oppressed the Dalit "untouchables." But he also knew that biblical texts were used by Europeans to justify slavery right down to the late nineteenth century. Such issues as the status of scriptures in the various traditions, he told me, needed to be sorted out in a process that would take generations. What Christians knew was the revelation of God's love for all humankind, particularly for the poor and outcast. Overall, on Dupuis's reading of the basic texts and the core of Christian tradition, salvation is the concern of God (*ho patêr* in the New Testament), who is distinct and transcendent, as well as immanent. It would not be easy for the language of logic and conceptual knowledge to bridge the gap between the God of Christian dogma and either the Absolute of the Vedas or the agnosticism concerning God in Buddhist Scriptures. One testament to the difficulty is to be found in the analysis of Christianity and Indian traditions in the huge volume edited by Dupuis's Gregorian University colleagues and published six years after his death, *The Catholic Engagement with World Religions*.[31]

Wendy Doniger has captured that metaphysical chasm between East and West brilliantly in the title of one of her books on Indian religion, *Dreams, Illusion and Other Realities*. What seems "real" in Western Christianity appears to be an "illusion" in India, Doniger shows. Dupuis knew that the Jewish, Muslim, and Christian doctrine of God the creator undergirds a very different ontology than that generated by Indian philosophy and religion. But an implication of the monotheistic Trinitarian

---

31. See Pataskar, Anand, and Shelke, "Hinduism and Christianity," in Becker and Morali, eds., 459–86 (with special attention to the appendix to that chapter by Karl J. Becker and Gavin D'Costa).

God of Christian tradition necessarily implied, he wanted to show, that God as *Logos* and *Pneuma* could be recognized as present everywhere both *before, during,* and *since* the Christ-event and the founding of the church. That said, the enduring mission of Christians is to proclaim that God's paradigmatic revelation lies in Jesus the Christ and that God's way of acting in this Jesus is the foreshadowing of how God will save all the world—only through the process of dying to self does humanity encounter the Divine in whom we move, live, and take up our being. But when the language of dying to illusion appears in other traditions, the reality to which one awakes is conceptualized quite differently from what is portrayed by Christianity and its "realistic" view of creation and of the "re-creation" that will occur at the eschaton as prefigured in the resurrection of Jesus.

CDF found problematic Dupuis's construal of a Trinity in which the *Logos* of God, who is the ultimate criterion of value and truth in *all* creation, is thought to be present also in other religious traditions. In Dupuis's construal of God's relation to the world, wherever there is authentic value and truth, there the *Logos tou Theou* ("the Word of God") is present. For Dupuis, the core Christian doctrine is that the unsurpassable expression of that *Logos* is the self-giving love (*agapê*) of God revealed in the life, teaching, death, and resurrection of Jesus. It is toward that *agapê* that the Spirit of God (*ho pneuma tou Theou*) moves everyone who follows conscience, the teachings of religion, or the wisdom of a culture. Christic revelation is unique and unsurpassable, according to Dupuis, in that God's very being is present in the incarnation, teaching, and paschal mystery of Jesus. This however does not mean that only in historical Christic revelation is Truth to be found. If a given religion is the vehicle that leads an individual toward selflessness and compassion, attributes of *agapê*, Dupuis suggests, it may be because that tradition rests in the *Logos* present wherever there is truth and because the *Pneuma* is operative. This does not seem too far from the spirit of the First Letter of John where we read, "because love is from God; everyone who loves is born of God and knows God. Whoever does not love does not know God, for God is love" (1 John 4:7–8).

Is that too optimistic? We should recall that the man who experienced Belgium's devastation during and after two world wars and who lived under Hitler's domination for nearly five years was no naïve optimist about the human potential to do evil and deceive ourselves with ideologies. He was fully aware that the Holocaust of the Jews in World War II showed that neither Christianity as a whole nor Catholicism in particular could deny complicity in the crimes of that period. We spoke several times about revelations of the sexual abuse of minors that have occurred in our own day. Dupuis was saddened but not surprised by these scandals and, although he died before the revelations of clerical corruption in his native Belgium in 2010 and 2011, I doubt if he would be surprised by them. Indeed, I have often wondered if his relative silence on the ecclesiological implications of his thought stemmed from his sense that church authorities were often compromised and corrupted by the need to toe a party line with which in their hearts they may disagree in order to maintain their positions of privilege. Christianity, he knew, participates in the ambiguity and deserves the suspicion to which all human institutions must be subjected. A man with no *deus ex machina* view of God's redemptive activity, neither was Dupuis confident of our power to save ourselves. While Jesus was a teacher in Dupuis's Christology, much more basically he was uniquely God's Son sent to save the world.

What was perhaps unforgivable to many of his critics, however, was the way in which Dupuis's silence about the role of the church can be taken as an indication that he had a minimalist view of the church. When I read *Dominus Iesus*, chapters 4–6 (i.e., sections 16–22) on the role of the church in the mystery of salvation today, with the benefit of eleven years of hindsight, I cannot escape thinking that Dupuis's silence was taken by the CDF to mean that the church played a minimal role in the universal economy of salvation for him. And that this, in the eyes of CDF, made his undoing necessary.

In proposing a view of how the *Logos* and the *Pneuma* have been and are active in the whole of creation and are luring the cosmos to a fulfillment foreshadowed in the Resurrection of Jesus, Dupuis articulates a high Christological, Pneumatological, and Trinitarian doctrine, but it is fair to say that his ecclesiology is not high enough for his critics, and that this is CDF's main problem with his work.

Is this perceived lacuna a fatal flaw in his writings? I am tempted to say that if he wrote too little about the role of the church, then *Dominus Iesus* has exaggerated it. The reader will decide.

What Dupuis articulated from the mid-1980s till his death was a Christocentric Trinitarian soteriology that gave other religious ways the "benefit of the doubt" by proposing that we see God's hand in them when they produce holy, committed, loving, wise, justice-seeking men and women. Having experienced the reality of other traditions producing such people, he tried to find a language in Christian tradition that did two things: (1) retained faith that the Word of God, which is itself God, had become incarnate uniquely and unsurpassably in Jesus of Nazareth, and that Jesus the Christ revealed God's salvific will; that the "event" that was his life is constitutive in bringing about human salvation by embodying God's salvific plan (*mysterion*) uniquely for all the world; and (2) proposed an explanation of how elements of God's nature, truth, wisdom, and saving power were not confined to Israel and historic Christianity but had been and still are active in other religious ways and cultures.

The epilogues that follow are the central matter of this book and defend his work. They also criticize the documents of the CDF. How they came to be in the book you hold and not in his own last book requires an explanation.

THE SITUATION OF DUPUIS IN LATE 2000

In the fall of 2000, nine years after Dupuis first told me that his work was being reviewed unfavorably in high places and after nearly twenty months of wrangling over the response of Dupuis to CDF questions, Dupuis and his critics at CDF were still in radical disagreement about a statement in regard to his book, *Toward a Christian Theology of Religious Pluralism*. Jesuit Superior General Peter Hans Kolvenbach had done all he could in the period between 1997 and 2000 to protect Dupuis. Among other things, Dupuis's friend and colleague at the Gregorian, Gerald O'Collins, had been appointed to help him prepare his defense. In September of 2000, when CDF issued its doctrinal Declaration *Dominus Iesus*, it did not mention Dupuis by name. It was nonetheless clear to everyone that Dupuis and other so-called "theological pluralists" were its object.

On Saturday, 21 October 2000, Jacques told me, my wife Linda, and Stephen Bevans during a quiet dinner in a restaurant near the Gregorian that CDF had tried to get him to ratify their statement before *Dominus Iesus* was released. The text they presented required him to acknowledge both the doctrine contained in the CDF text and "grave deficiencies" in his writings. He saw himself, however, as the victim of critics who misconstrued what he had written. Nor could he refrain from finding serious problems in *Dominus Iesus*. We told him that evening that he was in good company if he had problems with the document because we heard rumblings that several high Vatican officials did as well. We mentioned that earlier in the week at the conference that Steve and I had attended (to commemorate the tenth anniversary of John Paul II's encyclical *Redemptoris Missio*), Cardinal Kasper had given an interesting answer to a question on why he had not referred to *Dominus Iesus* in his talk on the uniqueness and universality of Christ.[32] Kasper said that he preferred to quote the Bible and the documents of Vatican II, whose reception had stood the test of time. *Dominus Iesus*, he said, was by contrast a recent document. His deadpan delivery brought the audience to its feet with applause. Dupuis enjoyed our report that another cardinal in the audience was visibly uneasy.

We moved on to saying that Claude Geffré, O.P. had been one of the speakers at the conference, where he spoke of Jesus as God's "concrete universal," entering into the paradox of God's universal Word, the *Logos* of the universe, becoming flesh in Jesus of Nazareth.[33] Dupuis said, "Geffré visited me and we talked all this afternoon. We can't find any significant difference between our positions on Christ and the religions, yet he speaks in the Urbaniana's Aula Paulo Sesto in the presence of cardinals, archbishops, bishops, professors, and students beyond counting. Me they accuse of heresy!"

After he had finished his favorite entrée (broiled sole with lemon and butter), Jacques pushed his plate back, picked up his glass of Frascati wine and told us a poignant story. "After my session at CDF, I came back to my room and found the proofs for the seventh edition of *The Christian Faith* waiting for me to correct."[34] As he began looking over these pages and going to original sources to be sure new materials and introductions were correct, he found they invariably were accurate. "My memory has not failed me and I realized that my accusers were amateurs. I knew the

---

32. Kasper, "Unicity and Universality of Jesus Christ."

33. Geffré, "La prétension du Christianisme á l'universel."

34. Dupuis, *Christian Faith in the Doctrinal Documents of the Catholic Church*. This more than eleven hundred thirty-six-page book is a meticulously organized compendium of the core doctrinal documents of the church from the late second century through the contemporary period. As competence in Latin has diminished among priests, bishops, and even theologians, it is the English-speaking Catholic Church's most trusted summary of dogmatic pronouncements.

Catholic dogmatic tradition better than they did, and I knew I was faithful to it. If I am a heretic, so is John Paul II."

He went on to recount how he was taken aback by a question from Cardinal Ratzinger about a point in the CDF objections to *Toward a Christian Theology of World Religions*. He reported saying to the Cardinal, "But, your eminence, it would take hours to answer that question. It's already in my responses to CDF's interrogatories. Did you read them?" Ratzinger's answer convinced Dupuis that either his responses had not been read carefully or, possibly, not at all. Neither had the cardinal absorbed what he had written in the book they were proposing to condemn. Dupuis was despondent.

I said, "But that's the equivalent of a going to a Supreme Court hearing and learning that the Chief Justice had not read the briefs!"

Jacques smiled weakly and exclaimed in French, "*Exactement!*" Ratzinger appeared to be relying, Dupuis said, on what (then Archbishop, now Cardinal) Bertone and (then Father, now Cardinal) Amato had reported about his work. I, of course, have no way of knowing if this is true. If it is, the next thing Dupuis reported takes on added significance. "CDF picked on me to signal the limits of the debate that they would permit the Asian theologians to carry on. I became a symbol, and the deeper dimensions of my actual work were never fully considered."

Dinner over, we walked Jacques back to the Gregorianum. We watched the diminutive man let himself in through a small door in the right side of the immense front door of the university's main building and headed toward Piazza Venezia to catch a bus back to the Collegio del Verbo Divino where we were staying.

Four months later, in late February 2001, the axe fell: publication of a CDF Notification, which alleged now that there were—instead of the "grave deficiencies" depicted in an earlier version—"notable ambiguities and difficulties on important points" in his work. Dupuis later told me over the phone that the epilogues he wanted to insert in *Christianity and the Religions* could not be published. His superiors had forbidden it. (It was never clear to me whether it was the superiors at the Gregorianum or at the Generalate who forbade it.) Given the difficulties the Jesuits were having in these very days with CDF displeasure expressed toward the work of two other Jesuit confreres (and Orbis authors), Jon Sobrino and Roger Haight, I can understand why the Jesuit superior general did not relish a direct assault by Dupuis on *Dominus Iesus*, particularly since the

Vatican had gotten very touchy about negative reactions to that document and was known to be suspicious of what they considered to be passive resistance on the part of not just the Jesuits but also of other religious orders to Vatican policies.[35]

In the months before meeting in Rome in the fall of 2000, Jacques and I had talked several times by phone, and I formed the impression that he was sinking into depression. When we met for dinner that October evening, my fear was confirmed. Subsequently, Jesuit confreres at the Gregorian, who had remained loyal to him when others virtually shunned him, confirmed that his psychological withdrawal had begun already with the inception of rumors that CDF was beginning a formal process of examining his work. Learning of his state of mind, Father Kolvenbach made the trip from Borgo Santo Spirito to the Gregorianum several times to try to help Dupuis. He was assuming the role of pastor and brother to a confrere. Nothing, however, helped. Already in his late 70s, Jacques could not rally. He became physically ill several times over the next two years.

In October of 2002, I was again in Rome on business and made a point of inviting Jacques and Gerry O'Collins to dinner. Noting his depression, I once again told him that he had, in effect, won and that the Notification was simply CDF's way of saving face. Intellectually, he accepted it, but emotionally he was exhausted and still felt ill handled. A year later, on 5 December 2003, although he was deeply touched by the large number of his students, friends, and others who attended the public celebration of his 80th birthday in the *Aula Magna* of the Gregorian University, he told me that his health was not good and stated his desire that I find a way to publish those epilogues. We talked by phone several times in the next year, and he repeated that he was not well.

On the 28th of December 2004, his confrere and friend, John Navone, SJ, called to say that Jacques had died earlier that day. He had fallen and hit his head on a table in the refectory and died of what would be diagnosed as a brain hemorrhage that resulted from the fall.

Requiescas in pace, Jacobe.

---

35. See Burrows, "Catholics, Carey's 'Means' and Mission," 133, 135–36, I give background for this assertion.

2

The Declaration *Dominus Iesus*
and My Perspectives on It

JACQUES DUPUIS, SJ

THE READERS OF THIS book[1] and of the articles that I have written on the subject these last two years [i.e., since 2000], will have noted that nowhere do I make any reference to the questioning about my 1997 book, to which I have been submitted by the Congregation for the Doctrine of the Faith [hereafter referred to as the "CDF"] since late 1998. The reason for this complete silence is the top secrecy that was enjoined on me by the Congregation and which out of loyalty I observed strictly. This complete silence is no longer possible, as I should justify the positions held in this new book in relation to the Declaration *Dominus Iesus* of the Congregation for the Doctrine of the Faith, dated 6 August 2000 and published on 5 September 2000. As I mention at the end of the Introduction, the present book, *Christianity and the Religions* [hereafter referred to in notes as *Christianity*] was completed on 31 March 2000. Subsequently, only some small corrections, suggested by five censors and readers, were introduced. However, I must now compare my own positions with the affirmations of the document. Hence this Epilogue. It goes without saying that my remarks on and eventual dissent from some positions of the Declaration are expressed in a spirit of constructive fidelity to Christ's

---

1. "This book" refers to and was written to become an epilogue to Fr. Dupuis's *Il cristianesimo e le religioni: dallo scontro all'incontro*, Queriniana, 2000; English translation, *Christianity and the Religions: From Confrontation to Dialogue*, Orbis, 2002. Footnotes and everything printed in square brackets in the text have been inserted by the editor to clarify the context and meaning of the chapter, especially for persons not versed in the Latin terminology used by the author and CDF.

revelation, to the authentic Christian tradition, and to the Church's doctrinal authority.

THE BACKGROUND

A letter of Cardinal Ratzinger to Fr. Peter Hans Kolvenbach, the Jesuit General, dated 26 September 1998, informed him that the Congregation for the Doctrine of the Faith had taken on June 10 the decision to proceed to a *contestazione* [literally, "objection"][2] to my book *Verso una teologia cristiana del pluralismo religioso* [Queriniana, 1997; English translation, *Toward a Christian Theology of Religious Pluralism*, Orbis, 1997; hereafter referred to as *Toward*]. A first document included with the letter was the report of the ordinary assembly of the members of the Congregation in which the decision was taken. This Report stated, along with other accusations, that: "In the work of Fr. Dupuis are found grave errors and doctrinal ambiguities on doctrines of divine and Catholic faith, regarding revelation, soteriology, Christology and the Trinity . . ."

A second document consisted of nine full pages of questions which I had to answer under complete secrecy (*strettamente riservato*) ["strictly confidential"] within three months. On Christmas Day I sent 188 pages in answer to the questions. There followed a silence of seven full months, at the end of which on 27 July 1999 Fr. Kolvenbach received another letter from Cardinal Ratzinger, in which the Cardinal expressed dissatisfaction with my answers; these were considered inadequate for "preserving the doctrine of Catholic faith from errors." Attached to the letter was an "annex" of eleven pages, containing a "Doctrinal Judgment" on my book, with a new set of questions to be answered, again under complete secrecy, within three months. On 1 November 1999 I sent sixty pages more of answers to the questions of the Congregation. This was followed again by a long silence, which this time lasted ten months.

On 4 September 2000, I was summoned to the CDF together with my Fr. General [Kolvenbach] and Professor Gerald O'Collins of the Gregorian University who would act as my advocate, for an official meet-

---

2. In the CDF's 1997 "Regulations for Doctrinal Examination" (III, 8) the *contestazione* (a presentation of objections to an author's work) follows a determination of the Congregation at two of its regular weekly meetings that there are (a) "preliminary" grounds to suspect unsound doctrine and (b) a determination by "one or more Consultors or other experts in the particular area" under consideration that an intervention is advisable.

ing with Cardinal Ratzinger, his Secretary Archbishop Bertone and Fr. Angelo Amato of the Salesian University, consultor of the Congregation. Incidentally, this was the first time I ever met the Cardinal and his secretary. During this meeting I was expected to sign a fifteen-page draft of a *Notification*[3] about my book, which was foreseen for publication in *L'Osservatore Romano* on September 7th, that is two days after the publication of the Declaration *Dominus Iesus*, which took place on the 5th. At the end of a tense session of two hours it became clear that the text submitted to my approval contained false accusations against my book. No quotations from my text, not even references to page numbers of the book, were provided to substantiate these accusations.

The draft of the Notification consisted of eight propositions. Each of these began by stating either a doctrine "to be firmly believed" or a truth "taught by Catholic doctrine." In six of the eight propositions (nn. 2–6, 8) after the basic truth had been recalled, there followed erroneous opinions to be rejected, as being either "contrary to the Catholic faith" or unacceptable to Catholic doctrine." To these, lengthy explanations were added, expanding on the meaning of the condemnations. Here is the list of the eight fundamental truths recalled in the eight propositions:

1. It must be firmly believed that Jesus Christ, Son of God made man, crucified and risen, is the unique and universal mediator of the salvation of humankind.

2. The doctrine that proclaims that Jesus of Nazareth, Son of Mary and Word of the Father, is the unique (*unicamente*) Savior of the world, must be firmly believed.

3. It must be firmly believed that Jesus Christ is the mediator, the completion and the fullness of revelation, that is, of all that God has willed to communicate and has in fact communicated of his salvific intentions and of the mystery of his own life, to the whole of humankind in the course of history.

4. It is conformed to Catholic doctrine to affirm that the seeds of truth and of goodness existing in the religions of the world are a

3. As used here, the word "Notification" (in Italian, *Notificazione*) refers to an official document issued by the Congregation for the Doctrine of the Faith to alert members of the church about errors, problems, or deficiencies that the CDF finds in the work of theologians. If one goes to CDF's websites, one can find a number of past Notifications. See http://www.vatican.va/roman_curia/congregations/cfaith/doc_doc_index.htm.

certain participation in the truths contained in the revelation of/ in Jesus Christ.

5. The faith of the Church teaches that the Holy Spirit operative after the resurrection of Jesus Christ, is always the Spirit of Christ sent by (*dal*) the Father, who works salvifically in both Christians or non-Christians.

6. It must be firmly believed that the Church is sign and instrument of salvation for all men.

7. The doctrine of the Church teaches that the followers of the religions of the world are ordained (*ordinati*) to the Church and are all called to be part of her.

8. According to Catholic doctrine, one must hold that "whatever the Spirit brings about in human hearts and in the history of peoples, in cultures and religions, serves as a preparation for the Gospel" (RM 29).

I gave my assent to these propositions as they stood, while being aware that some of them could be understood in different ways, about which the doctrine of faith did not seem to decide. As for the opinions to be rejected accordingly—which understandably were being attributed to my book—they either misrepresented what I actually wrote or interpreted it in a way which went against my intention and meaning. This was particularly evident in the explanations added to the main text of the various propositions. It was clear that I could not subscribe to such false accusations; and I did not. The text was thus dismissed, although it had already been approved by the Pope as early as 16 June and ordered by him to be published. The impression at the end of the meeting was that Cardinal Ratzinger would have a new text composed for a Notification, to be presented to the members of the CDF for their approval at their next ordinary assembly, at the end of October. At the time of writing [these pages] I do not know whether a new Notification is to be expected soon, or whether for different reasons the idea of a Notification has been postponed or simply dropped. In this situation I can address myself in this Epilogue only to the Declaration *Dominus Iesus*.[4]

4. When the Notification was revised and published on 26 February 2001, Fr. Dupuis wrote an extensive response both to inadequacies in the substance of the Notification and defects in the canonical process by which the Congregation for the Doctrine of the

It must be noted that the Declaration abstains from mentioning the names of any theologians who hold the opinions it means to condemn. In such a situation one can easily claim not to find his own opinions represented in the text of the document, and conclude that one is not in any way targeted for disapproval. I do not intend to take this attitude. I will rather distinguish between allegations which do not seem in any way directed at my book and could not honestly be raised against it, and other allegations which, partly though not exclusively, seem to be made against my text, even while they seem to misunderstand and misrepresent it. The former allegations I will not consider here; the latter allegations I intend to discuss in order to further explain the opinions which I have retained and tried to justify in the present book before the publication of *Dominus Iesus*, but which I still consider sustainable even after its publication. In this Epilogue, I will try once again to dispel misunderstandings and misinterpretations that seem to be persistent. In doing so, I will mostly follow the order of the Declaration itself, and where necessary will refer to the page numbers either of my previous book (*Verso una teologia cristiana del pluralismo religioso*, Queriniana, 1997 / *Toward a Christian Theology of Religious Pluralism*, Orbis, 1997, or of the present one (*Il cristianesimo e le religioni* / *Christianity Among the Religions*, Orbis, 2002).

INTRODUCTION TO *DOMINUS IESUS*

The Introduction of *Dominus Iesus* (4) refers to "relativistic theories," which "seek to justify religious pluralism, not only *de facto* [as an empirical reality] but also *de iure* (or "in principle"). The text makes no distinction between different meanings which the expression "religious pluralism in principle" may take on, nor does it take a position on the question whether religious pluralism may exist *de iure divino* (i.e., "by *divine* law"). Instead, DI immediately takes for granted that the terminology of pluralism intends to place all religious traditions on one and the same level, thus reducing Christianity to being simply one religion among others. This *a priori* definition and condemnation of religious pluralism *in principio* ("in principle") is prejudicial to the Catholic theologians who believe—not without good theological reason—that, provided it be correctly understood, religious pluralism *in principio* need not be opposed to

---

Faith arrived at the final version. Fr. Dupuis's reactions are contained in a document he entitled *Epilogue 2* and is contained in the following chapter of this book.

the Christian faith. The expression is used by these theologians to mean that the uniqueness of Jesus Christ as universal Savior does not exclude a positive meaning of the other religions in God's plan for humankind.

According to *Dominus Iesus* 4, the theory of religious pluralism—in the one meaning presumed by the text—is based on the denial of certain truths of faith, of which the main ones are enumerated: "the definitive and complete character of the revelation of Jesus Christ, the nature of Christian faith as compared with that of belief in other religions, the inspired nature of the books of Sacred Scripture, the personal unity between the eternal Word and Jesus of Nazareth, the unity of the economy of the Incarnated Word and the Holy Spirit, the unicity and salvific universality of the mystery of Jesus Christ, the universal salvific mediation of the Church, the inseparability—while recognizing the distinction—of the kingdom of God, the kingdom of Christ, and the Church, and the subsistence of the one Church of Christ in the Catholic Church."

What strikes one in this list is the underlying presupposition that upholding these doctrines of Catholic faith necessarily implies affirming them as absolute exclusive possessions. Does affirming and reaffirming the Catholic Christian identity, which seems to be the main intent of this document, necessarily imply denying the existence elsewhere of comparable authenticity, if not identical values? To give some examples: Does the Catholic doctrine of the complete character of the revelation of Jesus Christ need to deny a priori the existence of some divine revelation elsewhere? Does the nature of "Christian faith" need to exclude the existence elsewhere of any divine faith, whereby the other religions are reduced to holding "beliefs" of mere human origin, unable to carry saving faith? Each of these seemingly exclusive claims made in *Dominus Iesus* will have to be examined hereafter. But it is important to note from the outset the exclusivist mindset of the document, even where it admits that some questions may remain open to theological investigation.

The roots of the problems mentioned above are found, according to *Dominus Iesus* 4, in "certain presuppositions of both a philosophical and theological nature." The theological ones include "the difficulty in understanding and accepting the presence of definitive and eschatological events in history; the metaphysical emptying of the historical Incarnation of the Eternal Logos, reduced to a mere appearing of God in history. . . ." The document is aware that these and other presuppositions "may evince different nuances," but it is nevertheless convinced that on their basis "certain theological proposals are developed . . . in which Christian revelation and the mystery of Jesus Christ and the Church lose their character of absolute truth and salvific universality, or at least shadows of doubt and uncertainty are cast upon them."

This "absolute" statement fails to distinguish between different possible ways of understanding the definitiveness or non-definitiveness, the absoluteness or non-absoluteness of some historical events. Surely upholding the meaning of the mystery of Jesus Christ and of the Church need not depend merely on the use or non-use of some ambiguous terms. Let us also remark in passing that in this text, as in the very title of the document, the mystery of Jesus Christ and that of the Church seem regrettably placed on one and the same level of unicity and universality in the mystery of divine salvation, apparently forgetting that the Church is a derived, related mystery, which finds its significance exclusively in the mystery of Jesus Christ. Surely between Jesus Christ and the Church a distance ought to be maintained, lest we multiply absolute claims and affirmations.

DIVINE REVELATION IN JESUS CHRIST

The document states that, as a remedy for the relativistic mentality, it is necessary to affirm the "definitive and complete character of the revelation of Jesus Christ." Unhappily both terms are open to misunderstandings, as they could be interpreted as forgetting the gap that remains between the historical divine revelation which took place in Jesus Christ and God's final revelation at the *eschaton*. However complete the historical revelation in Jesus Christ may be, it belongs to the "already," not to the "not yet." While it is decisive as God's full historical manifestation, it is not definitive—the term is not used by *Dei Verbum*[5]—as will be God's final manifestation at the end of time in the *eschaton*; it is complete, then, but not fully achieved. I have called the fullness of God's revelation in Christ a "qualitative" fullness, in order to stress its transcendent and unique character as originating from him, who is God's Son made man; for that reason that fullness is unsurpassed and unsurpassable in history. This, however, does not imply that it comprehends and exhausts the entire mystery of God, which remains hidden to be fully manifested at the *eschaton*. This is why I

5. *Dei Verbum* is the Latin title of the Second Vatican Council's "Dogmatic Constitution on Divine Revelation."

have said that the fullness of revelation in Jesus Christ, though of a unique intensity and depth, is not "quantitative," meaning thereby that it does not disclose fully God's mystery (cf. *Cristianesimo*, 120–24, [E.T., 129–32]).

The scriptural arguments introduced by *Dominus Iesus* to justify the affirmation of the definitive and complete character of revelation in Christ (Matt 11:27; John 1:18; Col 2:9–10) do not prove it; nowhere in these texts is it said that God is already fully known through revelation in Jesus Christ. In Col 2:9–10 the context is not that of the Incarnation but of the resurrection; this difficult text seems to refer to the real transformation which the humanity of Jesus has undergone through the resurrection, by which the divine life becomes concentrated in him to spread to the baptized. Even if the text were interpreted to mean that Christ *possesses* the "fullness of deity," it would still not be said that he has *already revealed* the divine mystery fully. The texts of Vatican II cited here by the document (DV 2 and 4), where the Council speaks of "fullness of revelation" and of revelation being "completed and perfected") in Jesus Christ surely do not overlook the final achievement of revelation and God's full appearing which remains in store for the *eschaton*. *Dei Verbum* 4 marks well the distinction between the "already" and the "not yet," stating: "The Christian economy, since it is the new and definitive covenant, will never pass away; and no new public revelation is to be expected before the glorious manifestation of our Lord, Jesus Christ." That, as the encyclical *Redemptoris Missio*[6] states in article 5, that in Jesus Christ God "has made himself known in the fullest possible way" possible in history, is of course true. That "he has revealed to mankind who he is," or that he has "made his name known" does not, however, imply that the fullness of his mystery has already been manifested, for while divine revelation through the mystery of the Incarnation is unsurpassable in character as a historical revelation, it has its own innate limitations which will be overcome only at the *eschaton*.

Nevertheless, *Dominus Iesus* goes on to affirm that "the theory of the limited, incomplete, or imperfect character of the revelation of Jesus Christ, which would be complementary to that to be found in other religions, is contrary to the Church's faith" (DI 6). No distinction whatever is made here between different possible ways of understanding a certain

---

6. *Redemptoris Missio* is Pope John Paul II's encyclical letter "On the Permanent Validity of the Church's Missionary Vocation."

"complementarity" between Christian and other revelation. The statement excludes a priori the possibility of distinctions and qualifications.

According to the document, the position which upholds some limitation of Christian revelation is in "radical contradiction" with the Christian faith. In Jesus Christ is contained "the full and complete revelation of the salvific mystery of God"; similarly, in him the "truth about God" is found "unique, full and complete." There are two affirmations here: (1) in Jesus Christ the full revelation of the mystery of God is contained; and (2) in him is also fully revealed God's saving plan of salvation for humankind. The argument advanced to prove these assertions is repeated twice. Notwithstanding the limitations of the historical event of Jesus, and even while the divine mystery "in itself remains transcendent and inexhaustible," nevertheless Jesus's words and deeds "have the divine Person of the Incarnate Word . . . as their subject"; or again, "he who speaks or acts is the Incarnated Son of God." Therefore ("for this reason," "because"), it necessarily follows that in his revelation God's mystery is fully known and God's plan of salvation fully disclosed. In him, moreover, "the truth about God is not abolished or reduced because it is spoken in human language."

There would be much to say about this paragraph, and mostly about the Christology underlying it. But let us start with the affirmations themselves. Is it consistent to hold at one and the same time, on the one hand, that the divine mystery remains "transcendent and inexhaustible," even after revelation in Jesus Christ, and, on the other, that God's mystery is fully revealed through his historical event? I quoted John Paul II in *Cristianesimo* (123 [E.T., 132]) to the effect that "every truth attained [by the Church on the basis of revelation in Jesus Christ] is but a step towards that fullness of truth which will appear with the final Revelation of God" (*Fides et Ratio*, art. 2).[7] As for our full knowledge of the plan of God for the salvation of humankind after Jesus' revelation, one may not forget that Jesus himself admitted to not knowing the day of the end (cf. Mark 13:32; Matt 24:36). Exegetes think that he probably shared the mistaken persuasion of his day that the end was close at hand. Yet, surely the day and the hour of the end belong to the plan of God, though not being contained in the revelation already brought by Jesus Christ. As for the vexing question of the way in which salvation in Jesus Christ works itself

---

7. *Fides et Ratio* is the Latin title of Pope John Paul II's encyclical "On the Relationship between Faith and Reason."

out in the case of people not sharing the Christian faith and not belonging to the Church—obviously a burning issue in any understanding of God's plan for humankind—the Second Vatican Council has plainly professed its ignorance, being satisfied to affirm that this happens through a way "known to God" (*modo Deo cognato* in *Gaudium et Spes* 22; cf. *Ad Gentes* 7).[8] Such knowledge is not included in Jesus' revelation of God's plan of salvation, even while it affects the overwhelming majority of humankind. These two examples should suffice to make us cautious in affirming, as *Dominus Iesus* does, that "the full and complete revelation of the salvific mystery of God is given in Jesus Christ."

Let us come to the Christology underlying the statements. To simply state that, because the person who speaks in Jesus is the divine person of the Son of God, his words possess the definitiveness and completeness of divine revelation, runs the risk of underestimating the genuine authenticity of Jesus' humanity which is by no way abolished by his personal identity with the Son of God. The human words and actions of Jesus remain authentically and specifically human; they do not in any way become more than human, or super-human, by being the human words and actions of the Son of God. To think otherwise would imply supposing, through a wrong understanding of the *communicatio idiomatum*,[9] that there took place in Jesus a direct communication of the divine knowledge to his human consciousness and intellect, and similarly an overpowering of his human will by the divine. This would amount to affirming absorption of the humanity of Jesus by his divine nature, resulting in a loss of his being authentically human. It must, on the contrary, be held, in compliance with the Christological dogma of the Church, that the personal identity of Jesus, at once God and man, implies no such mixing and confusion of the two natures. The way of operation of the human knowledge and the human will of Jesus has been through the centuries the object of much Christological debate and reflection. But, while we must affirm that, as he lived in his own human awareness his personal identity as the

8. *Gaudium et Spes* is the Latin title of the Second Vatican Council's "Pastoral Constitution on the Church in the Modern World"; *Ad Gentes* is the Latin title of the same council's "Decree on the Church's Missionary Activity."

9. *Communicatio idiomatum* (literally "communication of attributes") is a technical Latin phrase used in the discussion of the relationship of divine and human attributes in the "one person," Jesus of Nazareth, who was declared by the Council of Chalcedon (451) to be "fully human and fully divine."

Son of God and his unique relationship with the Father, Jesus was able to express the divine mystery in human words, in a way that far surpassed any possible revelation of the divine mystery through human words uttered by the prophets, one must still maintain that his human intellect could neither exhaust the mystery nor reveal it in its fullness. To suggest, on the other hand, that the words spoken by Jesus in revealing God were not subject to the limitations or fluctuations of human language is an *a priori* supposition, without foundation. Jesus spoke the Aramaic of his time and place, a language with its own riches and limitations, and the New Testament itself testifies to the difficulties encountered by the early church in conveying his message in another idiom.

The second paragraph of *Dominus Iesus* 6 ends, somewhat abruptly, by stating that faith requires us to profess that "the Word made flesh, in his entire mystery . . . is the source, participated but real, as well as the fulfillment of every salvific revelation of God to humanity." It is not said which other salvific revelation of God to humanity might be meant for inclusion here; whether, that is, the concept could possibly extend beyond the biblical revelation to other religious traditions. We shall come to this below. As to the Christ-event being the "participated but real" source of divine revelation, more could have been said to explain this "participated" character. Nothing is said about Jesus' total dependence upon and relatedness to the God, whom he called *Abba*, who is the original, non-participated source of all divine revelation. *Dei Verbum* 2 expressed the matter better by stating that Jesus Christ is "himself both the mediator and the sum total of revelation."

Dominus Iesus goes on to speak of the divine faith with which the human person ought to respond to God's self-revelation in Jesus Christ (DI 7). Here we meet what is perhaps the most regrettable statement of the entire document. A distinction is established between theological or divine faith and religious belief. In itself such a distinction has little foundation in the language of Christian faith and theology. Our act of divine "faith" is expressed in "believing"; we profess our Christian "faith" (*fides*) by "believing" (*credere*) in one tripersonal God, Father, Son and Holy Spirit. And while theologians have made use of this distinction in various ways, the way in which it is understood here is questionable. Divine faith, we are told, is a supernatural virtue infused by God which "involves a dual adherence: to God who reveals and to the truth which he reveals," or again "the acceptance in grace of revealed truth"; belief, on the other hand, "is that sum of experience and thought that constitutes the human treasury of wisdom and religious aspiration, which man in his search for truth has conceived and acted upon in his relationship to God and the Absolute." In other words, while faith is a divine supernatural gift, "belief" is a natural achievement of humanity. The tragic point, however, is that according to *Dominus Iesus*, divine faith is apparently proper to Christianity, while "in the other religions" only belief is to be found. It is true that John Paul II referred to the "belief" of the members of other religions, apparently abstaining from using the term "faith" in reference to them. But he certainly did not intend the distinction in the sense in which it is being put forward here by *Dominus Iesus*. In fact the Pope explicitly stated that "the firm belief of the followers of non-Christian religions— a belief that is also an effect of the Spirit of truth operating outside the visible confines of the mystical Body"; and he added that this belief "can make Christians ashamed at often being themselves so disposed to doubt concerning the truths revealed by God . . ." (*Redemptor Hominis* 6).[10] It would be falsifying the Pope's mind to attribute to him the distinction between Christian faith and non-Christian belief as intended by *Dominus Iesus*.

The sweeping statement made by *Dominus Iesus* is offensive to the religious life of the members of other religions. Does the text really imply that, while our Christian faith in the God who revealed himself to Abraham and declared his name to Moses is theological faith, the same when professed by Jews is only a human belief? And was John Paul II mistaken when in August 1985 he told thousands of Muslim young people at Casablanca: "We believe in the same God, the one God, the living God, the God who created the world and brings his creatures to their perfection"? Or did he mean that what is divine faith for us Christians is for Muslims only human opinion? There is no biblical justification for refusing to extend the existence of divine faith to the members of the other religions; in chapter 11 the Letter to the Hebrews, for instance, testifies that from the beginning of human history God's self-manifestation has met with the response of divine faith. If the distinction made here by *Dominus Iesus* between divine faith found in Christianity and human belief in the other religions were to be drawn to its logical conclusion, we would be back to a rigid interpretation of the axiom "Outside the Church there is

10. *Redemptoris Hominis* is the Latin title of the first encyclical letter of Pope John Paul II's pontificate, "Redeemer of Humankind."

no salvation," since, according to St. Paul and the Letter to the Hebrews, divine faith is a universal requisite for human salvation. Yet *Dominus Iesus* regrets that "this distinction is not always borne in mind in current theological reflections"—"theological faith being identified with belief in other religions, which is religious experience still in search of the absolute truth and still lacking assent to God who reveals himself"! This statement betrays an exclusive understanding of divine revelation and of theological faith, as if they were to be found only in the Christian tradition.

Coming to the sacred writings of other religions, *Dominus Iesus* 8 recognizes that some elements in these texts may be de facto for people instruments to "nourish and maintain their life-relation with God." In the words of Vatican II's *Nostra Aetate*,[11] they "often reflect a ray of that Truth which enlightens all men" (2). But there is no mention of the possibility of recognizing in them a word spoken by God, however initial and incomplete, the "ray of that Truth" being thus reduced to providing some natural light. Following in the footsteps of the document "Christianity and the World Religions" of the International Theological Commission (1997, § 91–92), *Dominus Iesus* goes on to observe that the Church's tradition reserves the term of "inspired texts" to the canonical books of the Old and New Testaments, "since they are inspired by the Holy Spirit" and "have God for their author."

"Inspiration" is thus affirmed as an exclusive privilege of the Bible. In this manner the document refuses to pass from the univocal concept of the word of God, of sacred scripture and divine inspiration, which has developed within the Christian tradition, to an analogical understanding of those concepts which would allow for the possibility of recognizing some divine, even though incomplete, revelation outside the Bible. The word of God is understood to be the exclusive prerogative of the Jewish-Christian tradition. While *Dominus Iesus* agrees, with John Paul II's encyclical *Redemptoris Missio* 55, that God "does not fail to make himself present in many ways, not only to individuals, but also to entire peoples through their spiritual riches, of which their religions are the main and essential expression," it does not agree that this divine presence may imply a divine revelation. That God could be thus present in so many ways and yet abstain from all revelatory activity would seem a very strange position to hold. And, whatever value the sacred books of other religions may have

---

11. *Nostra Aetate* is the Latin title of the Second Vatican Council's "Declaration on the Relations of the Church to Non-Christian Religions."

in directing and nourishing the existence of their followers, they are said to "receive from the mystery of Christ the elements of goodness and grace which they contain." How the elements of divine "truth and grace," found among peoples as a "secret presence of God" (*Ad Gentes* 9) even before the historical event of Jesus Christ, are derived and "received from the mystery of Christ," is left unexplained.

THE INCARNATE LOGOS AND THE HOLY SPIRIT IN THE WORK OF SALVATION

Dominus Iesus 9 points out two approaches to the mystery of Jesus Christ in contemporary theological reflection which are "in profound conflict with Christian faith" (DI 10). According to the first opinion, Jesus of Nazareth, being "a particular, finite, historical figure" does not reveal the divine "in an exclusive way, but in a way complementary with other revelatory and salvific figures." "The Infinite, the Absolute, the Ultimate Mystery of God would thus manifest itself to humanity in many ways and in many historical figures," of which Jesus would be one; or else, "Jesus would be one of the many faces which the Logos has assumed in the course of time to communicate with humanity in a salvific way"—all of which being presumably of equivalent worth. Here as elsewhere, the text mentions no name and one is left to wonder who might be the target of the accusation. As for myself, I have insisted that the finite, particular, historical character of the humanity of Jesus—which cannot be denied— need not imperil his unique quality in conveying divine revelation and salvation, which is based on his personal identity as the Son of God. The opinion rightly rejected by *Dominus Iesus* ignores entirely the ontological foundation of the uniqueness of Jesus Christ in revelation and salvation.

The second opinion mentioned in *Dominus Iesus* 9 distinguishes two economies of the Word of God, one of the eternal Word and one of the incarnate Word. "The first would have a greater universal value than the second, which is limited to Christians." I have myself drawn the attention to this opinion and clearly declared it unacceptable. I referred to it as the "Logocentric paradigm," and insisted in both my previous book and the present one that there is but one divine economy of salvation, even though it has different aspects and elements always to be combined and viewed as interrelated (*Toward a Christian Theology of Religious Pluralism*, 195–98; *Christianity and the Religions*, 81–82, 182). Any accusation about holding two distinct economies of salvation, under this or whatever other form, if directed against me, misses the target.

Against such opinions which are "in profound conflict with the Christian faith," *Dominus Iesus* 10 recalls the faith in Jesus Christ the Son of God made man, as it is expressed in the writings of the New Testament. Texts to show it are not wanting. Let us, however, recall once more that Colossians 2: 9 has for its context not the mystery of the Incarnation—as *Dominus Iesus* supposes—but of the resurrection. As for Colossians 1: 19–20, the exact meaning of the text is not, as some translations (including the English text of DI 10) would have it, "In him all the fullness of God was pleased to dwell, and through him to reconcile to himself all things . . ."; but: "It pleased God to make the whole fullness (*pleroma*) dwell in him, and to reconcile everything by him and for him. . . ." There is no question—any more here than in Colossians 2: 9—of "the fullness of God" dwelling in Jesus through the incarnation. The "fullness" seems to refer to the universe being "filled" with the presence of God. The two texts of Colossians must be used with caution.

Dominus Iesus 10 goes on to quote the Christological profession of faith of the Council of Nicea (325), and the first part of the Christological definition of the Council of Chalcedon (451). Then follows a Christological text from *Gaudium et Spes* 22. Pope John Paul II is quoted next to the effect that "to introduce any sort of separation between the Word and Jesus Christ is contrary to the Christian faith. . . . Jesus is the Incarnate Word—a single indivisible person. . . . Christ is no other than Jesus of Nazareth; he is the Word of God made man for the salvation of all." (*Redemptoris Missio* 6). This doctrine is perfectly clear. Let us take note, however, of the term used here by the Pope (and italicized in the quotation): what is said to be "contrary to the Christian faith" is to introduce a separation between the Word of God and Jesus Christ; this does not preclude the possibility of really distinguishing between the Word of God as such and the Word of God as incarnate in Jesus Christ. For the Word abides eternally in God's mystery, while the mystery of the Incarnation is a historical event, particular and contingent.

There follows in *Dominus Iesus* 10 a text which needs to be quoted entirely:

> It is likewise contrary to the Catholic faith to introduce a separa-
> tion between the salvific action of the Word as such and that of the

Word made man. With the incarnation, all the salvific actions of the Word of God are always done in unity with the human nature that he has assumed for the salvation of all people. The one subject which operates in the two natures, human and divine, is the single person of the Word. Therefore, the theory which would attribute, after the Incarnation as well, a salvific activity to the Logos as such in his divinity, exercised "in addition to" or "beyond" the humanity of Christ, is not compatible with the Catholic faith.

Here I find myself personally concerned, though partly misinterpreted. It is therefore necessary to clarify my position in contradistinction to what is intended by the text of *Dominus Iesus*. To begin with, the text of *Dominus Iesus* speaks of a separation being introduced between the action of the Word as such and that of the Word made man. As already mentioned above, I have never spoken, either in the previous book or in the present one [i.e., *Christianity and the Religions*] of any separation between any two distinct aspects that make up the one unique plan of God for the salvation of humankind; on the contrary I have insisted everywhere that the different aspects of the one divine plan, though really distinct, cannot in any way be separated from each other as though they represented different economies of divine salvation. A distinct operation of the Word of God as such is a different matter. Though in no way separated, the Word in his divinity and the humanity of Jesus and his human operations, assumed in the unity of his person, remain distinct according to the Church's Christological dogma.

Secondly, *Dominus Iesus* 10 states that "all the salvific actions of the Word of God are always done in unity with the human nature that he has assumed . . ." I suppose that by "unity" is meant here the "communion" between the two natures of Christ of which the Council of Chalcedon (451) speaks and the harmony between the divine and human action taught by Constantinople III (681)—to which, strangely, *Dominus Iesus* makes no reference: "Each of the two natures wills and performs what is proper to it in communion (*in communione*) with the other" (Denzinger 558).[12] Clarifications are, however, required regarding the communion of

12. "Denzinger 558" here refers to § 558 in the collection of theological definitions and texts of the Catholic church begun by Heinrich Denzinger century and updated periodically since then. See Denzinger and Schönmetzer, *Enchiridion Symbolorum: Definitionum et Declarationum De Rebus Fidei et Morum*. It is apropos to note that Fr. Dupuis, assisted by Fr. Josef Neuner, SJ, is the editor of the comprehensive compendium of official Catholic doctrinal statements, *Christian Faith in the Doctrinal Documents*

the two natures and actions. The term "communion" (*koinonia*) needs to be understood here as an analogical term, used in an extended sense. "Communion" exists primarily among persons, as for example between the persons of the divine Trinity or among members of the Church community. When the term is used with reference to the two natures and actions of Jesus Christ, its meaning can only be analogical. There is no question in this case of two subjects or persons living and acting in communion with each other. The term can, moreover, have different meanings, depending on different kinds of actions performed by Jesus Christ in the "communion" of his two natures.

Undoubtedly, all the human actions of Jesus are the human actions of the person of the Logos who is personally their agent or acting subject; but not all the human acts of Jesus are the human expression of a divine power operating through them, for which the human nature serves as a "conjoined instrument" (*instrumentum conjunctum*). Such instrumental value of the human actions of Jesus in relation to the divine action is at work wherever the salvific divine power is expressed through the will, the words, gestures, and actions of Jesus, as is the case in his miracles of healing. In such cases, a much deeper (analogical) "communion" and cooperation of both natures is verified than is the case with the ordinary, merely human acts of Jesus: Jesus walks, sleeps, eats, and so on—although even these actions belong personally to the Word as their subject and agent.

The texts of Leo the Great to which *Dominus Iesus* 10 refers in a note call for some explanations. The texts in general refer to the actions of Jesus in which the divine power finds expression through a human act. St. Leo affirms clearly the (analogical) "communion" that exists between the two natures in the performance of such actions. The Letter of Leo to Flavian of Constantinople (449) (First *Tomus*, i.e., "Tome") expresses it thus: "Each of the two natures performs the functions proper to it in com-

---

of the Catholic Church. Dupuis, who is viewed by many Catholic theologians to have the best comprehensive understanding of official dogmatic theological tradition of the church, was correcting proofs for the seventh edition in the tumultuous September-October 2000 period when he had to respond to inquiries from the Congregation for the Doctrine of Faith. Dupuis told me several times that CDF's "watchdogs" needed to refresh their understanding of the complex background of texts in the Denzinger compendium, which he had virtually memorized. Denzinger, he said, should not be used in crude, proof-text fashion; its formulae came out of an historical context and that context needed to be taken into account.

munion with the other (*cum alterius communione*), the Word does what pertains to the Word and the flesh what pertains to the flesh" (Denzinger 294). There is here question of those actions "common" to both natures, in which each nature contributes what belongs to it, according to its own specific character. St. Leo tries to explain what is the specific contribution of each nature in such actions; that is, what each nature is really doing in (analogical) "communion" with the other.

St. Leo's letter to Emperor Leo (458) (Second *Tomus*, Denzinger 317–18) is, however, more explicit on this count than the first letter had been. St. Leo affirms here the inseparability of the two natures in the actions of Jesus and the absence of any confusion between them; yet he is asking "what belongs to each of the two natures" (*quid cuiusque formae sit*) in accordance to the specific character (*qualitas*) of each (Denzinger 317). He affirms clearly that the Word loses nothing of his divinity through the Incarnation (*decesserit Verbo*). The unity of the two natures is such since the Incarnation that "what belongs to God is not done without the man, nor is what belongs to the man done without God" (*nec sine homine divina, nec sine Deo agerentur humana*).

To the two Tomes of Leo cited above, to which *Dominus Iesus* 10 refers in a note, another text of Leo the Great can be added, which throws further light on the subject. The *Sermo* 64, 4 (PL 54, 360B, to which Hünermann's edition of Denzinger refers on p.176) explains in some detail, with reference to concrete actions of Jesus, what is done by the divinity and what by the humanity, within the (analogical) "communion" between both natures. One extract of this Sermon deserves to be quoted: "Even though the Word of God and the humanity [of Jesus] be one person, and both natures have [share] common actions, the proper quality of the actions must nevertheless be considered, and one must discern in the contemplation of a sincere faith . . . what there is that the flesh does not perform without the Word, and what there is that the Word does not perform without the flesh" (*Licet Dei Verbi et carnis una persona sit, et utraque essentia communes habeat actiones, intelligendae tamen sunt ipsorum operum qualitates, et sincerae fidei contemplatione cernendum est... quid sit quod caro sine Verbo non agit, et quid sit quod Verbum sine carne non efficit* [360B]). In this text as elsewhere, St. Leo has in mind those human actions of Jesus through which a divine power comes to expression. The last sentence, however, leaves the door open for actions of the Word being done without the cooperation of the flesh: one must also consider *quid sit quod Verbum sine carne non efficit* ("what it might be that the Word does without the flesh").

It does not therefore follow that St. Leo necessarily excludes actions done by the Word as such even after the Incarnation—actions done without the cooperation of the human nature, though always in communion with it. In such actions of the Word, a divine power would be operative without necessarily being expressed through the human nature of Jesus. It must in fact be affirmed clearly that even after the Incarnation the Word of God continues to fulfill some operations without the cooperation of the human nature assumed by him in time. One case in point is the Word's function in the divine act of creation (and conservation of what is created), of which the Prologue of John's Gospel speaks explicitly: "All things were made through him" who was in the beginning with God (John 1:1–3). Is it not an a priori assumption to state, as *Dominus Iesus* 10 does, that "with the Incarnation all the salvific actions of the Word of God are always done in unity with the human nature . . ."; if by this is meant that all salvific actions are necessarily expressed through the humanity? That the communion between the two natures is always present is certain. But does this necessarily exclude the possibility of any saving action of the Word, not being expressed through his humanity (cf. DI 10)—or, as I have put it, exercised "beyond" (*oltre*) the humanity? If the function of the Word in the divine act of creation continues without the cooperation of Jesus' humanity—which originally was non-existent—why should the possibility of any saving action of the Word as such be a priori excluded, especially if scriptural foundation is not lacking for affirming such activity of the Word as such?

Relying on notable exegetes, I have shown (see *Cristianesimo*, 131–33 [E.T., 124]) that the Prologue of John's Gospel knows of such saving activity of the Word as such. The Word of God, eternally present in the divine life, has also been universally present in human history since creation. He acted as Mediator in God's act of creation: "All things were made through him. . . . In him was life and the life was the light of men" (John 1:3–4). St. John goes on to say that "the Word was the true light which by coming into the world enlightens every man" (John 1: 9). One must not read in this "coming into the world" of the Word of God, the mystery of the incarnation, of which John 1:14 will speak thereafter. There is question here of a metaphorical coming into the world similar to that which the Sapiential literature of the Old Testament attributed to the personified divine attribute of the Wisdom of God: ". . . In the whole earth, and in every people and nation I have gotten a possession. Among all these I sought a resting place" (Sir 24:6–7). Throughout human history, therefore, and well before the Incarnation took place, the Word of God has been "the true light which by coming into the world enlightens every man." St. John goes on to say that "to all who received him, who believed in his name, [the Word] gave power to become children of God" (John 1:12). The Word of God has throughout human history performed a proper saving action. Exegetes further explain that this enlightening, saving action of the Word of God, prior to the incarnation, continues thereafter, as the Word's specific action, even though with the mystery of the Incarnation something new takes place by way of the concentration of divine revelation and salvation in the Word as incarnate in Jesus Christ. The distinction between a saving action of the Word as such and the saving act of the Word as incarnate in Jesus Christ seems to find here a secure biblical foundation.

Let it be made clear once more that the concentration of the mystery of salvation through the Incarnation—which is spoken of here—does not imply a separation between two economies of the Word, as such and as incarnate, but a distinction between two inseparable aspects of the Word's saving action. Nor does the saving action of the Word as such take anything away either from the centrality of the Christ-event in the divine plan for human salvation, or from the universality of its saving operation. I have insisted everywhere that the saving action of the Word as such must always be viewed as essentially relational to the historical saving event of Jesus Christ, which represents the apex of God's personal engagement with humankind and the hermeneutical key for understanding all dealings of God with humanity. As for the universality of the saving power of the Christ-event, it is based on the transhistorical character which Jesus' humanity has acquired by passing from the state of kenosis to its risen state. Due to this real transformation of Jesus' human existence, the saving power of the Christ-event transcends all limits of time and space and is universally operative. This universality knows no restriction whatsoever, and therefore the question of an economy of the eternal Word having "a greater universal value" (DI 9) than has the economy of the Word incarnate, does not even arise. There is but one divine economy with distinct aspects, equally universal and inseparable in their saving action.

Dominus Iesus 11 insists rightly on the "unicity of the salvific economy willed by the One and Triune God" having to be "firmly believed," . . . "at the source and center of which is the mystery of the Incarnation of the Word, mediator of divine grace . . ." By quoting St. Paul, it also rightly stresses the primacy of the mystery of Christ in God's plan for humankind, in both creation and redemption. Quoting *Gaudium et Spes* 45, it shows how the Church's magisterium reasserts the salvific mediation of the Son of God made man, who died and was risen: "This salvific mediation implies also the unicity of the redemptive sacrifice of Christ, eternal high priest."

Dominus Iesus 9 had rejected the opinion of an economy of the Word different from that of the Word incarnate and having a greater universal value. I recalled above that I myself have refused what I called the "Logocentric paradigm," which results in two different economies of salvation. *Dominus Iesus* 12 rejects similarly the idea of a double economy of salvation, this time of the Holy Spirit and of the Incarnate Word, among which that of the Spirit would have a more universal breadth than that of Jesus Christ. Similarly, in my two books I have personally rejected what I have called the "Pneumatocentric paradigm" (See *Toward*, 195–98, and *Christianity*, 81–82, 182), which would result in two parallel economies of salvation, respectively of the Spirit and of Jesus Christ; I insisted that Christocentrism and pneumatology represent two inseparable aspects or elements in one unique economy of salvation.

Against the position of a double economy, of Christ and of the Spirit, unacceptable to the Catholic faith, *Dominus Iesus* 12 states that according to the New Testament the mystery of Jesus "constitutes the place of the Holy Spirit's presence and the principle of the Spirit's effusion on humanity, not only in messianic times . . . but also prior to his [the Word of God's] coming in history." Unhappily the two texts from Scripture that are supposed to establish the effusion of the Spirit on humanity having its principle in the mystery of Jesus, even prior to the Word's coming in history, have a limited proof value. First Corinthians 10: 4 affirms that the Spirit was conferred on Israel in view of the coming of the Word into the flesh, not that it was conferred on the chosen people through the humanity of Jesus Christ. That the "Spirit of Christ was present" in the prophets when in advance they testified to the sufferings to be endured by Christ (1 Pet 1:10–12) leaves entirely open the problem of knowing in what sense a preexistence of Christ prior to the Incarnation needs to be understood. Do the revealed word and the faith of the Church imply a real preexistence, even from eternity, of Jesus' humanity, or do they affirm more soberly that the mystery of the Incarnation was intentionally present eternally in God's mind and in his plan for humankind?

The texts put forward in *Dominus Iesus* 12 to sustain that Jesus Christ is the principle of the presence and of the gift of the Spirit prior to the incarnation, must be dealt with carefully. How would or could the humanity of Jesus Christ be the channel of the communication of the Holy Spirit, even before that humanity began to exist in history through the Incarnation of the Word? Surely the Creed of the Council of Constantinople, in which the presence and action of the Holy Spirit in the prophets of the Old Testament is affirmed, does not imply that the Spirit was being conferred on them by a preexistent Christ; it simply states that the Holy Spirit "has spoken through the prophets" (Denzinger 150).

Dominus Iesus 12 rightly states, with reference to Vatican II, that "the entire work of building the Church by Jesus Christ the Head, in the course of the centuries is seen as an action which he does in communion with his Spirit" (see LG 3–4).[13] And similarly, quoting *Gaudium et Spes* 22, *Dominus Iesus* notes that "the salvific action of Jesus Christ, with and through his Spirit, extends beyond the visible boundaries of the Church to all humanity." *Dominus Iesus* 12 concludes that the connection between the salvific mystery of the incarnate Word and that of the Spirit is to be understood in the sense that the Holy Spirit "actualizes the salvific efficacy of the Word made man in the life of all people," either before or after the incarnation. This must not be understood to deny any salvific action of the Spirit which would not flow from the communication made of him, at all times and in all places, by the risen Christ. For, on the one hand, the Old Testament affirms a specific saving action of the Spirit in history before the Incarnation of the Word; the Second Vatican Council itself clearly states, with reference to St. Leo the Great, that "without doubt the Holy Spirit was at work in the world before Christ was glorified" (AG 4), obviously without implying that the Spirit was already being conferred by the humanity of the incarnate Word. On the other hand, to limit the action of the Spirit after the Christ-event exclusively to his communication by the risen Christ and to reduce his function to that of actualizing the saving efficacy of the Christ-event, seems to turn the Holy Spirit into

13. *Lumen Gentium* is the Latin title of the Second Vatican Council's "Dogmatic Constitution on the Church."

a mere "vicar" of Christ, whereby damage is done to the fullness of his specific saving action, such as it flows from his personal character in the divine life. In *Christianity and the Religions* (178–82), I have drawn the attention to the real danger existing in the Latin tradition of an excessive Christocentric concentration of the mystery of salvation which would end up holding a kind of "Christomonism," such as has often been denounced by the Eastern tradition. One does not see why the saving action exercised by the Spirit before the historical event of Jesus Christ should, after the event, be so constrained as to be exclusively conveyed and communicated by the risen humanity of Jesus; not any more in fact, than, after the mystery of the incarnation, the saving action of the Word of God needs to be so constrained as to be operative only through the humanity of Jesus. Surely—and I have stressed it insistently—the Christ-event is at the center of God's historical engagement with humankind, and the key of interpretation of all his personal dealings with them throughout history, in accordance to the one and unique economy of salvation; but this unique plan of salvation is made up of distinct aspects and elements, never separable from each other because they are always reciprocally relational, yet at the same time really distinct.

Dominus Iesus 12 ends up recalling—rightly—"the truth of a single economy," as it is expressed in the recent magisterium of the Church. In so doing, it somewhat strangely attributes—as does *Redemptoris Missio* 28—to the Holy Spirit the "sowing of the seeds of the Word present in various customs and cultures, preparing them for full maturity in Christ." This does not seem to correspond to the Logos theology of the early fathers of the Church, for whom the *Logos spermatikos* referred to the Word of God himself sowing his seeds among people, thus rehearsing in advance the mystery of his own personal coming into the world. Should not the sowing of the seeds of the Word continue even today to be attributed to the Word himself? In view of the economy of salvation being one, the present magisterium states that the Holy Spirit "is not an alternative to Christ nor does he fill a sort of void which is sometimes suggested as existing between Christ and the Logos" (RM 29). It is hard to guess what theological theory may be intended here. But surely to hint at a perduring saving action of the Spirit, essentially related to the Christ-event, as has been suggested above, does not lead to considering the Spirit as an alternative to the Logos, nor to his filling a void left open by the Christ-event. In fact, the positive stress of *Redemptoris Missio* is that, "whatever the Spirit brings about in human hearts and in the history of peoples, in cultures and religions, serves as a preparation for the Gospel and can only be understood in reference to Christ . . ." (RM 29). I too have repeatedly affirmed the necessary reference to Christ, where I spoke of the inter-relatedness of the various aspects that make up the one divine economy of salvation, while at the same time avoiding what may be seen as a one-sided Christological concentration.

In conclusion, *Dominus Iesus* 12 states that "the action of the Spirit is not outside or parallel to the action of Christ. There is only one sal-vific economy of the One and Triune God, realized in the mystery of the incarnation, death and resurrection of the Son of God, actualized with the cooperation of the Holy Spirit, and extended in its salvific value to all humanity and to the entire universe . . ." A more definite Trinitarian perspective would have helped in being more precise and comprehen-sive. Surely God (the Father) was saving his chosen people before the Incarnation of the Son, according to the Bible. Divine saving activity was therefore operative before it came to be realized in Jesus Christ. That in him it is realized means that with him it has come to a climax. The Father is, in fact, the great Absent One in this section of the text of *Dominus Iesus*. Yet, according to the New Testament, even in and after the Christ-event the Father still remains the original, fundamental Savior: "In Christ it was God who was reconciling the world with himself" (2 Cor 5:19). The primary cause of salvation remains the Father: the title "Savior" is attributed primarily to him (1 Tim 2:4; 4:10); Jesus Christ bears the title conjointly, but in a derivative way. A Trinitarian perspective recalling ex-plicitly that the origin of the mystery of salvation is in the person of the Father, would have helped to show with greater precision in which sense the mystery is realized through the Christ-event and actualized in the gift of the Spirit, without necessarily excluding a personal permanent action of the Word as such and of the Spirit of God.

UNICITY AND UNIVERSALITY OF THE SALVIFIC MYSTERY OF JESUS CHRIST

This section starts off by stating that the unicity and the salvific universal-ity of the mystery of Jesus Christ is a truth to be "firmly believed as a con-stant element of the Christian faith" (DI 13). Among the New Testament texts cited to illustrate this doctrine, not all have, however, the same probative value. Acts 4: 12 does not seem to justify a general, universal statement, for, as I argued in *Christianity and the Religions* (37–38), the context of Peter's declaration is exclusively intra-Jewish and inter-Jewish. We are on better ground with 1 Tim 2:4–6 where the unicity and the salvific universality of Jesus Christ are clearly stated: "[God] desires all men to be saved and to come to the knowledge of the truth. For (*gar*) there is one God, and there is one mediator between God and men, the man Christ Jesus, who gave himself as a ransom for all . . ." Incidentally, in this text, too, salvation is understood to find its origin in God (the Father), the man Jesus Christ functioning as "Mediator" between God and men, that is as the bearer of the salvation that comes from God. After having cited abundantly from the New Testament, *Dominus Iesus* 13 confirms the doctrine of the uniqueness and universality of Christ the Savior with a quotation from *Gaudium et Spes* 10.

The conclusion is stated in *Dominus Iesus* 14: "It must therefore be firmly believed as a truth of Catholic faith that the universal salvific will of the One and Triune God is offered and accomplished once for all in the mystery of the incarnation, death, and resurrection of the Son of God." That it is "accomplished once for all" in the mystery of Jesus Christ, does not exclude, as I have insisted above, that it was already operative before him; it means that in him it has come to a climax and has been "realized." *Dominus Iesus* 14 invites theologians to explore, under the guidance of the Church's magisterium, "if and in what way the historical figures and positive elements of [other] religions may fall within the divine plan of salvation." The quotation from *Lumen Gentium* 62 does not, unhappily, seem quite relevant: that a "manifold cooperation" to the unique mediation of Jesus Christ is possible is affirmed by *Lumen Gentium* to uphold the cooperation of the Virgin Mary, invoked in the Church under the title of Mediatrix, with the one mediation of Jesus Christ. No mediation of other religions in the mystery of salvation seems to be intended in the Vatican II text.

We come closer to what is in view with the quotation from *Redemptoris Missio* 5, where, addressing himself directly to the context of the unique and universal mediation of Jesus Christ, Pope John Paul II recognizes explicitly—though with great caution—the possibility of other, derived, mediations: "Although participated forms of mediation of different kinds and degrees are not excluded, they acquire meaning and value only from Christ's own mediation, and they cannot be understood as parallel or complementary." The "participated mediations" seem to include the possibility of a mediating role of the religious traditions in the salvation of their members. *Dominus Iesus* 14, while stating that the content of such participated mediation should be explored more deeply, voices the same caution: it must remain always consistent with the principle of Christ's unique mediations. The conclusion in *Dominus Iesus* 14 is: "Hence, those solutions that propose a salvific action of God beyond the unique mediation of Christ would be contrary to Christian and Catholic faith." This conclusion is rather unexpected. The sentence cannot be understood to exclude all saving action of God operating before the Incarnation of the Son, without passing through the mediation of Jesus's humanity. Nor should it be understood as excluding all direct divine saving action outside the humanity of Christ after the Incarnation; such direct divine act of salvation does not bypass the unique mediation of Jesus Christ, it simply is part of the freedom of action of the divine power. God is not constrained in his action by the ordinary channel of his own choosing. As for what *Dominus Iesus* has to say regarding the possibility of a participated mediation of the religious traditions in the order of salvation, we shall return to it later.

Meanwhile, *Dominus Iesus* 15 proclaims the unicity, universality, and absoluteness of the salvific event of Jesus Christ. With insistence and emphasis it repeats that "Jesus Christ has a significance and a value for the human race and its history, which are unique and singular, proper to him alone, exclusive, universal and absolute." Against those who would find such proclamation of exclusive and absolute claims redundant, improper and derogatory to other religions, the document claims that "such language is simply being faithful to revelation, since it represents a development [from] the sources of the faith themselves. From the beginning, the community of believers has recognized in Jesus a salvific value such that he alone . . . bestows revelation (cf. Matt 11: 27) and divine life (cf. John 1:12; 5:25–26; 17:2) to all humanity and to every person." It can, however, be asked whether the knowledge of the Father which only the Son can convey (cf. Matt 11: 27) is the only possible form in which divine revelation can reach to people; whether, that is, the eminent and in that sense unique knowledge of God which is conveyed by the Son incarnate excludes every other possible form of divine revelation. As for the meaning of John 1:12, I have observed earlier that, according to a reliable reading of the text, the Word can, before the incarnation, give to people who have received him the "power to become children of God." John 1:12 does not then refer to God's salvific action through Jesus Christ, the Son incarnate, who will be spoken of in verse 14 and after. The claims of unicity about Jesus Christ in the New Testament appear more subtle and sober than *Dominus Iesus* 15 would have us believe; it has not been shown convincingly that they exclude all possibility of divine revelation apart from him.

The terminology used in *Dominus Iesus* 15 is in part problematic. While some of the terms are based on the sources of the Christian faith, others can be seriously questioned. I have myself spoken of the "uniqueness" (in a singular sense) and of the "universality" (as constitutive) of the divine revelation and human salvation conferred upon humankind by the Christ-event. But I have affirmed these positively—not in an exclusive way—leaving the door open to the possibility of other divine revelation and saving action; I have moreover intentionally abstained from using the term "absolute." Not without serious theological reasons and not without some authority behind me.

"God alone is the Absolute," Pope John Paul II wrote in *Fides et Ratio* 80. It is true that the Pope had affirmed earlier, in *Redemptoris Missio* 6 (quoted in DI 15), that the "uniqueness of Christ . . . gives him an absolute and universal significance . . ." It must be noted that the use of the term "absolute" is quite novel and unusual in documents of the magisterium dealing with the revealing and saving significance of Jesus Christ and of the Christ-event. It is used neither by *Dei Verbum* nor by *Gaudium et Spes* 45, quoted here by *Dominus Iesus* 15. The term has been spread in recent times. It must, however, be kept in mind that God—not Jesus Christ in his humanity—is the ultimate, original source of revelation and salvation. As the ultimate, original source, God is the absolute Revealer and Savior, while the Son incarnate in his human existence is for us the bearer, the conveyer of the divine revelation and salvation. What is absolute is by definition necessary, while the created is by nature contingent. While, then, God is the absolute Revealer and Savior, the created humanity of Jesus, the Son incarnate, is not. And while the use of the term "absolute" is quite proper in relation to God, it seems less appropriate when applied to Jesus Christ in his humanity. The mystery of the Incarnation of the Son of God, as we know, was not necessary for the salvation of human-kind—*pace* St. Anselm; it was an entirely free choice on the part of God. This is so true that for centuries theology has asked why the Incarnation of the Son of God took place in history: *Cur Dens Homo?* ("Why Did

God Become Man?") or better, *Cur Verbum Caro?* ("Why Did the Word Become Flesh?")—a question that even today has not received a fully satisfactory answer. The question, however, reminds us that the humanity of Jesus is contingent, not necessary; freely created by God, it is not absolute, even while it is assumed in the unity of the person of the Son of God for the salvation of humankind. As St. Paul makes clear: "In Christ it was God who was reconciling the world with himself" (2 Cor 5:19).

UNICITY AND UNITY OF THE CHURCH

Under this heading I offer some comments on the first two paragraphs of *Dominus Iesus* 16, which treat directly the union of the Church with Jesus Christ in the mystery of salvation. This topic will return under the section entitled "The Church and the Other Religions in Relation to Salvation," but it will be only mentioned there rapidly to support the affirmation according to which the Church is the "universal sacrament of salvation" (DI 20). It is therefore necessary to comment here on what *Dominus Iesus* 16 has to say about the union of the Church with Jesus Christ.

The reason why I limit myself to this topic is that the rest of the section (DI 16–17) is not directly relevant to my own concerns, or even, it may be added, to what is the main theme of the document itself. The main theme of *Dominus Iesus* is the unicity of Jesus Christ and the Church for salvation in the context of other religions; that is, generally speaking, the document is primarily concerned with the relationship which exists between Christ, the Church and the religions. However, the main part of the present section of *Dominus Iesus* treats directly the problem of Christian ecumenism, that is of the relations between the Church instituted by Jesus Christ and the various Christian Churches as they exist today, as well as of the mutual relations between these Churches themselves. In my own work, I have been concerned with asking what relation may exist between the mystery of salvation in Jesus Christ, the Church instituted by him, and the many world religions as we know them in today's world. I was not asking—except for some passing reference—where, that is, in *which* Church existing today, the one Church instituted by Jesus Christ may be found, and to what extent it may—or may not—also be present in another Christian Church or community. Dealing as I was with a Christian theology of religions, not with the problem of Christian ecumenism, I was satisfied with taking the Church as one reality and asking what precise role the Church providentially exercises in conveying salvation in Jesus Christ to people not belonging to her as members, and what saving function the other religious traditions might have in conveying the same salvation to their own members. *Dominus Iesus* deals with these questions in a later section, and I will return to them then.

The problem of Christian ecumenism to which the present section of *Dominus Iesus* is largely devoted, no matter how important it may be in itself, will not be my concern here. Commentators on *Dominus Iesus* have in fact been quick to ask why the problem of Christian ecumenism has been introduced into a document whose primary concern and purpose was different. And they did not fail to observe that this aspect of the document has met with sharp criticism on the ecumenical scene because of its restrictive interpretation of the ecumenical ecclesiology of Vatican II and its lack of ecumenical sensitivity.

In the first two paragraphs of *Dominus Iesus* 16, on the union of the Church with Jesus Christ, the document states that "the fullness of Christ's salvific mystery belongs also to the Church, inseparably united to her Lord." This affirmation is based on the Pauline doctrine of the Church as the Body of Christ. The text insists that, "just as the head and the members of a living body, though not identical, are inseparable, so too Christ and the Church can neither be confused nor separated, and constitute a single 'whole Christ.'" Therefore, "in connection with the unicity and universality of the salvific mediation of Jesus Christ, the unicity of the Church founded by him must be firmly believed as a truth of Catholic faith." In other words Jesus Christ instituted but one Church to be the "universal sacrament of salvation." To this universal function of the Church we must return later.

Before passing on, it should, however, be noted that *Dominus Iesus* here abstracts entirely from an important question that has to do with the "fullness of Christ's salvific mystery belonging also to the Church." That is the question of the necessity or not, of belonging to the Church in order to share in the salvation in Jesus Christ. The notorious axiom according to which "Outside the Church there is no salvation" (*extra ecclesiam nulla salus*),which for centuries was understood in a rigid and exclusive manner by the official doctrine of the Church, cannot simply be silently passed over. To establish the unicity of the Church instituted by Jesus Christ, *Dominus Iesus* 16 appeals in note to Pope Boniface VIII's Bull issued in the year 1302, *Unam Sanctam* (Denzinger nn. 870–872).

It does not mention that this text explicitly states, as being part of the doctrine of faith, that "outside [the one, holy, Catholic and apostolic Church] there is neither salvation nor remission of sins" (Denzinger 870). Mercifully, the Bull of Boniface VIII, as historical criticism has shown, needs to be handled carefully as to its dogmatic value, for more than one reason. While it may be understood to state the doctrine of faith on the unicity of the Church instituted by Jesus Christ, its rigid and exclusivist stand on the necessity of belonging to the Church for salvation, though later repeated by the Council of Florence ([which took place in the years 1431–1445] Denzinger 1351), has since been officially revoked by later Church Magisterium. Witness to this is the Letter of the Holy Office to the Archbishop of Boston under Pope Pius XII (Denzinger 3866–72). This document, while continuing to uphold the axiom as a "dogma" of the Church, explains that explicit belonging (*reapse*) to the Church as members is not required for salvation; belonging to it by implicit desire (*voto et desiderio*) suffices. The need and meaning of such implicit desire will be discussed below.

Meanwhile, let it be noted that it would have been in order for *Dominus Iesus* in this section to take its distance from an axiom that, in its rigid form, has for centuries been detrimental to the faith itself and derogatory to the religious life of people not belonging to the Church and to the religious traditions to which they belonged. In a later section, *Dominus Iesus* 21 makes a quick allusion (in footnote 82), to the axiom. Quoting it in the wording of the Lateran Council IV (year 1215, cf. Denzinger 802), *Dominus Iesus* suggests that the axiom should be interpreted as affirming that, even in the case of people not belonging to the Church as members, the grace which comes to them from Christ "has a relationship with the Church" (DI 21). To the question of this relationship I shall turn later. Meanwhile, let it suffice to note the determination of *Dominus Iesus* to retain, even if under a different form, an axiom that, in the mind of many theologians today, would better be put to rest. The International Theological Commission,[14] in its document "Christianity and the World Religions" (§ 67), shows the same propensity to retain the traditional axiom—by sheer coincidence, we may ask? It goes so far as to claim, against the evidence, that in *Lumen Gentium* 14 the Council

14. The International Theological Commission (ITC) was created on 11 April 1969 by Pope Paul VI to advise the Holy See (in particular, the Congregation for the Doctrine of the Faith) on "doctrinal questions of major importance."

Vatican II has made the axiom its own, and goes on to propose a rather far-fetched interpretation of the axiom, which, it believes, would do away with its rigid, exclusivist edge: the axiom would address only Catholics, for whom it would have a parenetic value. Against such unconvincing niceties belied by historical evidence, the safer course is simply to abandon the infamous axiom, while regretting that it remained in place for centuries in the Church's official doctrine.

THE REIGN OF GOD AND THE CHURCH

It will be noted that for this section I take the liberty of changing the order of terms in the heading of *Dominus Iesus.* The point is not without importance. The heading as it is given in *Dominus Iesus,* "The Church: Kingdom of God and Kingdom of Christ," suggests that the Reign of God is to be understood in relation to the Church which provides its foundation and *raison-d'être.* It could even hint, against the will of *Dominus Iesus,* that the Church is simply identified with the Kingdom of God and of Christ. The truth is, on the contrary, that the Church finds its *raison-d'être* in the Reign of God and must be understood in relation to it: the Church is *for* the Kingdom, at its service, not the Kingdom for the Church. Even a cursory reading of the Gospels makes it abundantly clear that the Reign of God, not the Church is the decisive point of reference, the paramount concern in the mind of Jesus himself. The mission of Jesus consisted in announcing the "good news" (*euaggelion*)of the Kingdom of God (Mark 1:15); that of the Church after him will be to announce the same "Gospel" (Mark 16:15). As for salvation, in Jesus' mind it consists in entering into the Reign of God through an act of faith in the God of life and an act of love. For Jesus, in fact, belonging to an ethnic or religious group—be it the Church herself—is irrelevant for entry into the Kingdom; conversion of the heart is what matters. The Church's relation to the Reign of God must then be envisaged in this perspective.

The text of *Dominus Iesus,* it must be said, is ambiguous. On the one hand, the Church is said to be—after *Lumen Gentium* 5 and 3—"the seed and the beginning of the Kingdom" and "the Kingdom of Christ already present in history," On the other hand, "she is called to announce and to establish the Kingdom." But has not the Kingdom which she is called to announce been "established" not by the Church herself, but by God in Jesus Christ? The statements quoted from *Lumen Gentium* seem to imply—wrongly—that, inasmuch as the Kingdom is already present and operative in history, it is identical with the Church, and that it belongs to her to "establish" it; the growth of the Kingdom towards its eschatological fullness is then seen as the growth of the Church herself towards her fullness.

Dominus Iesus 18 admits that there is some fluidity in the meaning of the expressions Kingdom of heaven, Kingdom of God and Kingdom of Christ in Sacred Scripture and the Fathers of the Church, as well as in the documents of the magisterium; and, therefore, that there can be various interpretations of the terms. The main concern of *Dominus Iesus* 18 is to stress the "intimate connection between Christ, the Kingdom, and the Church," and the fact that, "while remaining distinct from Christ and the Kingdom, the Church is indissolubly united to both." To this end, *Dominus Iesus* 18 quotes an important extract from *Redemptoris Missio* 18. The context of the quotation is well known. Pope John Paul II addresses himself here to a certain tendency to propose a "horizontal" view of the Kingdom of God, reduced to "a purely human or ideological goal," whereby the Kingdom would lose its essential relationship to Jesus Christ and to the Church. In this context, the Pope reminds us that we may never overlook the fact that Jesus Christ is not merely the prophet of the Reign of God but that it is in him that God has established his Kingdom on earth. Similarly, the Church has an irreplaceable role to play for the spread and growth of the Kingdom in history. The stress in *Dominus Iesus* is, therefore, that one may never separate the Kingdom from Christ and the Church: "while remaining distinct from Christ and the Kingdom, the Church is indissolubly united to both." No separation, then, though no identification either; but a close union between the Church, Jesus Christ and the Kingdom of God, notwithstanding the distinction that endures between them.

The aim of *Dominus Iesus* is clearly to insist on this "intimate connection" on which the inalienable function of the Church with regard to the Kingdom of God will have to be based. This would explain why *Dominus Iesus* abstains from quoting the important passage of *Redemptoris Missio* 20 where the Pope affirms in unmistakable terms the equally important distinction between the Kingdom of God present in history and the Church. The Kingdom of God is a broader reality than the Church, to which the members of the other religious traditions also have access. It is the presence in the world of the universal mystery of salvation in Jesus

Christ. Against a longstanding theological tradition which simply identified the Kingdom of God on earth with the Church, the Pope declares: "It is true that the inchoate [historical] reality of the Kingdom can also be found beyond the confines of the Church among peoples everywhere, to the extent that they live 'Gospel values' and are open to the working of the Spirit who breathes when and where he wills (cf. Jn 3:8)" (RM 20). There, however, follows an important caution: "But it must immediately be added that this temporal dimension of the Kingdom remains incomplete unless it is related to the Kingdom of Christ present in the Church and straining towards eschatological fullness." Which goes to say that, although present everywhere and potentially operative as a universal reality, the Kingdom is nevertheless present in a privileged manner in the Church, and in any case keeps tending towards its eschatological fullness. One would have wished *Dominus Iesus* to quote this text of Pope John Paul II, which, besides stating that the "others" too belong to the Kingdom of God, opens the way for a broader view of the Church's function in relation to the Kingdom of God: Her mission "to proclaim . . . [it] among all peoples" is not identical to the spreading on earth of the Church herself.

This is not to say that *Dominus Iesus* overlooks altogether the distinction which exists between the Reign of God present and operative in history and the Church on earth. *Dominus Iesus* 19 reads: "To state the inseparable relationship between the [Church[15]] and the Kingdom is not to overlook the fact that the Kingdom of God—even if considered in its historical phase—is not identified with the Church in her visible and social reality." One does not see why the admission of a distinction between Church and Kingdom is tempered here by the consideration of the Church's "visible and social reality." To return to the distinction between two Churches, one visible and one invisible, one spiritual and one institutional, would go counter to the ecclesiology of *Lumen Gentium* 8 speaking of two distinct aspects of one ecclesial reality. The universal reality of the Reign of God in history is simply broader than the reality of the Church, under whatever aspect. *Dominus Iesus* 19 concedes somewhat

---

15. Following Dupuis, I have checked and corrected here the official English translation of *Dominus Iesus*, which mistakenly says "Christ" instead of "Church" in this quotation. The relevant portion of the official text in Latin reads: *Affirmatio autem conexionis nunquam separabilis Ecclesiam inter et Regnum minime significat ut praetereatur Regnum Dei—etsi in momento suo historico ipsum consideretur—non identificari cum Ecclesia in eius realitate visibili ac sociali* (DI 19). I have underlined *Ecclesiam* for emphasis.

reluctantly that the action of Christ and the Spirit outside the Church's visible boundaries "must not be excluded." Pope John Paul II seems to be more generous when he affirms that "the Kingdom is the concern of everyone: individuals, society, and the world. Working for the Kingdom means acknowledging and promoting God's activity, which is present in human history and transforms it" (RM 18). If all people—independently of their religious allegiance—are called to share in the task of promoting God's activity, it surely is an understatement to admit that the action of Christ and the Spirit outside the Church "must not be excluded." What needs to be affirmed is that such action is everywhere present and operative.

In concluding this section, let us observe that *Dominus Iesus* 19 affirms that, in considering the relationship between the Kingdom of God, the Kingdom of Christ, and the Church, "it is necessary to avoid one-sided accentuations." As a model of such one-sided accentuations the text refers to "conceptions which deliberately emphasize the Kingdom and which describe themselves as 'Kingdom-centered.'" *Dominus Iesus* 19 refers to the description of such Kingdom-centered conceptions made in *Redemptoris Missio* 17, which the Pope rightly rejects on more than one count—their horizontal view of the Kingdom, their reductionism with regard to the mystery of Jesus Christ, and their forgetfulness of the role of the Church in relation to the Kingdom (RM 17–18). "These theses," *Dominus Iesus* 19 concludes, "are contrary to Catholic faith because they deny the unicity of the relationship which Christ and the Church have with the Kingdom of God." While this is certainly true where the Kingdom-centered thesis described in *Redemptoris Missio* is concerned, it would be wrong to conclude that any Regnocentric or Kingdom-centered perspective on the Church's mission necessarily implies "one-sided accentuations" and needs therefore to be rejected as contrary to the faith. It must on the contrary be affirmed that a theologically well-founded and correctly argued regnocentric perspective is capable of opening new and broader horizons for the mission of the Church in relation to the Kingdom of God universally present in the world; such broader horizons must be encouraged and deserve to be further explored.

THE CHURCH AND THE OTHER RELIGIONS
IN RELATION TO SALVATION

This section of *Dominus Iesus* 20 starts out recalling the doctrine of faith ("firmly to be believed") that the Church, in which people enter through baptism, is "necessary for salvation," as this doctrine is expressed in *Lumen Gentium* 14. Anticipating a difficulty arising from the explicit mention of baptism as the "door" through which people must enter the Church (cf. Mark 16:16; John 3:5), the text adds immediately: "This doctrine must not be set against the universal salvific will of God" (cf. 1 Tim 2:4). As John Paul II puts it: "It is necessary to keep these two truths together, namely, the real possibility of salvation in Christ for all mankind and the necessity of the Church for this salvation" (RM 9). This means that the reception of the sacrament of baptism by individual persons cannot be placed on the same level of necessity as is attributed to the Church in general for the salvation of humankind. Baptism, which does not occur in the case of the vast majority of people, is not absolutely required by Mark 16: 16, which reads, "he who does not believe will be condemned." The necessity of the Church for the salvation of the world will have to be carefully determined; it is a collective necessity flowing from the function in the order of salvation which the Church derives from her union with Christ.

Dominus Iesus 20 goes on to explain, in the light of St. Cyprian,who is referred to in note 80, that the Church is "universal sacrament of salvation" (*Lumen Gentium* 48) because, "united always in a mysterious way to the Savior Jesus Christ, her Head, and subordinated to him, she has, in God's plan, an indispensable relationship with the salvation of every human being." One should not overlook the fact that, in his way of proclaiming the doctrine of an "indispensable relationship (of the Church) with the salvation of every human being," St. Cyprian was unwittingly laying the foundation for the rigid understanding of the axiom "outside the Church no salvation" (cf. *Toward*, 86–90). A more sober view of the "indispensable relationship" is required. *Dominus Iesus* 20 is right in stating clearly the "subordinate" character of the role of the Church for the salvation of all in relation to Christ. Unhappily, the expressions used for expressing its role positively remain notably vague and imprecise. The Church, we are told, has "in God's plan, an indispensable relationship with the salvation of every human being." What such a relationship consists of is not explained.

Quoting *Redemptoris Missio* 10, *Dominus Iesus* 21 adds that, for those who are not formally and visibly members of the Church, "salvation in Christ is accessible by virtue of a grace which, while having a mysterious relationship to the Church, does not make them formally part of the Church, but enlightens them in a way which is accommodated to their spiritual and material situation." The text of the Pope itself recognizes frankly the "mysterious" character of the relationship of the grace of the "others" to the Church, and makes no attempt to be more specific. On the other hand, the same text is equally vague with regard to the "accommodation" of the salvation of the "others" to their spiritual situation. Clearly, more needs to be said on the role which their "religious situation" may play in the mystery of their salvation. We need to return to this later.

Dominus Iesus 21 is satisfied to conclude that grace come to them from Christ and "has a relationship with the Church." In the same vein, *Redemptoris Missio* 18 spoke of a "unique and special relationship" between the Church and the Reign of God, which, "while not excluding the action of Christ and the Spirit outside the Church's visible boundaries, confers upon her a specific and necessary role; hence the Church's special connection with the Kingdom of God and of Christ." One cannot but be struck by the vagueness of the expressions used by the Church's magisterium to express the necessary relationship of all grace with the Church. This lack of precision and apparent inability to be more specific on the matter raises questions on which more needs to be said. Can the magisterium be satisfied to affirm a "mysterious relationship," a "unique and special relationship," and again an "indispensable relationship," if, as is apparent, it is unable to specify the nature of such a relationship?

With respect to the way in which the grace of Christ with its "mysterious relationship" to the Church, reaches individuals who are not her members, *Dominus Iesus* 21 is satisfied to repeat the admission of ignorance professed by the Council Vatican II: this happens "in ways known to God" (AG 7; cf. GS 22). Theologians are "encouraged" to seek to understand the question more fully, since their work "is certainly useful for understanding better God's salvific plan and the ways in which it is accomplished." No mention is being made of any successful attempt at a theological explanation. The concern of *Dominus Iesus* 21 is, instead, to point to theological theories that contradict the doctrine of the faith: "It is clear that it would be contrary to the faith to consider the Church as 'one way' of salvation alongside those constituted by the other religions, seen as complementary to the Church or substantially equivalent to her, even if these are said to be converging with the Church toward the eschatological kingdom of God." No name of any Catholic theologian holding this or a similar position is given—as usual. As a matter of fact, the statement covers different possible positions which ought to have been carefully distinguished in the document. It is one thing to admit that the other religious traditions—or at least some of their constitutive elements—can serve as "ways" or "channels" of salvation for their members; it is another thing to affirm that these ways are "substantially equivalent" to the way represented by the Church.

As for a possible "complementarity" between the Church and the other religious traditions as ways of salvation, it can also be understood in different manners, not all of which need to be viewed a priori as contradicting the Christian faith. And if revelation speaks of the "convergence" of all things in Christ in the *eschaton*, such an eschatological convergence between the Church and the religious traditions need not be excluded a priori, unless we should presuppose as a matter of faith that the other religious traditions are bound to disappear in the course of time in a world destined by God to become explicitly and exclusively Christian. The historical evidence seems to belie such a supposition. Nor does divine revelation and the role which it attributes to the Church suppose it.

Dominus Iesus 21 could not avoid saying something with regard to the role the other religious traditions might have in the order of grace and of salvation. Let us observe immediately that the document takes all the religions of the world *en bloc*—with the exception of Christianity—without making any distinction, not even, for instance, between the three Abrahamic religions and those not based in biblical revelation. We have had to observe earlier that, while Christianity possesses divine, theological faith, according to *Dominus Iesus*, the members of all other religions, Judaism and Islam included, would seem to possess only "religious beliefs," amounting to merely human opinions. This, we noted, is perhaps the most derogatory statement made by *Dominus Iesus* against other religions. It is especially offensive where Judaism and Islam are concerned, both of which share with Christianity divine, theological faith in the God of Abraham, of Isaac, and of Jacob—who, it must be added, is in fact none other than the God and Father of our Lord Jesus Christ.

Disregarding all distinctions between religions outside Christianity, *Dominus Iesus* 21 is satisfied to state that "certainly the various religious traditions contain and offer religious elements which come from God." These are seen as the "seeds of the Word" (in note 85), and "are part of what the Spirit brings about in human hearts and in the history of peoples, in cultures and religions" (RM 29). I have already mentioned that the sowing of the seeds of the Word should, according to the theology of the early fathers, be left to the action of the Word himself, not of the Spirit. The document admits that "some prayers and rituals of the other religions may assume a role of preparation for the Gospel in that they are occasions or pedagogical helps in which the human heart is prompted to open to the action of God." This statement calls for some remarks.

The only role that *Dominus Iesus* is prepared to assign to those elements of the other religious traditions which "come from God," consists in their being "occasions or pedagogical helps in which the human heart is prompted to be open to the action of God." Is there no contradiction between affirming, on the one hand, that the elements concerned "come from God" and, on the other hand, that they may be "occasions" prompting the human heart to open itself to the action of God? Do those elements come from God or from the human heart? In the first case, they cannot be reduced to serve as mere occasions leading to him. In the second, they cannot suffice to do so.

Nowadays some theologies of religions are prepared to attribute to them a positive role in the dispensation of divine grace. Not so *Dominus Iesus* 21, which continues: "One cannot attribute to these [elements], however, a divine origin or an *ex opere operato*[16] salvific efficacy, which is proper to the Christian sacraments." More observations are called for. The claim that one cannot attribute "divine origin" to the elements of the religious traditions concerned can bluntly be denied (witness DI 21 itself,

---

16. *Ex opere operato* (literally, "by the work [i.e., act or rite] having been performed") is used in Canon 8 of the "Canons on the Sacraments in General" at the Council of Trent (which was held in the years 1545–1563). For the Tridentine text, see Denzinger and Schönmetzer, eds., *Enchiridion Symbolorum*, 851 or Tanner, ed., *Decrees* 2:685. The phrase refers to the Council's teaching at Trent that one is mistaken to teach that "the sacrament confers grace not by the performance of the sacramental action itself [*ex opere operato*] but that faith in the divine promise by itself is sufficient for obtaining the grace . . ." The Tridentine canon is directed against the teaching of Martin Luther. Dupuis is discussing whether that phrase is appropriately used in denoting the efficacy of Christianity or another religion.

which has just affirmed that these elements "come from God"!) And who would deny that the "seeds of the Word" have a divine origin? Whether an *ex opere operato* salvific efficacy, such as is attributed to the Christian sacraments, can be affirmed where the same elements of the other religious traditions are concerned, is quite another matter. I have no knowledge of any Catholic theologian who has held such an opinion. Even so, rigid oppositions which do not correspond to the reality need to be avoided.

The *ex opere operato* efficacy attributed by the Catholic dogma to the Christian sacraments must not be understood as some sort of magic efficacy; this would make a parody of faith in the Christian sacraments. What faith professes is that in the celebration of the sacraments instituted by, or founded on, Jesus Christ, members of the Christian community come into contact, in a sacramental manner—that is through the signs— with the divine mystery of salvation realized in him. Whether these signs efficaciously produce grace in the celebrating members depends, however, in the last resort, on the subjective dispositions of these. In a similar manner, the reception of divine grace among members of other religions necessarily depends on their personal dispositions, that is on their readiness to open themselves to the gratuitous gift of divine grace. Whether in Christianity or outside of it, God does not, and cannot, force on people, against their personal will, a share in his own divine life. At this level of reception of divine grace, there is no difference, then, between Christians and the "others." The difference is in the way in which divine grace is being offered in one case and the other. And, while admitting clearly that the sacramental presence of the mystery of salvation attributed to the Christian sacraments is proper to them, it can still be held that some elements of the other religious traditions may, in some way, convey to their members the gift of divine grace. The way in which they "mediate" grace differs from that of the Christian sacraments; it is not, for that reason, to be denied.

According to *Dominus Iesus* 21, elements of the other religious traditions can in no way be channels of grace for their members. In reality, they are not even "occasions" for the working of divine grace, but merely "pedagogical helps" in which the human heart is prompted to open itself to the action of grace; that is, they may help to create in the person the dispositions necessary for the reception of divine grace, but can contribute nothing to its working. We may note in passing that *Dominus Iesus* is on this point even more restrictive than was the document of the International Theological Commission, "Christianity and the World Religions." There we read the following:

> The presence of the Spirit in the religions being explicitly recognized, it is not possible to exclude that they may, as such, exercise a certain salvific function . . . It would be difficult to think that what the Holy Spirit does in the hearts of individual persons would have salvific value, while that which the same Spirit brings about in the religions and cultures would not. The recent magisterium, however, does not seem to allow for such difference. The religions can, then, within the terms specified, be a means (*mezzo*)which helps for the salvation of their adherents . . . (§§ 84 and 86).

The "recent magisterium" referred to here is, no doubt, that of Pope John Paul II. It is sad to observe that the latest document from the Church's central doctrinal authority seems to undermine what the Pope has repeatedly suggested in recent years.

Dominus Iesus 21 ends by noting, with reference to the other religious traditions: "It cannot be overlooked that other rituals, insofar as they depend on superstitions or other errors . . . constitute an obstacle to salvation." Theologians know well that not everything in the other religious traditions and in their sacred writings is from God or can be considered as conducive to salvation. But they know too that the other traditions have no monopoly of superstitions, or even of idolatry. Not everything in Christian devotions or rituals is exempt from error. In the keen discernment which needs to be made in this matter, all should beware of applying a double standard—comparing what is best in one's own tradition with what is less good in the other. This has unhappily been common practice for centuries among Christians, even on the part of Church authorities. And this is not the least reason why a new assessment of the value of other religious traditions, which in turn will generate new attitudes towards their members, is needed today.

Previous paragraphs spoke of a "mysterious relationship" of all grace to the Church. *Dominus Iesus* 22 affirms plainly that "God has willed that the Church founded by [Christ] be the instrument for the salvation of all humanity." The reference made to Acts 17:30–31 to show this, is not very convincing, its context being that of the judgment. Nor do the texts referred to in the notes (LG and RM 11) use the term "instrument." I have noted earlier the vagueness of the expressions used by the recent magisterium to express the "mysterious relationship" of every grace to the Church, in the case of persons not belonging to her as members. The term "instrument," on the contrary, is quite clear. But it raises a question which I have discussed both in *Toward* (pp. 347–56) and in *Christianity* (pp. 182–90). The issue is whether it is possible to speak of a true mediation—in the theological sense—of the Church in the order of grace for non-members. The mediation of the Church towards her members expresses itself principally in the proclamation of the Word of God and the sacramental economy, "the table of the word and of the bread"—two elements which do not reach out to people outside the Church—to which can be added the sharing of Church members in the life of the community. As for the intercession on the part of the Church and her members for the salvation of the "others" and their good works done on their behalf, these do not seem to represent a true form of mediation in the theological sense. In Thomistic terms, the causality at work in intercession is of the moral and final order. It does not belong to the order of instrumental efficient causality. It is permitted, therefore, to think that the "universal instrumentality" of the Church in the order of salvation, of which *Lumen Gentium* 9 and *Redemptoris Missio* 9 speak, remains, in the case of people not belonging to her as members, in store as a hope for the future. "Oriented" as those people are, according to *Lumen Gentium* 16, toward the mystery of the Church, they are also prospective beneficiaries of her mediating action. The Church is "destined" by God to exercise a universal instrumentality of grace, as she is "called to announce . . . the Kingdom" of God (DI 18). The working out of her universal instrumentality and mediation of grace must be left to God's providence.

The truth of faith that the Church is willed by God as universal instrument of salvation—as *Dominus Iesus* 22 states—does not lessen the Church's respect for the other religions, but it rules out the "religious relativism" according to which "one religion is as good as another." This is plain truth; and while one may affirm that a certain mediation of grace is operative also in the other religious traditions, such mediation may not be placed on a level of equality with that which is at work in the Church, to whom, as Pope John Paul II says, Jesus Christ has entrusted "the fullness of the benefits and means of salvation" (RM 18). *Dominus Iesus* 22 concludes from this that, objectively speaking, the members of other religions, even though they can receive divine grace, "are in a gravely deficient situation" in comparison with the members of the Church. While fully appreciating the special benefits that Church membership entails in the order of salvation, Christians should be wary of underestimating and devaluating the endowments for salvation which the members of other religions may derive from their own traditions. Such benefits can only be rightly evaluated from the inside; and, if it is true, as Pope John Paul II has insisted, that the Holy Spirit has been and is universally at work not only in people, but in cultures and religions, there should be no surprise when we discover in the religious traditions traces of his action.

The "gravely deficient situation" of the "others," affirmed by *Dominus Iesus* 22, cannot but sound offensive to them, insofar as they too possess an authentic religious faith in the practice of which they find their way to God and discover the meaning of human life. Comparisons can be odious and Christians should not indulge in them readily. The International Theological Commission—unhappily—does indulge in a shaky comparison where, after stating that "the religions can . . . be a means (*mezzo*) which helps for the salvation of their adherents," it adds: "but they cannot be equivalent (*equiparare*) to the function which the Church exercises for the salvation of Christians and of those who are not" (ITC, "Christianity and the World Religions," § 86). Let us admit that, while we know what the Church is doing for the salvation of her members, we are in the dark as to what she does for the salvation of others. We are better informed, if we wish to be, about what their own religious traditions are able to do for them. The objectively "gravely deficient situation" of the "others," of which *Dominus Iesus* 22 speaks, is affirmed from a Christian viewpoint, apparently in ignorance of, and disregard for, what the other traditions can offer to their members.

There remains the subjective aspect of the question. *Dominus Iesus* seems to think that salvation primarily consists in the knowledge of truth: "salvation is found in the truth," the last paragraph of *Dominus Iesus* 22 says. In fact, the document, throughout, speaks almost exclusively of truth, of faith and of belief. One of the great absences in the whole document is love, *agape*. Yet, according to Jesus and the New Testament, what matters supremely is to love: "God is love, and he who abides in love abides in God and God abides in him" (1 John 4:16). The love of God and the love of others are inseparable: "He who does not love his brother whom he has seen, cannot love God whom he has not seen" (1 John 4:20). And it is on the love that they have shown or not shown to others that people will be judged on the last day (Matt 25:31–46).

What matters primarily for salvation, then, is not how close people have come to the fullness of truth, nor whether they have benefited from the means of salvation entrusted by Jesus to the Church, but how much they have loved. Love, as we know, is notoriously present among the poor; and this is one reason why Jesus told the poor: "Blessed are you poor, for yours is the Kingdom of God" (Luke 6:20). Speaking to his disciples he added: "Truly, I say to you, it will be hard for a rich man to enter the Kingdom of heaven. Again I tell you: it is easier for a camel to go through the eye of a needle than for a rich man to enter the Kingdom of God" (Matt 19:23–24). Jesus did not say: "How hard it will be for *non-Christians* to be saved!" *Dominus Iesus* 22 notes rightly that Christians may "fail to respond in thought, word and deed to the grace" of Christ; but it has begun by one-sidedly stressing the "gravely deficient situation" in which people who are not members of the Church find themselves objectively with regard to salvation. In the last resort, conditions required for reaching salvation are equal for all, even while in Jesus Christ people may "find the fullness of their religious life" (NA 2).

The last paragraph of *Dominus Iesus* 22 is devoted to interreligious dialogue. The text states, following many documents from the recent teaching authority, that dialogue is part of the Church's evangelizing mission, though it goes on to insist that the proclamation of the Gospel obtains the priority in that mission. And while "those who obey the promptings of the Spirit of truth are already on the way to salvation," "the Church, to whom this truth has been entrusted, must go out to meet their desire, so as to bring them to the truth." The supposition is that the Church "possesses" the fullness of truth, that she has a monopoly over it; her mission is to bring the others to it. There is no need here to ask again how the "fullness" of revelation in Jesus Christ needs to be understood cautiously. This has been discussed earlier. But there is need to note here the other half of the supposition, that is the seeming presumption of *Dominus Iesus* that the other religious traditions apparently have no truth to offer to their members. By contrast, the Second Vatican Council spoke repeatedly of the "elements of truth and grace" contained in the other religious traditions (cf. AG 9), and of the "seeds of the Word" enshrined in them (AG 11, 15). No wonder if, with its negative presupposition, *Dominus Iesus* 22 sees interreligious dialogue as "just one of the actions" of the Church. It says, too, that the Church must be "primarily committed to proclaiming to all people the truth definitively revealed by the Lord and to announcing the necessity of conversion to Jesus Christ and of adherence to the Church through baptism and the other sacraments in order to participate fully in communion with God, the Father, the Son and the Holy Spirit."

These are loaded terms—that is to say, "truth definitively revealed" and "necessity of adherence to the Church through baptism." Interreligious dialogue is, in sum, of little account in this document, and one wonders what can be found in it that may bring about between Christians and the "others" a true exchange and mutual enrichment, if we suppose that the Church has an exclusive monopoly of divine truth. The equality between the partners which interreligious dialogue presupposes is reduced in the text to "the equal personal dignity" of the parties involved; there is no room for comparing the "doctrinal content" of the various traditions, much less the position of Jesus Christ in relation to the founders of the other religions. Interreligious dialogue, as understood by *Dominus Iesus*, does not tolerate any comparison of doctrines. Rather the text is based on the Christian certitude of "possessing the whole truth" in comparison with a void of divine truth in the other traditions. It is not a "dialogue" but a "monologue." The document of the Secretariat for non-Christians, entitled "Dialogue and Mission" (1984),[17] expressed another view of interreligious dialogue, which it described as follows: "There is the dialogue in which Christians meet the followers of other religious traditions in order to walk together towards truth and to work together in projects of common concern" (§ 13, Gioia ed., pp. 569–70). Here the concern is not to point one-sidedly to the inequality between the partners but to the possibility of building up communion in the search for truth and in combined action for the sake of people, differences in religious allegiance notwithstanding. In *Dominus Iesus*, on the contrary, the "others" are expected to listen and to receive; they have nothing to contribute, to share or to give. It ends with the remark: "Thus, the certainty of the universal salvific will of God does not diminish, but rather increases the duty and urgency of the proclamation of salvation and of conversion to the Lord Jesus Christ" (DI 22).

The general conclusion of the document (DI 23) has a long quotation from *Dignitatis Humanae*[18]—an otherwise very important document

---

17. The text is available in Gioia, ed., *Interreligious Dialogue: The Official Teaching of the Catholic Church (1963–1995)*, 566–79.

18. *Dignitatis Humanae* is the Latin title for the Second Vatican Council's 1965 "Declaration on Religious Liberty."

of the Council. Speaking of Christianity as the way in which, by serving God, people "can be saved and reach happiness in Christ," the conciliar declaration says: "We believe that this one true religion continues to exist (*subsistere*) in the Catholic and Apostolic Church to which the Lord Jesus entrusted the task of spreading it among all people" (DH 1).[19] This formulation is doubly unfortunate. From the ecumenical viewpoint, to begin with, for it repeats the *subsistit in* of *Lumen Gentium* 8, on the presence of the Church instituted by Christ in the Catholic Church, which has received in *Dominus Iesus* 16 a restrictive interpretation, presumably intended here also. From the point of view of the theology of religions the passage is also unfortunate, for it seems to go back to the apologetic approach of past times (the tract *de vera religione* ["on true religion"] of former fundamental theology), and to disregard the positive affirmations of the Council on the presence of elements of divine truth and grace in the other religious traditions (cf. AG 9). The "fullness" of revelation in Jesus Christ, correctly understood, should not lead to overlooking, and seemingly denying, the presence of divine truth elsewhere. Surely a more sensitive formulation could have been found which, while expressing what is proper to Christianity, would have acknowledged the presence of divine gifts outside it.

The last statement of the document is borrowed from Pope John Paul II's encyclical *Fides et Ratio*. It affirms that "the truth, which is Christ, imposes itself as an all-embracing authority" (Fr. 92). The Pope is speaking from the viewpoint of the Christian believer and does not hide the problems and challenges which are met today by the "all-embracing authority" of the Gospel. Much less should Christians and the Church's official documents hide the challenges which the Gospel encounters when it comes into contact with the reality of other religious traditions. What to

19. Curiously Dupuis follows here the Flannery translation of the documents of Vatican II, which translates *subsistere* as "exists," although the tortured history of LG 8, whence comes DV 1's use of the word (see following note) makes me think "subsists" is better precisely since it brings the careful reader closer to those debates. The traditional, pre-Vatican II Roman viewpoint simply taught that the Church willed by Christ *is* the Catholic Church. Recent commentators have maintained that *subsistit in* really means *est*; cf. Becker, "Church and Vatican II's 'Subsistit in' Terminology." In "*Quaestio Disputata*: A Response to Karl Becker, SJ, on the Meaning of Subsistit In," Francis A. Sullivan, SJ, makes the case that *est* is the wrong equivalent for the purposely polyvalent *subsistit in*. Dupuis believed strongly that the tendency to return to the former usage exemplified a form of essentialism and objectivism that had had dire consequences in the past and that should be resisted today.

the Christian believer seems obvious truth does not appear as such to the sincere believer of another religion. We should all be wary of presuming that the truth of the Gospel is so plain that it ought to be accepted at first sight by every sincere person. Concrete reality belies such a persuasion which, in the past, has led to Christian intolerance. An open dialogue with the "others" in which Christians are prepared to listen and to receive would soon reveal the fallacy of such presumption. Practiced with sincerity, such dialogue would dispel all propensity to self-sufficiency and exclusivism.

IN CONCLUSION

Towards the end of the official meeting at the CDF on September 4, 2000. which I mentioned above, Cardinal Ratzinger asked me: "Would you be willing to declare that your book must be understood in the light of our Declaration *Dominus Iesus*?"—of which I had received an advance copy before the encounter. My answer was: "Eminence, I am afraid you are asking too much from me." This Epilogue to this new book—which further explains and clarifies my position—will help the reader to understand the meaning of my discreet but clear answer to the Cardinal Prefect of the CDF. It is time to state summarily the main reasons why I cannot find myself in agreement with the declaration *Dominus Iesus*.

I adhere without hesitation, nonetheless, to what is contained in the Declaration when it is certainly doctrine of the faith.

I regret, on the other hand, that the Declaration also contains half-truths, in the sense that, while one aspect of the truth is one-sidedly stressed, the complementary aspect is often overlooked altogether. The positive statements of Vatican Council II on other religions have practically been pushed to the way-side. I also regret that important statements of the Council receive in the Declaration a restrictive interpretation. One clear instance is the way in which the *subsistit in* of the one Church of Jesus Christ is restricted to the Catholic Church, thus failing to distinguish various degrees or modalities of "being Church." This exclusive interpretation has caused much damage in the field of ecumenism. I also denounce the document's drawing conclusions that do not follow necessarily from the doctrine of faith. One example is where, from the fact that the person who speaks in Jesus Christ is a divine person, *Dominus Iesus* concludes that the words of Jesus possess in themselves the "definitiveness and completeness of the revelation of God's salvific ways" (DI 6).

The apparent aim of the document is to reaffirm Catholic-Christian identity in the face of erroneous interpretations that are threatening the faith. I wonder whether the best method for affirming Catholic-Christian identity consists in making it clash abruptly with other opinions by way of exclusive and absolute statements. Some ability to self-criticize would lead to a different posture, including regret for past mistakes and intransigent attitudes. I believe that an alternative or even better way for discovering and strengthening one's identity would consist in a sincere dialogue with others. The theological method put to use in *Dominus Iesus* is purely dogmatic and *a priori*. It consists in listing quotations from the New Testament—often taken out of context and thrown in by way of the proof-text method—which are followed by other quotations from documents of the Council and of the recent magisterium. The concrete reality of today's religious pluralism is distressingly absent. No effort whatever has been made to meet this reality, to understand it and sympathize with it, as an indispensable first step for an inductive method of theologizing. The result of such ignorance is that the other religious traditions are seriously undervalued.

The CDF has allowed itself in this document to be carried away by fear, which is a bad adviser, and, paradoxically, can even hide a lack of faith. Hence the trenchant tone of *Dominus Iesus* and the often abusively exclusive character of its self-assertions. In sum, compared to the signs of hope which the open and receptive attitude of the Council Vatican II had given us, and which had been confirmed by statements and symbolic gestures of two popes, this document represents a serious step backwards in the ecumenical field as well as that of interreligious dialogue, whether with Jews or Muslims, or with whatever religion of the East. Much good will on all sides will be required to repair the damage.

In concluding, I may repeat a conviction which I have expressed repeatedly, I am deeply convinced that the Church must shun any way of proposing the faith that indulges in derogatory, exclusive evaluations of "others." There is a way of defending the faith that is counterproductive, inasmuch as, instead of making it attractive, it makes it appear restrictive and narrow. I am convinced that a broader approach and a more positive attitude, provided they be theologically well-founded, will strengthen the credibility of the Christian faith and help Christians themselves discover in the Christian message new dimensions and a new depth.

Here then are the reasons why I have thought it my duty to be critical of the document of the CDF. I am aware that this matter is a serious one, especially in view of the confirmation which the document received from Pope John Paul II. My observations, however, are prompted by a desire for a "creative fidelity" to the Christian message. While I propose them for discussion, I do so in full adherence to the revealed truth, and in communion with the living tradition and doctrinal authority of the Church.

26 November 2000
Solemnity of Christ the King

3

The CDF Process and Notification
and My Perspectives on Them[1]

Jacques Dupuis, SJ

A T THE END OF the tense session at the Congregation for the Doctrine of Faith on 4 September 2000, it had become clear that the draft of the Notification submitted then for my approval would have to be dismissed. In this situation I ventured to ask why a special Notification on my book was required since everything contained in it was already being said in *Dominus Iesus* from which the draft of the Notification was copying entire paragraphs. Why did the errors rejected in *Dominus Iesus* have to be attributed explicitly and especially to my book since, as they were found in the first draft of the Notification, they had proved to be false accusations. The answer of the Secretary of the CDF was that the bishop- and Cardinal-members of the CDF were insisting on having a Notification explicitly about my book in which the theses to be rejected would be pointed out. From this it was clear that there would be a follow-up and that a new draft of the Notification would be prepared.

Yet I waited till 6 December 2000 for further news. On that day I received a letter from my Father General (without any letter of Cardinal Ratzinger attached) with a new text of the Notification. This time I was requested to sign, without any further discussion or opportunity for cor-

---

1. As used here, the word "Notification" (in Italian, *Notificazione*) is an official document issued by the Congregation for the Doctrine of the Faith about errors, problems, or deficiencies that the CDF finds in the work of theologians. If one goes to CDF's websites, one can find a number of past Notifications on the work of other theologians, most notably in regard to the work of Roger Haight and Jon Sobrino. See http://www.vatican.va/roman_curia/congregations/cfaith/doc_doc_index.htm.

rections, and to send the document back without delay. Faced with this situation I asked myself three questions: (1) If the CDF wishes to publish a Notification about my book, why do they need my signature to do so? What use do they intend to make of my signature and how would they interpret it? (2) If I were not to sign the text submitted to me, what might be the consequences? (3) If I did sign the text, what might in turn be the consequences? After consulting with my superiors, and since I was left without an alternative, I acceded to the order to sign the text in the form in which it had been submitted to my approval. But, when sending it back, I attached a letter in which I explained the meaning which I was attributing to my signature. I wrote: "I understand that the meaning of my signature is that, in the future, both in talks and in my writings, I will have to take into account the text of the Declaration *Dominus Iesus* and of the Notification." As will be seen hereafter, the CDF interpreted my signature differently.

The question will be asked: why, after I had refused to sign the text submitted to me on 4 September 2000, did I agree to sign the revised text of 6 December 2000? What was the difference between one and the other? I have explained in the Epilogue 1 [chapter 2 in this book, entitled "The Declaration *Dominus Iesus* and My Work"] the main elements of the 4 September version of the text. In fact it remained substantially the same in the new version, consisting of eight propositions of faith or of Catholic doctrine, six of which were followed by opinions to be rejected as being either contrary to the faith or to Catholic doctrine; the long explanations following each proposition had been dropped. But the most important difference between the two versions of the text was to be found elsewhere. It consisted in the fact that, while in the 4 September version the "errors" mentioned in the text were directly attributed to my book, in that of 6 December this was no longer the case. Instead the text spoke now of some "ambiguities" in the book which could induce readers into "error." It is interesting to follow the change in the accusations made by the CDF through the various steps of the case.

I will distinguish five different steps:

1. the decision by the CDF to file a "Contestation" (*contestazione*) of the book (decision taken on 10 June 1998, communicated by Cardinal Ratzinger to my Father General, Peter Hans Kovenbach, SJ, on 26 September 1998);

2. the "Doctrinal Judgment" pronounced by the CDF (30 June 1999, communicated by Cardinal Ratzinger to Father General on 27 July 1999);

3. the first draft of the Notification (approved by Pope John Paul II on 16th June 2000, and presented at the official meeting with the authorities of the CDF to which I was called on 4 September 2000);

4. the second draft of the Notification (approved by the Pope on 24 November 2000, sent to Father General in a letter dated 6 December 2000 to be signed by me, which I sent back with my signature on 16th December 2000);

5. and the definitive text of the Notification (approved by the Pope on 19 January 2001, and published in *Osservatore Romano* on 27 February 2001, accompanied by an unsigned article entitled "Articolo di commento della Notificazione della Congregazione della Dottrina della Fede a proposito del libro di J. Dupuis *Verso una teologia cristiana del pluralismo religioso*").[2] It is to this final text that my comments hereafter will refer. As for the article commenting on my book, since it bears no signature I dispense myself from taking it into account.

It is instructive to observe the difference between the accusations made in the five documents just mentioned. The official record of the *Contestazione* (10 June 1998)—as I have mentioned in the Epilogue 1 [i.e., the previous chapter]—stated, among other accusations, that: "In the work of Fr Dupuis are found *grave errors* and doctrinal ambiguities on doctrines of divine and Catholic faith, regarding revelation, soteriology, Christology and the Trinity . . ." According to the covering letter of Cardinal Ratzinger (27 July 1999), the "Doctrinal Judgment" of the CDF "makes a list of the main affirmations of the author which are considered *erroneous,* or ambiguous and unsatisfactory." This is done "in order to protect the doctrine of the Catholic faith from errors, ambiguities and dangerous interpretations." The first draft of the Notification (4 September 2000) mentioned the "presence [in the book] of *grave errors* and ambiguities which oblige the CDF to intervene ... in order that readers may not be induced into

2. English translation: "An Article Commenting on the Notification of the Congregation for the Doctrine of the Faith in regard to the Book of J. Dupuis, *Toward a Christian Theology or Religious Pluralism.*"

error or doctrinal uncertainty." The second draft of the Notification (6 December 2000)—which I agreed to sign—no longer speaks of errors found in the book but, more soberly, of "grave ambiguities" and of "ambiguous formulations or insufficient explanations" which could lead the reader into "erroneous opinions." The text published in *Osservatore Romano* (27 February 2001) speaks similarly of "notable ambiguities and difficulties on important doctrinal points, which could lead a reader to erroneous or harmful opinions." One can thus see clearly that, while the previous texts attributed doctrinal errors directly to the book, the second draft of the Notification and its official text in *Osservatore Romano* mention only that "ambiguities" are found in the text which could induce readers into error. What ambiguities are intended is not specified in any way. What relation, if any, exists between the false opinions rejected in the February 2001 document and what I myself have suggested in my book, will have to be asked hereafter. Meanwhile, the important change in the accusations made against the book—from "grievous errors" to "some ambiguities"—explains why, in the later circumstances, I thought I could sign the text proposed to me in December 2000, while explaining in writing the meaning which I was attributing to my signature.

An important change has, however, been introduced in the official text of the *Osservatore Romano* as compared to the text which I agreed to sign in December 2000. Almost one entire paragraph had been added in the "Preface," which was absent in the text submitted to my signature. That paragraph states:

> This Notification was presented to Father Jacques Dupuis and was accepted by him. By signing the text, the author committed himself to assent to the stated theses and, in his future theological activity and publications, to hold the doctrinal contents indicated in the Notification, the text of which must be included in any reprinting or further editions of his book, as well as in all translations.

The difference between the meaning of the text to which, after consulting my superiors, I had given my signature and the interpretation which the CDF attributes to it in the official text, needs little explanation, since the difference between "taking into account" and being committed to "hold the doctrinal contents" is indeed great. The procedure followed by the CDF in adding to the text submitted to me for my signature, is of course questionable. And, while I do assent to the eight positive propositions of the Notification, in so far as they express the doctrine of the faith, I still consider myself entitled to discuss some of the opinions rejected by the CDF in six of the eight propositions mentioned above. Hereafter I will ask: In what sense are those opinions being condemned by the CDF? And, how do they differ from or compare with some opinions which I myself have expressed in my book? What follows contains therefore my reactions to the official text of the Notification, mainly concerning the "errors" mentioned in propositions 2–6 and 8. Where some significant change has been introduced in the text between the second draft of the Notification and its final official version, I will bring that into relief or otherwise take it into account.

Before broaching the subject, let me note the fact that, as footnote 1 of the final text of the Notification mentions, the "evaluation" which the Notification makes of my book "draws from the principles expressed in *Dominus Iesus.*" References to *Dominus Iesus* in the footnotes of the text are as many as ten. Other references are principally to recent documents of the magisterium. By way of contrast, there is not a single reference to the pages of my book, let alone any quotation from it, in the entire document. As for Holy Scripture, all references to it have been dropped between the first and the second draft of the Notification; and all issues about scriptural exegesis are conspicuously absent.

Omitting the "Preface," I will cite the text of each of the eight propositions before making my comments.

I. ON THE SOLE AND UNIVERSAL SALVIFIC MEDIATION OF JESUS CHRIST

The text of the Notification reads:

> 1. It must be firmly believed that Jesus Christ, the Son of God made man, crucified and risen, is the sole and universal mediator of salvation for all humanity.

> 2. It must also be firmly believed that Jesus of Nazareth, Son of Mary and only Savior of the world, is the Son and Word of the Father. For the unity of the divine plan of salvation centred in Jesus Christ, it must also be held that the salvific action of the Word is accomplished in and through Jesus Christ, the Incarnate Son of the Father, as mediator of the salvation for all humanity. It is therefore contrary to the Catholic faith not only to posit a separation between the Word and Jesus, or between the Word's salvific

activity and that of Jesus, but also to maintain that there is a salvific activity of the Word as such in his divinity, independently of the humanity of the Incarnate Word.

Let me first note, with regard to proposition 1, that the role which the deutero-Pauline epistle (1 Tim 2:5) attributes to Jesus Christ is that of "mediator" between God (the Father) and the whole of humankind. I myself have insisted all along on the Pauline Trinitarian perspective which stresses the fact that the Father, not Jesus Christ as the Son incarnate, is the fountain and source of our salvation. Jesus Christ acts as the "mediator" between the Father and humankind. In him, as Paul himself says, "it was God [i.e., the Father] who was reconciling the world to himself" (2 Cor 5:19). Jesus Christ is mediator in a unique manner inasmuch as he unites in his own person divinity and humanity. That he is the "unique and universal mediator" does not, however, exclude, in the words of Pope John Paul II, the possibility of "participated forms of mediation" that "acquire meaning and value *only* from Christ's mediation" (RM 5). Whether this possibility is verified in the case of other religious traditions must be examined separately.

That Jesus Christ, Son and Word of the Father, is the only Savior of the world (proposition 2), must also be viewed in Trinitarian perspective. It does not obscure the fact that the person of the Father is the fontal source, and the primary cause of universal salvation. The saving action of Jesus Christ is the human expression in the Son Incarnate of the divine act of salvation which has its source in the person of the Father. I have shown that in the New Testament the term "Savior" is attributed originally to the Father, and in a derivative way to Jesus Christ. That Jesus Christ is the "only Savior" must not, then, be understood as denying the primary role of the Father as the original source of salvation. Instead, it must be understood to mean that he is the only man in whom all humankind finds divine salvation. The reason for this is the personal identity of Jesus Christ with the Son of God who became incarnate in him. As such, he is the "sacrament of God's salvation." It is worthwhile recalling that the Council of Trent, in canon 7 of its "Decree on Justification," affirms that "the efficient cause is the merciful God [i.e., the Father] who gratuitously washes and sanctifies," while Jesus Christ is called the "meritorious cause" (Denzinger 1529) of justification-salvation. I have personally preferred to use for Jesus Christ the term "universal, constitutive Savior," rather than "unique and only Savior," so as not to seem to exclude *a priori* the possibility of other "human figures" playing some role in the order of salvation for members of other religions. It goes without saying that such a role cannot be equalized with that of Jesus Christ; what can be attributed to such "saving figures" is that they are for followers of other religions "indicators" of a way along which they may meet the mystery of salvation in Jesus Christ.

The Notification remarks that "for the unity of the divine plan of salvation centred in Jesus Christ, it must . . . be held (*ritenuto*) that the salvific action of the Word is accomplished (*attuata*) in and through Jesus Christ." The need to maintain unity in the divine plan of salvation is beyond questioning, and any suggestion of two divine plans of salvation must be rejected. I have myself insisted repeatedly on this requirement of faith. What this unity of the divine plan requires us to hold is, however, less clear, and the text of the Notification rightly abstains from speaking here of a question of faith but rather of a truth to hold. The fact is that the principle of the necessary unity of the divine plan has been used in the past to defend exclusive positions now long rejected. It has been invoked to sustain the principle "Outside the Church there is no salvation," on the grounds that for the unity of the divine plan there could be but one "ark" of salvation, that of the Church. More recently the same principle has been used to deny the existence of any salvific value in the other religious traditions. The existence of elements of grace in the traditions themselves (those urging its acceptance seem to fear) would destroy the unity of the divine plan, since such endowments of grace are to be found only in Christianity. This goes to show that, while the principle of the unity of the divine plan of salvation in Jesus Christ clearly belongs to the faith, what its application entails is less evident.

The Notification concludes from the unity of the plan of God in Jesus Christ to the need to *hold* that "the salvific action of the Word is *accomplished* in and through Jesus Christ," and consequently that it is contrary to the Catholic faith to posit a *separation* between the Word and Jesus, and similarly between the salvific activity of the Word and that of Jesus. Regarding the necessity of the saving activity of the Word being "accomplished" (*attuata*) in and through Jesus Christ, let me observe that, if this were to be affirmed as a universal principle valid for all times, it would amount to denying the existence of any salvific action of the Word before the incarnation. The humanity of Jesus did not exist before the incarnation of the Word in history, yet the Word of God has been active throughout salvation history before the incarnation, as the Prologue of John's Gospel clearly testifies. Instead of saying that the "actuation" or "accomplishment" of the salvific activity of the Word is necessarily linked solely to the incarnation—which would make the incarnation necessary or even co-eternal with the Word of God—one should admit that, while the Word has been salvifically active throughout salvation history, a new "concentration" (Xavier Léon-Dufour) of his saving action takes place through the incarnation and is present in the humanity of Jesus Christ. The humanity of Jesus Christ expresses in history the saving activity of the Word of God and of God through him. As will be seen below, a salvific action of the Word as such can also perdure after the incarnation of the Word and the resurrection of Jesus. If, on the contrary, one were to postulate a real preexistence of Jesus Christ's humanity to account for the saving action of the Word previous to the incarnation, one would reduce the historical mystery of the incarnation to a mere human theophany of the Word of God, thus emptying the incarnation of the Word of God of its true historical significance and density. Moreover, a real pre-existence of the Incarnate Son's humanity would jeopardize faith in his being consubstantial with us in humanity. His humanity, enjoying a real and not merely intentional pre-existence would differ dramatically from ours. We have existed intentionally—in the divine plan—but certainly not really or physically.

Let me further recall once again that I have never spoken of any *separation* either between the Word and Jesus Christ or between the action of the Word and the saving action of Jesus Christ. I have affirmed the perduring *distinction* that exists between the Word-as-such and the Word-as-incarnate in the humanity of Jesus. Christological dogma affirms in all clarity that "the *distinction* between the natures was never abolished by their union but rather the character proper to each of the two natures is preserved as they come together in one person and one hypostasis" (Denzinger 302, citing the Council of Chalcedon). What the Council of Chalcedon states in 451 in regard to the two natures is similarly affirmed by the Third Council of Constantinople (in 680–681) in regard to the activities proper to both natures: "The difference of natures in that same and unique hypostasis is recognized by the fact that each of the two natures wills and performs what is proper to it in communion with the other" (Denzinger 558). Theologically speaking, it must be affirmed that the relationship by which the human nature and action of Jesus Christ subsist by the *esse* ("being") of the Word of God, is not a reciprocal relation. That is to say, the being of the Word of God and his action cannot be made to depend on the personal union of the human nature of Jesus with the Word of God entailed in the mystery of the incarnation. The expression used by the Fathers when they spoke of a "theandric" action must, therefore, be treated cautiously and understood correctly: there is no question of a hybrid action of the two natures, one semi-divine and semi-human, but of a communion between the two natures in their respective mode of action.

The Notification goes on to state that it is contrary to Catholic faith "to maintain that there is a salvific activity of the Word as such in his divinity, *independent* of the humanity of the incarnate Word." Let me recall that whenever I have spoken of an activity of the Word as such perduring after the incarnation and the resurrection of Jesus Christ, I was always careful not to consider such perduring action as *independent* from the Word incarnate in Jesus Christ. On the contrary, I stressed the *communion* which necessarily exists between the two natures in all actions of the Word and of the Word incarnate. That communion of the two natures is stressed by the Council of Chalcedon and is repeated by the Third Council of Constantinople: "Each of the two natures wills and performs what is proper to it *in communion* with the other" (Denzinger 558). The formula is borrowed from Pope St. Leo the Great, who wrote: "Each of the two natures performs the functions proper to it *in communion* with the other (*cum alterius communione*): the Word does what pertains to the Word and the flesh what pertains to the flesh" (Denzinger 294). I have also shown that St. Leo the Great holds the possibility of the Word as such performing actions "without the flesh." Elsewhere I have expressed the communion between the two natures in terms of the essential *interrelatedness* that exists between the action of the Word as such and his action though the humanity assumed by him in Jesus Christ. To hold an action of the Word as such to be *independent* of the action of the Word in the humanity of Jesus Christ would amount to affirming two different economies of salvation—one in the Word as such and another in the Word as incarnate in Jesus Christ. I have always rejected such position which I stigmatized as upholding "parallel economies" of salvation, that is, a "Logocentric paradigm" in competition with the Christocentrism of the Christian faith.[3] There are not two economies of salvation, one of the Word and one of Jesus Christ, but there is an interrelatedness of two complementary aspects in one divine economy, in which the two natures always act in mutual communion. The question must, however, be asked whether we humans are entitled to impose limits to God's freedom of action in order to simplify, in accordance with our own human concepts, the unity of the divine plan of salvation. This unity is an essential requirement of faith, but its implications remain open to further investigation.

It may be useful to recall that Fathers of the Church had no scruple in affirming a saving activity of the Word as such. Witness St. Athanasius who wrote:

> It is he, the holy Word of the Father, omnipotent and absolutely perfect, who is present in all things and extends his power everywhere, illuminating all things visible and invisible, containing and enclosing them and gathering them in himself; he leaves nothing deprived of his power, but gives life and protection to everything, everywhere, to each individually and to all together. (Athanasius, *Discourse against the Gentiles,* 42: *Sources chretiennes,* n. 18 bis, 191)[4]

Before Athanasius, while commenting on Matthew 11:27, St. Irenaeus explained that God's revelation through the Word "has a general reference to all time." He wrote:

> The Word "will reveal" refers not merely to the future, as if the Son had begun to reveal the Father only after he was born from Mary, but has a general reference to all time. For the Son, assisting his creation from the beginning, reveals the Father to all, to whom he wishes, when he wishes, and as the Father wishes. That is why, in all and through all there is one God the Father, and one Word and one Spirit and one salvation for all who believe in him. (Irenaeus of Lyons, *Adversus Haereses,* Book IV, Chapter 6, section 7; *Sources chretiennes,* n.100, 454–55)

3. See Dupuis, *Toward,* 195ff.

4. Dupuis cites and translates the standard French edition. In older English editions the document by Athanasius is entitled, "Against the Heathen."

ON THE UNICITY AND COMPLETENESS
OF REVELATION OF JESUS CHRIST

The text of the Notification reads:

> 3. It must be firmly believed that Jesus Christ is the mediator, the fulfillment and the completeness of revelation. It is therefore contrary to the Catholic faith to maintain that revelation in Jesus Christ (or the revelation of Jesus Christ) is limited, incomplete or imperfect. Moreover, although full knowledge of divine revelation will be had only on the day of the Lord's coming in glory, the historical revelation of Jesus Christ offers everything necessary for man's salvation and has no need of completion by other religions.

> 4. It is consistent with Catholic doctrine to hold that the seeds of truth and goodness that exist in other religions are a certain participation in truths contained in the revelation of or in Jesus Christ. However, it is erroneous to hold that such elements of truth and goodness, or some of them, do not derive ultimately from the source-mediation of Jesus Christ.

The first affirmation of proposition 3 according to which Jesus Christ is "the mediator, the fulfillment and the completeness" of divine revelation combines numbers 2 and 4 of the Constitution on Divine Revelation, *Dei Verbum* ["The Word of God"], of the Second Vatican Council. As such, it is beyond discussion. The rest of the proposition, in which various opinions contrary to the faith are mentioned, has known fluctuations through the various documents of the process against my book: the *Contestazione,* the *Doctrinal Judgment,* the two previous drafts of the Notification, and the present official text. Without entering into details, let me say that the present text is more sober and more precise than the previous documents. As I have discussed at length the way in which the fullness of revelation in Jesus Christ must be understood, I can afford here to be brief.

What then must be concluded regarding divine revelation in Jesus Christ? When the document states that "the historical revelation in Jesus Christ offers everything necessary for man's salvation," this is an understatement. In fact, revelation offers infinitely more, since strictly speaking, "implicit faith" is sufficient for the possibility of salvation in Jesus Christ. In Jesus Christ, on the contrary, is found the deepest possible revelation of God in history; the divine revelation found in him is at once unsurpassed and unsurpassable, its unique quality being due to the personal identity of Jesus Christ as God's Son made man who lived in his human consciousness his interpersonal relationship with his Father in the mystery of God's inner life. As he lived in his human consciousness his unique personal relationship with his *Abba,* the Son of God incarnate could reveal the divine mystery in a way altogether beyond the reach of any prophet inspired by God and his Spirit. In this sense we can and must speak of Jesus Christ as the fullness of God's revelation in history. All this notwithstanding, divine revelation in Jesus Christ remains nevertheless "limited, incomplete (and) imperfect." But these terms must be correctly understood.

That it remains *limited* is due to the innate limitations of Jesus Christ's human consciousness, which by definition cannot exhaust the divine mystery. No human consciousness or intellect, even that of the Son of God made man, can fully comprehend the divine mystery; this only the divine consciousness or knowledge can do. That it is *incomplete* refers to the fact that revelation took place in history and therefore remains oriented to the final completion of divine revelation in the *eschaton.* It would be wrong to reduce the eschatological completion of divine revelation to the mere end-result of the process through which, helped by the Holy Spirit, the Church must continuously grow through history in her comprehension of the divine revelation she has already received in Jesus Christ. The *eschaton* will on the contrary consist in a final, definitive revelation or self-disclosure of God in Jesus Christ which will mark at once the completion and final achievement of the history of salvation and the advent of the fullness of God's Reign, in which God will be all in all. That the historical revelation in Jesus remains *imperfect* is to be understood in the sense that it leaves many elements of the divine plan of salvation for humankind unknown to us: for instance, when salvation history will be completed at the Lord's coming in glory, which Jesus himself admitted to not knowing, or in which way salvation in Jesus Christ reaches out—"in ways known to God," says the Second Vatican Council (GS 22), admitting its own ignorance—to the great majority of the human family who have not known him.

That revelation in Jesus Christ "has no need of completion by other religions," as proposition 3 goes on to affirm, may be true but should be understood correctly. It need not exclude the possibility or even the fact that a divine revelation contained in the sacred books of other religious traditions may bring out some aspects of the divine mystery even more forcibly than does the Christian revelation. This notwithstanding, the fullness of revelation in Jesus Christ, understood as here above, leaves no void needing to be filled by revelation in other religious traditions, without which its "fullness" would be lost. In order to combine those two aspects—which at first sight may appear contradictory—I have spoken of a complementarity, which is reciprocal but "asymmetrical," between Christian revelation and revelation elsewhere.[5] *Reciprocal* means that other divine revelations may indeed stress some aspects of the divine mystery in such a way that Christian communities themselves may derive profit and enrichment from contact with them through interreligious dialogue. The "fulfillment theory," according to which only natural human endowments can be found in the other religious traditions, says therefore too little; it would reduce interreligious dialogue to a one way traffic to which the other traditions would have nothing to contribute. On the other hand, this reciprocal complementarity must be understood as *asymmetrical* in the sense that the revelation in Jesus Christ leaves no void to be filled by other revelations, as though without their contribution it would fall short of the "fullness" of divine revelation in history which Christian faith claims for it.

Proposition 4 refers to Catholic doctrine, not to doctrine of the faith. It affirms that the "seeds of truth and goodness" found in the other religious traditions "are a certain participation in truths contained in the revelation of or in Jesus Christ." There seems to be a certain obsession with interpreting any positive divine endowments in the other traditions as only shadows or adumbrations of the fullness contained in the Christian revelation. Do the other traditions contain only "seeds" of something which once grown becomes foreign to them, without divine fruits ever being produced within them? I prefer to say that those elements of truth and goodness are in themselves true, even though partial, disclosures of the infinite divine mystery which has been fully revealed to us historically in Jesus Christ. That is to say, they participate in the Truth which is God. In fact, the Second Vatican Council attributes the presence of the "seeds of the Word" in the religious traditions to a "hidden presence of God" (AG 9). And the early Fathers of the Church assigned them to the universal active presence of the Word of God.

---

5. See Dupuis, *Toward*, 326–29; *Christianity*, 132–37; 255–59.

I do not see why it should be necessary to hold that such elements "derive ultimately from the source-mediation of Jesus Christ." Proposition 4 refers here to *Lumen Gentium* 16 and 17 and to *Redemptoris Missio* 10. These texts do not seem to affirm what CDF is here trying to derive from them. The "seeds of the Word" were present and operative before the humanity of Jesus Christ existed and before his "source-mediation" could come into play. Moreover, the expression "source-mediation" *(mediazione fontale)* is somewhat misleading. The mediator is not the fontal source of the elements of truth and goodness found in the other religious traditions. The fontal source or ultimate cause is God the Father; Jesus Christ acts on God the Father's behalf and initiative as mediator between God and humankind. It is from God that the elements of truth and goodness found in the traditions ultimately derive. In the last resort God is the Truth who in history has been fully manifested in Jesus Christ.

III. ON THE UNIVERSAL SALVIFIC ACTION OF THE HOLY SPIRIT

The text of the Notification reads:

> 5. The Church's faith teaches that the Holy Spirit, working after the resurrection of Jesus Christ, is always the Spirit of Christ sent by the Father, who works in a salvific way in Christians as well as non-Christians. It is therefore contrary to the Catholic faith to hold that the salvific action of the Holy Spirit extends beyond the one universal salvific economy of the Incarnate Word.

In the current Western tradition it would seem that one can hardly refer to the "Spirit of God" without having immediately to add that this Spirit is the "Spirit of Christ," lest one should be accused of falling short of the faith. However, while the meaning of the expression "Spirit of God" is abundantly clear, this is not the case with the expression "Spirit of Christ." That the Spirit is "of God" (i.e., the Father) means that the Spirit "proceeds" from God the Father within the divine life and is sent by him on his mission to the world. That the Spirit is "of Christ" is less clear, if one thinks of how views differ between the various Christian traditions, Western and Eastern. For the Orthodox the expression cannot mean that the Spirit "proceeds" *also* from the Son in the divine life *(filioque)*, though it can mean that the Son contributes to the sending of the Spirit on his mission. The principle of the correspondence between the ontological and the economic Trinity is therefore not understood in a consistent manner in the various Christian traditions.

The text of proposition 5 speaks of the "Spirit of Christ sent by the Father," not by the risen Christ. However, the meaning of the expression "Spirit of Christ" seems to refer directly to the sending of the Spirit by the risen Christ. The text, then, amounts to stating that the Spirit is sent by the Father and the Son. That the risen Christ will send the Spirit to his apostles is clearly affirmed by Jesus himself in the Gospel of John 5:26 and 16:7. Yet other texts in John attribute the sending of the Spirit simply to the Father: the Father will send the Spirit to the apostles on the request of the Son ("in my name"), who will act as intercessor for them with the Father (John 14:16; 14:26). The Father is the primary cause of the sending of the Spirit, as he is of the Spirit's eternal procession from him. If from St. John we pass on to St. Paul, chapter 8 of the Letter to the Romans suffices to show that the Father is for Paul the principal cause of the sending of the Spirit: The Spirit is repeatedly called the "Spirit of God" (the Father) (Rom 8:9; 8:11 [twice]; 8:14), while only one verse in the chapter speaks of the "Spirit of Christ" (8:9). The expression used by proposition 5, "the Spirit of Christ sent by the Father," must then refer to the Spirit being sent by the Father and the risen Christ, according to the Western understanding of the divine missions; these correspond to the "processions" in the divine life. In view of the plurality of views and expressions in the New Testament itself with regard to the sending of the Spirit, the question may legitimately be asked whether there may not exist, even after the incarnation of the Son of God in Jesus Christ and the glorification of his humanity, a mission of the Holy Spirit in the world, the origin of which would simply be the person of the Father.

That the Holy Spirit was present and active throughout salvation history well before the historical incarnation of the Son is beyond doubt and has been felicitously stressed by the recent Church magisterium. It is equally beyond doubt that the humanity of Jesus Christ could play no role in this active presence of the Spirit before it began to exist through the mystery of the incarnation. The incarnation itself was brought about by God through the power of the Spirit; the Spirit prompted Jesus in all key-moments of his earthly career; it is still by the power of the Spirit that God raised Jesus after his death on the cross. In all these instances the Spirit acted as sent by God the Father without any mediation of the humanity of Jesus in the mission of the Spirit. The question now under consideration is whether such direct mission of the Spirit from the Father can continue after the Resurrection of Christ, or must we, on the contrary, affirm as *doctrine of faith* that after the resurrection of Jesus the sending of the Spirit passes always and necessarily through the mediation of Jesus' risen humanity? Can then the salvific action of the Holy Spirit "extend beyond the one universal salvific economy of the Incarnate Word"? I must note in passing that, put in these terms, the question is poorly posed. For we know that there is but one divine economy of salvation, of which all the various elements must be seen in their unity. Let us then ask more precisely whether there may persist after the resurrection of Jesus a salvific action of the Spirit without him being sent by the risen Christ.

The question of the *filioque* is in fact involved here. It is well known that the *filoque* (*kai tou uiou*) clause was added to the Nicene-Constantinopolitan profession of faith in the Western tradition in 381. It is less known that a recent document published by the Pontifical Council for Promoting Christian Unity, entitled "Clarification on the Greek and Latin Traditions regarding the Procession of the Holy Spirit" (1995), has stressed anew the "monarchy" of the Father, "principle without principle, . . . sole source (*pēgē*) of the Son and of the Holy Spirit." The document adds: "The Holy Spirit therefore takes his origin from the Father alone . . . in a principal, proper and immediate manner." The same document also affirms that the clause of the *filioque* may be left out in the Creed, even in the Latin rite: "The Catholic Church has refused the addition of *kai tou uiou* to the formula *to ek tou Patros ekporeuomenon* of the Symbol of Nicaea-Constantinople in the Churches, even of Latin rite, which use it in Greek. The liturgical use of this original text remains always legitimate in the Catholic Church" (*Information Service* [of the Secretariat for Promoting Christian Unity], n. 89, 1995 (II–III) 88–92). We may note in passing that the Declaration *Dominus Iesus* (n. 1), while quoting the entire text of the profession of faith, leaves out the clause *filioque*. The restoration of the original form of the Creed in the liturgy is bound to raise questions as to the perduring dogmatic value of the *filioque* in the doctrine of the Latin Church. To what extent does the clause *filioque* remain doctrinally binding regarding the eternal procession in God of the Holy Spirit and, consequently, his historical mission?

It is commonly said nowadays that the only doctrine of faith which continues to divide the Orthodox Churches from the Roman Catholic Church, is the meaning which they attribute to the ministry of the bishop of Rome as successor of Peter, and specifically the question of the universal jurisdiction and of personal infallibility of the "Roman Pontiff." If this is the case, it would seem that the *filioque* question is on the way to being reduced from a dividing dogma of faith to a *theologoumenon* on which opinions are divided but also freely open to discussion. Can it not then be admitted by Catholic theologians that there may exist a mission of the Spirit from the Father which does not necessarily pass through the mediation of the risen humanity of Jesus Christ, any more than his eternal procession needs to be affirmed as also "from the Son (*filioque*)"? The Spirit would then be seen more clearly as "another Paraclete" sent by the Father to continue the work of Jesus Christ after he has achieved his own mission and returned to the Father. Elsewhere I have quoted Orthodox theologian Paul Edvokimov, who writes as follows:

> The Word and the Spirit, "the two hands of God," according to the expression of S. Irenaeus, are inseparable in their action of manifesting the Father, and yet they are infinitely distinct. The Spirit is not subordinated to the Son, nor is he a function of the Son; he is the second Paraclete. Between the two economies of the Son and the Spirit there is reciprocity and mutual service, but Pentecost is not simply the consequence or a continuation of the Incarnation. Pentecost has its full value by itself, *it represents the second act of the Father*. The Father sends the Son, and now he sends the Holy Spirit. His mission being completed, Christ returns to the Father so that the Holy Spirit may come down in person." (*L' Esprit Saint dans la tradition orthodoxe*, Le Cerf, Paris 1969, 88–89)

The expression "two economies of the Son and the Spirit" should of course be avoided, and I have rejected everywhere the idea of two divine economies, which would destroy the unity of the divine plan of salvation. But, apart from that, the Oriental and Orthodox traditions have rightly pointed out the danger in the Latin tradition of a "Christomonism" which would unduly curtail the saving activity of the Holy Spirit, reducing the Spirit to being a "vicar" or a "function" of Christ, thereby depriving him of the integrity of his specific saving action. It is legitimate then to ask whether after the resurrection the saving activity of the Spirit needs to be viewed as necessarily dependent upon and exclusively bound to the communication which the risen Christ makes of him to the Church and to the world.

Nor does it seem to result from the writings of the Fathers that the sanctifying activity of the Spirit is exclusively bound to the communication that the risen Christ makes of the Spirit. Witness to this is an ample description which Basil of Caesarea makes of the effects of the action of the Spirit in us (*De Spiritu Sancto,* IX, 22–23; *Sources chretiennes,* n. 17 bis, 322–31). Even more than being communicated to us by the risen Christ, it is the Spirit who leads us to see the "Image of the Invisible [the Son]" and through him makes us contemplate the "ineffable beauty of the Archetype [the Father]." St. Basil writes: "He (the Spirit Paraclete), like a Sun laying hold of a very pure eye, will show you in himself the Image of the Invisible. And in the blissful contemplation of the Image, you will see the ineffable beauty of the Archetype" (329). Elsewhere he writes: "Our spirit, enlightened by the Spirit, fixes its eyes on the Son and in him, as in an image, contemplates the Father" (*Letter* 226, 3; *PG* 32, 849A). And again: "The Spirit, being present to each of the subjects able to receive him, as if he were alone, utters sufficiently for all, grace in fullness: those enjoy it who share in it, in so far as is possible for their nature, but not as much as he himself is able to give himself to be shared" (327).

A saving activity of the Holy Spirit would then be possible without the Spirit being necessarily communicated by the risen Christ, though never without being essentially related to him in the unique but complex divine plan for the salvation of humankind. The divine plan is indeed complex, but not monolithic, any more than the unity of the intrinsic divine mystery excludes a plurality of inter-related divine persons. It is the eternal mind of God that determines the unity-in-complexity of the manifold divine action *ad extra* in the plan of salvation. According to that plan the Spirit is undoubtedly communicated to the Church and to the world by the risen Christ, but this way of communication need not be the only possible way of action of the Holy Spirit, even after Christ's resurrection and glorification. A direct intervention of the Spirit sent by the Father does not in any way contradict the one universal salvific economy of God for humankind.

IV. ON THE ORIENTATION OF ALL
HUMAN BEINGS TO THE CHURCH

The text of the Notification reads:

> 6. It must be firmly believed that the Church is sign and instrument of salvation of all people. It is contrary to the Catholic faith to consider the different religions of the world as ways of salvation complementary to the Church.

> 7. According to Catholic doctrine, the followers of other religions are oriented to the Church and are all called to become part of her.

That the Church is "necessary for salvation" and that she is "universal sacrament of salvation" (proposition 6) is clearly taught by the Second Vatican Council and must be considered a doctrine of faith—not, however, it goes without saying, *before* its foundation by Jesus Christ and the Holy Spirit. According to the divine plan, there ought to be present in the world a universal sign of what God has done and continues to be doing for the whole of humankind in Jesus Christ. This divine will does not, however, obscure the fact that, even after the foundation of the Church, such a sign has not been available for centuries to entire continents and even today remains unknown to the vast majority of humankind. The plan of God is subject in its concrete realization to historical circumstances and contingencies. The difficulty arises when to the term "sacrament" that of "instrument" is added, as is the case in *Lumen Gentium* 9 and *Redemptoris Missio* 9. I have shown that the recent magisterium uses very vague expressions, such as "mysterious relationship" or "indispensable relationship," to describe the role played by the Church in conferring the grace of salvation to people who are not Church-members. It looks as if the magisterium were embarrassed when it comes to specifying what precisely the Church is doing for the salvation of those people. Proposition 6 adds, however, the term "instrument," following thereby the Declaration *Dominus Iesus* (22), which affirms plainly that "God has willed that the Church founded by [Christ] be the *instrument* for the salvation of *all* humanity."

It should not be forgotten that the "instrument" of the Church was non-existent for incalculable generations of human beings before the coming of Jesus the Christ and that it still remains unavailable today to the majority of contemporary people. Keeping this in mind would engender a more sober view of the *necessity* of the Church as *universal* instrument of salvation.[6] It must in fact be asked, first, whether the term "instrument" is appropriate for describing the function of the Church for salvation, especially in the case of people who are not her members. Does not the term suggest material efficacy? A difficulty arises inasmuch as one would expect an instrument to exercise an "instrumental" causality—which does not seem to be the case in relation to the saving grace of non-members is concerned.

One can perhaps speak of "instrumentality" in a loose sense, to express the kind of "mysterious relationship" between grace outside the Church and the Church herself, affirmed by the recent magisterium. But if one takes the terms in their precise, technical meaning, it is hard to see how instrumentality can be applied to the Church's action in regard to grace and salvation outside her ranks. I have thought it necessary to distinguish between the action of the Church in word and sacrament by which she reaches out to her members, and her "intercession" on behalf of the others in view of their salvation. The first is of the efficient order, the other of the moral and final order. The Church intercedes for the salvation of people outside her ranks, and God saves. Precise talk will help here for accurate theology. I have suggested that in the case of non-members of the Church, a mediatory function of the Church—by way of "instrumentality"—is left in hope of an eventual future when, that is, the Church will be in a position to announce Jesus Christ to them and they will be able to share in the Church's sacramental economy at the "table of word and bread." In so far as they remain "oriented" towards the Church to which Jesus Christ has entrusted, as John Paul II has said, the "fullness of the benefits and means of salvation" (RM 18), they are potential beneficiaries of an "instrumental" mediation of the Church, but they are not members.

Proposition 6 goes on to say that "it is contrary to the Catholic faith to consider the different religions of the world as ways of salvation complementary to the Church." Let us note that the wording of this sentence in the first draft of the Notification (4 September 2000) was much more severe in its condemnation; it read: "It is contrary to the Catholic faith to consider the Church as one way of salvation, even though the most eminent, beside those constituted by the various religions of the world, which would thus be substantially equivalent or complementary to the Church

---

6. Dupuis discusses this and associated matters in this section at length and with great nuance in *Toward*, 347–57; and *Christianity*, 197–217.

in the order of salvation." It should be plain why I refused to sign a text in which such flagrant error was directly attributed to my book.

Coming to the present text of the Notification, it may be noted that the reference to *Redemptoris Missio* 36, is wrong. The only reference which remains is to *Dominus Iesus* 21–22. Let me recall in what sense I have affirmed a "complementarity" between the Church and other religious traditions as ways of salvation. I have spoken of the other religious traditions as eventually exercising a mediation of "substitution," where the mediation of the Church cannot reach people who are not her members. I have also borrowed the expression "participated forms of mediation of different kinds and degrees" from Pope John Paul II, which, as the Pope goes on to affirm, "acquire meaning and value *only* from Christ's own mediation, and . . . cannot be understood as parallel or complementary to his" (RM 5). In view of this, what "complementarity" can be affirmed between the Church and the religious traditions as ways of salvation? As stated above, I have called that complementarity "reciprocal and asymmetrical."[7] The meaning of these terms has already been explained here. They are devised for preserving at once the uniqueness and transcendence of the Christian way, which does not need to be complemented by other ways, and the reality of participated ways of substitution found in the other traditions. Both affirmations need to be held together, even if some tension is involved. To keep the first to the neglect of the other would betray an *a priori* exclusivist attitude tantamount to denying *a priori* that the other religious traditions may contain "elements of truth and grace" conducive to the salvation of their members. To uphold the second to the detriment of the first would lead to denying the uniqueness of Jesus Christ as universal Savior and the necessity of the Church as "universal sacrament of salvation."

Proposition 7 is presented not as doctrine of the faith but as Catholic doctrine. That the followers of other religions are "oriented" to the Church is clearly affirmed by Vatican II (LG 16). It is worth recalling again that by using that expression the Council was intentionally departing from the pre-Conciliar doctrine of the members *in voto* [i.e., "by desire"] of the Church. The Council affirmed that, though not being members of the Church, the members of other religions are nevertheless "oriented" (*ordinantur*) towards her. This, as I have explained, is due to the fact that the

---

7 See Dupuis, *Christianity*, 255–58 for his explanation of asymmetrical complementarity.

Church has received from Christ "the fullness of the benefits and means of salvation" (RM 18).

That the members of other religious traditions "are *all* called to become part of her [the Church]" needs to be understood correctly. Before mentioning the universal call of people to become part of the Church, the Notification would have done well to note that by God's grace they are already members of the "Reign of God," universally present and operative in the world, in which all people of good will share together with Christians the mystery of human salvation in Jesus Christ, through a participation in the paschal mystery in ways known to God (GS 22). This belonging is more fundamental and consequential than is membership in the Church. Concerning the calling to the Church, *Lumen Gentium* 13 affirms that "all are called (*vocantur*) to [the] Catholic unity of the People of God . . . and belong (*pertinent*) or are oriented (*ordinantur*) to it in different ways: the Catholic faithful, others who believe in Christ, and finally all are called (*vocati*) by God's grace to salvation." The Council does not seem to have attributed a distinct meaning here to the two terms of "orientation" and "calling." In any case, the Council does not pronounce on the concrete realization of the calling of the members of other religious traditions to the Church.

It is one thing to say that the members of the other religious traditions are *ideally* called to membership of the Church in the overall plan of God for humankind. It is quite something else to say that *concretely* this call to membership vocation can, must, or will be *realized*.[8] To claim that would contradict the obvious global reality of the world as we know it, in which out of more than six billion human beings four and a half billion have not heard of Christ and the Church or are in a position to adhere to the Christian faith! It would also suppose a fundamentalist interpretation of the "great commission" given by the risen Christ to the apostles in the Gospels of Matthew and Mark. How would it be possible to believe in the present world that *all people are concretely called* to become *explicitly* Christian in a way that makes their salvation depend on it? Such a belief would betray a monolithic view of God's plan of salvation for humankind. God would have devised but one valid path of salvation and those from among the vast majority of humankind who are actually saved outside the

8. In conversation with me Fr Dupuis once added the phrase "or would be penalized for *not* becoming Catholic Christians, since there are many important and understandable reasons why someone might not recognize the obligation of joining our Church."

one path would all have to be viewed as representing singular exceptions to a rigid rule established by God. The "ways known to God" (AG 7; GS 22) by which, according to his own design, God saves outside the Church would then be altogether overlooked and denied. God and his design of salvation for humankind would be reduced to the dimension of mean human ideas, forgetting that God, as Scripture testifies, is "greater than our hearts" (1 Jn 3:20)—and greater than our concepts.

V. ON THE VALUE AND SALVIFIC FUNCTION OF THE RELIGIOUS TRADITIONS

The text of the Notification reads:

> 8. In accordance with Catholic doctrine, it must be held the "whatever the Spirit brings about in human hearts and in the history of peoples, in cultures and religions, serves as a preparation for the Gospel (cf. Dogmatic Constitution *Lumen Gentium* 16)." It is therefore legitimate to maintain that the Holy Spirit accomplishes salvation in non-Christians also through those elements of truth and goodness present in the various religions; however, to hold that these religions, considered as such, are ways of salvation, has no foundation in Catholic theology, also because they contain omissions, insufficiencies and errors regarding fundamental truths about God, man and the world.
>
> Furthermore, the fact that the elements of truth and goodness present in the various world religions may prepare peoples and cultures to receive the salvific event of Jesus Christ does not imply that the sacred texts of these religions can be considered as complementary to the Old Testament, which is the immediate preparation for the Christ event.

Proposition 8 is presented as Catholic doctrine, not as doctrine of faith. It refers to *Redemptoris Missio* 29, holding that "whatever the Spirit brings about in human hearts and in the history of peoples, in cultures and religions, serves as a preparation for the Gospel." The Pope is referring to *Lumen Gentium* 16. Let us note, however, that the text of Vatican II does not exactly correspond to that of the Pope. The Council states: "Whatever good or truth is found among them [those who do not know the Gospel of Christ and his Church] is considered by the Church to be a preparation to the Gospel" (see Eusebius of Caesarea, *Praeparatio evangelica*, 1, 1; *PG* 21, 28AB). It is not said that those elements of truth and goodness are brought about among them by the Holy Spirit. Elsewhere the Council attributes the presence of such elements to a "secret presence of God"(AG 9). And we know that the early Fathers of the Church assigned the presence in other traditions of "seeds of the Word" to the universal active presence of the Word of God. As to the view according to which such endowments are considered a "preparation to the Gospel," it supposes the Fathers' opinion according to which the Gospel is the one and only way devised by God for the salvation of humankind, to the effect that anything outside which would be conducive to salvation must be viewed as leading to it. If, however, other religious traditions exercise some salvific function for their members in accordance with the plan of God, even if in essential relationship to the Christian way, the expression will appear one-sided and inadequate.

The text of proposition 8 goes on to say that "it is therefore legitimate to maintain that the Holy Spirit accomplishes salvation in non-Christians also through those elements of truth and goodness present in the various religions." The text admits therefore that the elements of truth and goodness found in the other traditions exercise a positive role in the mystery of the salvation of their members. It attributes this to the working of the Holy Spirit. Why, it may be asked, are the religious traditions *not* then called "ways of salvation" for their members? I have observed elsewhere that the magisterium seems reluctant to draw that conclusions from what otherwise it affirms strongly.[9]

A question may nonetheless be asked: Who is the agent of salvation according to this text? The Notification has affirmed earlier that Jesus Christ is the only Savior of humankind; it has also stated that the Holy Spirit always acts as communicated by the humanity of the risen Christ. How do these affirmations square with what is now being claimed regarding the Holy Spirit's apparently specific and proper work? In a Trinitarian perspective, I have explained that, according to revelation, the Father is the principal cause, the fontal source of the mystery of salvation in all cases and circumstances. One wonders why the text under consideration seems once more to abstract from the fontal causality of the Father, thus obscuring the Trinitarian aspect of the mystery of salvation, which reflects outside the intrinsic life of the Godhead, the threefold interpersonal communication of which God's inner mystery is made up. God the Father

9. Dupuis, *Christianity*, 182–85.

is the one who fundamentally saves; Jesus Christ is in his humanity and in the historical event of his human life, death and resurrection, the primordial sacrament of God's saving action; the Holy Spirit renders the saving value of the Christ-event present and actual in all times and places.

While admitting that the elements of truth and goodness contained in the other traditions play some positive role in the Holy Spirit's action of salvation on behalf of their members, the text hastens to add that considering those religions "as such are ways of salvation, has no foundation in Catholic theology." Here it is worth taking note of the fact that the text of Notification 2, submitted for my signature in December 2000, was harder. It said that, "There is no foundation whatever in Catholic *doctrine* for holding that those religions, considered in themselves *and in their globality* are ways of salvation. . . ." Note that "Catholic doctrine" has been softened to "Catholic theology." It may well be asked *which* "Catholic theology" the document is talking about; for the time is gone when there was only one! Furthermore, let me note that I have never claimed that the other traditions are *in their globality* ways of salvation. I have drawn attention to the Document entitled "Dialogue and Proclamation" (1991),[10] which reads as follows: "Concretely, it will be in the sincere practice of *what is good in their own religions* and by following the dictates of their conscience that the members of other religions respond positively to God's invitation and receive salvation in Jesus Christ" (§ 29).

What I have maintained is that the elements of truth and grace present in the traditions can be the channels through which God reaches out to their members with his salvation. Where the *saving figures* of those traditions are concerned, I have been cautious in describing the role they may play as that of *indicators of a way* along which their followers will be able, [albeit] unknowingly, to encounter the mystery of salvation in Jesus Christ. This is a far cry from a sweeping statement about the saving power of other traditions *in their globality.* Yet, the "omissions, insufficiencies and errors" contained in those traditions notwithstanding—of which, moreover, these traditions do not have the monopoly—I have shown that

10. "Dialogue and Proclamation" was issued by the Pontifical Council for Interreligious Dialogue on 19 May 1991. It is also contained in Gioia, ed., *Interreligious Dialogue*, 608–42. Fr Dupuis was an advisor to the PCID while "Dialogue and Proclamation" was being drafted, and in 1993 Fr Dupuis published a lengthy commentary on the document, "A Theological Commentary: Dialogue and Proclamation" in Burrows, ed., *Redemption and Dialogue*, 119–58.

it is possible to hold that the other religions are, as such and in themselves, as many *"gifts of God to the peoples of the earth"* (see Odasso, *Bibbia e religioni*). To this end, it is necessary to distinguish in the religions of the world between what in them comes from God and is always a gift of God to people, and what comes from human beings—including distortions, falsifications or even corruption. Let us beware of attributing to God what comes from human beings, or to human beings what comes from God! And the same discernment must be imposed upon Christianity.

The second paragraph of Proposition 8, while admitting that the elements of truth and goodness present in the religions "may prepare peoples and cultures to receive the salvific event of Jesus Christ," insists that this "does not imply that the sacred texts of these religions can be considered complementary to the Old Testament, which is the immediate preparation for the Christ event." The question has in fact been asked, not only whether those sacred books could perhaps "complement" the books of the Old Testament, but even "replace" them. Just as the Old Testament was for the Jews a preparation for the Christ-event, it has been suggested, the sacred writings of other religious traditions would have served as a preparation for the same event for the peoples of the other traditions. From this standpoint, there is more than one sacred history oriented to the Christ-event. This notwithstanding, to the question of a possible substitution of the Old Testament by other sacred writings, my answer has been that the Old Testament has a unique function to play in the unfolding of God's self-disclosure to the world. The reason which I gave for this is the very reason proposed by Proposition 8, namely, that the Old Testament is—according to the Christian typological interpretation—the immediate preparation for the Christ-event in history. Account must, nevertheless, also be taken of the fact that the Old Testament has taken into itself myths, legends, and stories from other religious traditions. The New Testament, and St. Paul in particular, have likewise made use of pre-Christian, non-Jewish literature.

While taking into account these various elements, I have distinguished three phases in the progressive and differentiated revelation of God to humankind: (1) the scriptures of religious traditions belonging to the cosmic economy of salvation, which contain an "initial" word spoken by God through prophets and seers; (2) the Old Testament, which records the history of Israel, which the Christian faith interprets as the immediate preparation in history for the Christ event; and (3) the New Testament, in which the official record of the Apostolic Church's faith in Jesus Christ and the Christ-event is contained.

This different grading in the unfolding of divine revelation notwith-standing, a reciprocal, "asymmetrical complementarity"—such as has been affirmed above between the different modalities of mediation of the mystery of salvation—can be said to obtain between the various modes of divine revelation—cosmic, Jewish, and Christian. All are interrelated in the overall plan of God's self-disclosure to humankind. Revelation and salvation go hand in hand at every step.

Unlike earlier versions, the final, official Notification no longer ac-cused my book of errors against the faith or against Catholic doctrine. Instead it spoke of "ambiguous statements and insufficient explanations" which could lead the reader into "erroneous or harmful opinions." I blush with shame when I imagine that I might be leading my readers into "er-roneous or harmful opinions." What was therefore expected from me is that I should offer all the necessary explanations and clarifications so as to dissipate all possible ambiguities. I have already tried to comply with this request in two articles, one in Italian and the other in English, which I have mentioned in the Introduction to *Christianity and the Religions.*[11] The book itself and the two Epilogues [which I wanted] attached to it have pursued the same end. It is true that in the process I have not thought it necessary to alter substantially my theological position; I have rather strengthened it and clarified it with further considerations, precisions and qualifications. The fact is that I have not been convinced that my views and proposals contradict the faith or the Catholic doctrine at any stage, while they develop new perspectives capable of leading to a theology of religions and of religious pluralism at once more open, more credible and appealing.

I was aware of suggesting what I have called a "qualitative leap," which would lead beyond what remains even today the official teach-ing of the Church's magisterium, though I meant the new vision to be deeply anchored in the Church's living tradition and to build upon it. I was convinced that the official doctrine of the Church does not claim to fix boundaries beyond which theological research is forbidden to venture, but to draw guidelines and to indicate pointers along which theology may think and reflect anew, in the present context, on the ineffable divine

11. See Dupuis, "La teologia del pluralism religioso revisitata"; and "Truth Will Make You Free: The Theology of Religious Pluralism Revisited."

mystery, which has been progressively disclosed to humankind through-out history and, "in these last days," "fully revealed" in Jesus Christ. The outcome has been what I have called an "inclusivist pluralism," which, while having nothing in common with the pluralistic paradigm of the so-called "pluralist theologians," would attempt to show how the Christian faith and doctrine can combine the faith-affirmation of the uniqueness of Jesus Christ as universal Savior and the theological apprehension of a positive role and significance in the divine plan for humankind of the other religious traditions. I once more submit my endeavors to the consideration of my theological peers and to the judgment of the Church's doctrinal authority.

There can be no doubt that the Christian identity must be preserved in its integrity in the process of encountering and entering into dialogue with the other religious traditions. There is no dialogue in a void or in a flux of personal religious persuasions. But the sincere affirmation of the Christian identity need not imply exclusivist statements by which any positive significance in God's eternal design for humankind, assigned to the other traditions by God, is *a priori* denied. Christianity and the Church do not have the monopoly of the truth and of the benefits and means of salvation, even if they have received in Jesus Christ the "fullness" of revelation and from the risen Lord the fullness of the means of salvation. Absolute and exclusive statements about Christ and Christianity, which claim the exclusive possession of God's self-disclosure or of the means of salvation, distort and contradict rather than corroborate or enhance the Christian message and the Christian image. The fullness of revelation in Jesus Christ does not imply the denial of divine revelation elsewhere. Rather, it may be stated that it *suggests* it. Similarly, God's saving action need not be expressed exclusively through the sacramentality of Jesus Christ's humanity and of the Church, even while these—on different planes to be clearly distinguished—are viewed as central and pivotal in the one plan of salvation, eternally devised by God. Our one God is three, and the communion-in-difference that characterizes God's inner life is reflected and operative in the one plan which, eternally and of common accord, Father Son, and Holy Spirit have devised for their dealings with humankind in revelation and salvation. The plurality of religions, then, finds its last source in a God who is love and communication.

Let me end by quoting the statement which Father Hans-Peter Kolvenbach, Superior General of the Society of Jesus, addressed to the entire Society on the day of the publication by the Congregation for the Doctrine of the Faith of the Notification about my book (26 February 2001):

> With the Notification just published by the Congregation for the Doctrine of the Faith, a long and important inquiry has ended. The book of Father Jacques Dupuis, professor emeritus at the Pontifical Gregorian University, which has been justly recognized for the seriousness of its methodological research, the richness of its scientific documentation, and the originality of its exploration, dares to venture into a dogmatically fundamental area for the future of the interreligious dialogue. The Notification itself recognizes the intent and the efforts of Father Jacques Dupuis to remain within the teaching of the Catholic Faith as enunciated by the Magisterium. In line with the orientations of the document *Dominus Iesus*, the Notification clearly establishes the limits of this teaching to which the author has tried to adhere, even if he has not always succeeded. Thus, the Notification helps the reader to interpret the book according to the doctrine of the Church. On this solidly established dogmatic basis we hope that Father Jacques Dupuis can continue his pioneer research in the field of interreligious dialogue which in his recent Apostolic Letter *Novo Millennio Ineunte,*[12] John Paul II encourages as a challenge for the evangelisation in the third millennium.

7 March 2001

---

12. *Novo Millennio Ineunte* is the Latin title of the encyclical letter of Pope John Paul II at the conclusion of the Jubilee Year 2000 (dated 6 January 2001).

4

A Concluding Personal Postscript
on a Conservative Revisionist

WILLIAM R. BURROWS

I HAD NO GREATER privilege as an editor at Orbis Books for twenty years than working with Jacques Dupuis on the four books he published with us. At the risk of tiring the reader, I would like to describe my debt to him and what he taught me may be helpful in coming to a positive judgment on the work of a man whom I believe is fundamentally both deeply conservative, yet, in the best sense of the word, the epitome of what David Tracy means when he speaks about theological "revisioning."

When I began work on the first of those books, I had just encountered the unpublished writings of the Maryknoll theologian William Frazier on the saving significance of the death of Christ and the meaning of human death and the impact on Christian identity of a culture that tried to ignore death. The reflections of Dupuis and Frazier helped me confront the paradox that the supreme revelation of God in all four gospels was the death of Jesus. Yes, I had long ago heard the sage comment of Martin Kähler (1835–1912) that the gospel of Mark was basically an extended passion narrative with a long introduction made up of isolated literary units. Extending that insight, all four gospels give their interpretation of his mission and significance by narrating the life of Jesus, singling out those events and sayings that offer insights into the passion and resurrection. But it is one thing to know such facts *about* Scripture. It is another to have the Spirit work in your heart, moving you to understand the words as they become the Word addressed to yourself. Reading Jacques Dupuis and Bill Frazier forced me to attend to the biblical narratives and epistles, and I felt that push and pull of the Spirit. Together the three invited me to transcend the conundrums of rationalism by embracing the Mystery of Jesus as the Christ. I hope to acknowledge my debt to Bill Frazier in a forthcoming book on mission, church, and culture. I wish now to lay out the reasons that I think Dupuis's critics—including those at the Congregation for the Doctrine of Faith—have not fully grasped what he was about.

A BRIEF THEOLOGICAL AUTOBIOGRAPHY

At the risk of solipsism, I must recount my own theological autobiography. I write not because I view myself as important, but because it will give some background on why I think Dupuis's critics have not fully engaged him. And I suspect that my path is not greatly unlike that trod by many others who have tried to resolve the tension between the wisdom and truth of Tradition and Scripture with the insights of contemporary comparative theological, religious and philosophical studies

When I worked on the first two books by Dupuis that Orbis published I was faced with the fundamental question of Christian theology since the 1800s: Are the Scriptures reliable? And for Catholics especially: What are we to make of Tradition as developed in the Ecumenical Councils of the first five centuries and its subsequent elaboration by the official (especially the recent papal and Vatican II Conciliar) *magisterium*? These are, on the one hand, of course, the questions raised by biblical criticism as it began in the Enlightenment and continues down to our own day; and on the other hand, the question of the teaching authority of councils and popes. The papal magisterium dealt with these issues in the nineteenth century in the *Syllabus of Errors* (1864) from Pope Pius IX, and in the early twentieth in *Lamentabili Sane Exitu* (1907) and *Pascendi Dominici Gregis* (1910), both from Pope Pius X.

By the end of the Second Vatican Council, all three documents were understood by most historically conscious Catholics to be relics that required so much separation of wheat from chaff as to be practically useless. They had also postponed the day that the wider Catholic community would deal with the Enlightenment by nearly a century. It was our fate—in a single generation—to absorb and deal with issues Protestants had been dealing with since the beginning of the nineteenth century. By way of articulating a personal judgment on the context of the century between the *Syllabus* and the close of Vatican Council II and the major themes running through the papacies of Paul VI, John Paul II, and Benedict XVI, let me run the risk of a generalization that I think is warranted but for which I will not provide documentation here. The central concern of Rome during this entire century and a half has been the steady progress of an historicist and reductive-rationalist approach to exegesis, theology, and church. Progressives see *Gaudium et Spes*, Vatican II's document on the church in the modern world as emblematic of turning a new page, one in which modernity is accepted and the church declared an end to that war. This is the famous argument about a "spirit of the Council" (which progressives see encapsulated especially in *Lumen Gentium, Gaudium et Spes, Nostra Aetate, Dignitatis Humanae*, and *Dei Verbum*), which was betrayed by the three post-Conciliar popes, on the one hand, and those who, on the other hand, argue that a more careful reading especially of *Lumen Gentium* (arguably the most important document of the Council) militates for a more conservative "hermeneutic" of the Council. As the arguments have proceeded, the so-called "Bologna School" (represented by the late Giuseppe Alberigo, Joseph Komonchak, and Alberto Melloni—all, for the record, friends of mine), according to the "Renewal in Continuity" School (represented by Joseph Ratzinger, Agostino Marchetto, Roberto de Mattei), have exaggerated the *nova* introduced by the Council. I personally find that John W. O'Malley's *What Happened at Vatican II* makes a more convincing case for there being real *nova* amidst the *vetera*, but my view on this is less important than what the dispute reveals. Namely that Rome has been engaged in a battle with "reductionist modernism" for more than a century, against which background the "Continuity School" wants to paint the Bologna School as, if not "modernists," at least uncritical progressives who ignore traditional elements in the new documents. Both Komonchak and O'Malley would agree that the battle with modernist reductionism has been an important battle. And at the risk of offending many of my Protestant friends, I would add, if one wants to know the stakes, one needs only look at much of contemporary Lutheranism, Presbyterianism, Anglicanism, Methodism, and Congregationalism in the United States to see what happens when progressives win decisively. For my liberal friends, the picture revealed in these churches is a happy one. Alas—influenced as I have been by an open sort of Evangelicalism modeled in authors like Richard Mouw, Andrew Walls, David Bosch, Christopher J. Wright, N.

T. Wright, and Paul Hiebert, as well as in Pentecostal historians such as Allan Anderson, Grant Wacker, and Gary McGee—I judge that the angels are with Catholics who keep the extremes in a healthy kind of dialectic tension. Here I think of Bernard Lonergan, Karl Rahner, Yves Congar, David Tracy, Elizabeth Johnson, Terrence Tilley, Stephen Bevans, Sandra Schneiders, Robert Schreiter, and Joseph Komonchak. They are part of Lonergan's "not numerous center" who realize that we are in the midst of "a crisis not of faith but of culture. There has been no new revelation from on high to replace the revelation given through Christ Jesus. There has been written no new Bible and there has been founded no new church to link us with him. . . ."

And in the midst of all the roiled waters of cultural change, as Lonergan goes on to say,

> There is bound to be formed a solid right that is determined to live in a world that no longer exists. There is bound to be formed a scattered left, captivated by now this, now that new development, exploring now this and now that new possibility. But what will count is a perhaps not numerous center, big enough to be at home in both the old and the new, painstaking enough to work out one by one the transitions to be made, strong enough to refuse half-measures and insist on complete solutions even though it has to wait.[1]

Truth be told, I do believe that in the nearly century and one-half since the death in 1874 of the exegete and theologian David F. Strauss, those churches and theologians that believed that they should tilt to the *nova* of the new exegesis often slipped over into something resembling Unitarianism or Deism. To be sure, that faith provides praiseworthy ethical insights and philosophies, and it is usually on the side of just causes, but it is only historically connected to Christian Tradition, living one might say off the capital piled up in earlier centuries. In them Jesus is not the Son of God, Savior, and the first fruits of the eschatological reign of God. Rather he is a teacher whose really important teaching revolves around ethics. Dupuis, to my mind, is a quintessential member of the not numerous center. Not as someone who sought the center as an ideal reached by compromise, but someone who was comfortable with the dialectic of competing "truths" while he dwelt in a house of faith capa-

---

1. Lonergan, "Dimensions of Meaning," 266–67.

cious enough to tolerate uncertainties while holding on to its dynamic Christomorphic core. One of the Society of Jesus' greatest contributions was forming men of that generation: Dupuis himself, John Courtney Murray, Teilhard de Chardin, Karl Rahner, Bernard Lonergan, and Henri de Lubac. They explicate the magisterium and sometimes paint wondrous pictures of the convergence of all in Christ, the great Alpha and Omega. They are also comfortable in the act of critically correlating the expanding frontiers of human knowledge with the Catholic-Christian faith.

While most in my generation of students preparing for the priesthood were not taught dogmatic theology in the strict sense of that word, as these theologians and philosophers were, I did receive a licentiate in theology at the Gregorianum in the post-Conciliar years of 1969 to 1972. Despite a lot of reservations at the time, I have been grateful ever since, to the extent that I think that the disappearance of the core curriculum we followed is a great loss. Whether you bought everything or not, you were introduced to a two-millennium-year-old tradition that was presented and—in the lectures of such teachers as Juan Alfaro, Zoltan Alszeghy, Francis Sullivan, Maurizio Flick, and René Latourelle—explicated over against contemporary criticisms and intellectual currents.

Under the aegis of the corps of Jesuit professors at the "Greg," I grappled with the dogmatic tradition of the church in rooms whose windows and doors had been opened by the late Pope John XXIII. I didn't always enjoy the encounter, to be honest. In fact, I was often bored. So bored that in the six or eight weeks we were given to prepare for our licentiate exams, I began devouring mystery stories at a prodigious rate, forty in about six weeks, many of them by Alistair MacLean, as well as lives of Jefferson, Madison, and Hamilton borrowed from the American Information Service Library on Via Veneto. I just couldn't be bothered to memorize the answers to the seventy-five theses that comprised the *Examen Peculiare ad Licentiam de Universa Sacra Theologia* ("The Special Examination for the Licentiate in the Universe of Sacred Theology") that we were expected to defend and explain.[2] But, despite my last-minute balking, my teachers had made an impression on me, in particular Juan Alfaro, probably the greatest teacher I encountered in my entire life.

2. For purists who know there were one hundred, not seventy-five theses at the Greg, one of the many, sometimes cosmetic, post Vatican II reforms reduced them in number for my cohort, although the was carried out in an almost Machiavellian maneuver that combined the disappearing theses into the remaining ones.

Luckily, I managed to pass the STL exam with a fairly good grade. More importantly, I came to judge that the central magisterium of the Catholic Church is, in fact, the best and most integrated interpretation of Christian faith on offer. And I realized that, despite all the serious historiographical problems with the way papal office is sometimes claimed to have originated and its powers invested in a monarchical structure, the continuation of the Petrine ministry in the popes of Rome had guarded and passed on Christian faith better than any other means in Christian history. That conviction has stayed with me, without my ever having been tempted to modern-day, creeping infallibilist interpretations of the authority of every utterance of holders of that office.

During my last year in Rome (1971–72), I wrote a *tesina* (a mini-thesis) for my licentiate under the direction of John Navone, SJ. Navone was an excellent director, encouraging me to write clearly on a topic that expanded my theological reach considerably. A visit to his office might be interrupted as he took a phone call from Franco Zeffirelli or Gore Vidal, but to me this young Oregon Jesuit's insertion into the Italian arts scene was an example of the way I thought a priest and theologian ought to live. The topic I had chosen for my *tesina* was "Process and Finality in the Theology of John B. Cobb, Jr." Overly ambitious for what was the Roman equivalent of a master's degree, it necessitated my immersion in the works of the great Anglo-American philosopher Alfred North Whitehead (1861–1947) and John Cobb, Jr. (b. 1925 in Japan to Methodist missionary parents). Before and during my years in Rome, I also kept up my studies of my other great *magister*, Bernard Lonergan, whose *opus* had helped me understand the dilemmas of a church whose defenders had been arriving, as he put it so memorably, "on the scene a little breathlessly and a little late,"[3] ever since Kant and the Enlightenment ushered in historical consciousness and its ambiguous enshrinement of the physical sciences as the epitome of understanding in a new temple of knowledge. (It may be worth noting in passing that my reading of Lonergan, Cobb, and Whitehead all took place outside of the classrooms in which I studied Christian history, Bible, and theology.) Later still liberation and feminist theology made a big impact on me, but interreligious, philosophical, and cosmological concerns have always dominated my intellectual life.

---

3. Lonergan, *Insight*, 733.

These three giants (Whitehead, Lonergan, and Cobb) plunged me into a world marked by the polarity of seemingly timeless Christian doctrine and at every level of reality, "process"—the growing together of sub-atomic elements to form everything from quarks to amoebas, from religious traditions to civilizations, from earthworms to galaxies millions and millions of light years in extent. Everything, I came to realize, is formed in a process marked by ongoing "creativity." But that creativity is purchased at the price of the continual destruction and recombination of the stuff of the universe, a "stuff" that is not inert elements but a reverberation of entities that behave like waves and particles, *events* of greater and lesser duration and complexity, *events* in which being from the sub-atomic to the macrocosmic level explodes into being, coheres, grows, and passes away to become the wherewithal of *new events* in a fourteen- to fifteen-billion-year-old cosmos. In that worldview, one has to take evolution seriously and think through Christian doctrine on a pan-cosmic scale. Teilhard de Chardin influenced both me and many others then and now to envisage and hope for the convergence of world process in Christ. John Navone (today a friend whose writings and person I admire greatly and who merits the title, "Initiator of Narrative Theology"[4]) kept me grounded in the concreteness of the great biblical narratives as I wrote on Cobb and Whitehead. The Divine *Logos* of this dynamic world process was the Word that was incarnate in Jesus, and I was a fledgling member of a society that took its name from it, the Society of the Divine Word.

THE DILEMMA OF AN HISTORICALLY CONSCIOUS THEOLOGY OF RELIGIONS

I went from Rome to teach theology as a missionary in Papua New Guinea for five wonderful years from 1972 to 1977. This plunged me into the entire issue of cultural adaptation of Christianity at a level I had never imagined I would face. When I returned to the United States and began doctoral work at the Divinity School of the University of Chicago, its marvelous interdisciplinary curriculum plunged me deep into the entire question of Christianity and "other" religious traditions. When I finished my thesis in 1987 ("The Roman Catholic Magisterium on 'Other' Religious Ways"—a study of the four fundamental texts of the Second

---

4. See, among others, two of Navone's signature books, *Towards a Theology of Story* and *The Jesus Story: Our Life as Story in Christ*.

Vatican Council), I was convinced that: (1) the so-called "pluralists" were right—*on philosophical and history-of-religions grounds*—about the relativity of the world's great religious Ways, but also that relativity did not obligate one to accept "relativism," since the universe was clearly marked by gradients of value and only dialogue could clarify such issues; (2) that the pluralist position, at least as articulated by John Hick, was not reconcilable with Christian doctrine as summarized in my four Vatican II texts, nor with the Bible; and (3) that those who proposed a straightforward pluralist position were propounding the view that Western university professors were the arbiters of truth, a proposition I found quite dismal, given the academy's penchant for crippling analysis and lack of a sense of the poetry of the cosmos and its history as a meaningful Whole.

The members of my dissertation committee (Langdon Gilkey, 1919–2004; David Tracy, b. 1939; Anne Carr, 1934–2008; and Joseph Mitsuo Kitagawa, 1915–1992) urged me to publish the thesis. Kitagawa, an historian of religion and a leading expert on Asian religions, particularly liked the fact that—while recognizing the depths of the challenges posed by religious plurality—I also brought into relief the weakness of the Western pluralist position by judging that the pluralists presupposed the superiority of Western academic methods. That position (though it has become a common place since then, was not much propounded then) I said in my dissertation, was a *de facto* argument that academics knew what the various traditions were *really* about better than insiders in the several traditions themselves. At another level I was wrestling with something Kitagawa said during the session in which my thesis topic was approved: "The problem with Catholic teaching is that it is marked by too much authoritarianism and too little 'religious' authority," an enigmatic statement of a Japanese Christian saturated in Asian wisdom that seems as true today as it did in April of 1981. He counseled me not to get hung up on the typically liberal Catholic critique of the authoritarianism. Instead he advised me to try to discern what was authoritative and passed on vital tradition to a new age . . . despite the authoritarian dress in which it came.

I remember responding to a telephone call from my director inviting me to his office a few days after submitting the hundred-plus pages that were the central chapter of my dissertation. Gilkey thumped the chapter on his desk. I was expecting criticism, but Langdon said with a big smile, "If you're right about what Vatican II says, and I think you are, that Knitter fellow is wrong." Paul Knitter, I remind the reader, was and is one of my closest friends. Once we were both confreres in the Society of the Divine Word, and for thirty years we have been conversation partners on these issues. Together we helped nurture forty books into print in the Faith Meets Faith Series, for which Paul served as general editor. Paul, his wife Cathy Cornell, my wife Linda, and I have season tickets for the Roundabout Theatre in New York City, which brings us together regularly. Paul's insistence that truth must be judged by its practical fruits in liberating human beings from oppression continues to serve me as an important reminder of the limits of theory in this area.

It was heady stuff to be told by my advisors that I had written something discerning. When I finished my thesis, in fact, there was scarcely a gap between Paul Knitter and me. At an historical or phenomenological level, I judged that there was no way to demonstrate the superiority of any religion. From what humanity knows on the basis of *empirical* evidence, no world religion can demonstrate its superiority over the others. It has to appeal to faith to do so, which means it cannot argue its position convincingly in the public square. Second, I came to realize that the issue of an apparent "incommensurability" among the religions make comparisons difficult if not impossible.[5] Third, the effect of the first two perspectives means that, in a post-Kantian world, religious "truth" is inevitably relegated to the realm of "mere" opinion and belief, unreliable and, from a scientific point of view, untestable in any meaningful empirical manner. The problem I had with my advisors' encouragement to publish my thesis, however, was that I couldn't resolve the conflict within me either by choosing Christian faith over academic rationality or by embracing academic rationality over faith.

The pluralists, as characterized by my *Doktorvater* Langdon Gilkey, held that "rough parity" marked the relationship of the great religions of

---

5. By "incommensurability" (literally, "difficult to measure or compare") I mean that to compare doctrines of salvation, for example, by comparing the use of the Sanskrit word *moksha* and the New Testament Greek word *soteria*—both of which are usually translated "salvation"—is to ignore differences in context and connotation so immense as to make the comparison almost worthless. Reading the work of my friend David Carpenter on "revelation" in the Christian theologian Bonaventure and the Vedic commentator Bhartṛhari convinced me of the futility of trying to make sense of Indian and Christian religious traditions without careful study of every level of each. As used within the religious universe of each tradition, in other words, what is referred to by the word "salvation" appears an incommensurable reality.

the world.[6] This rough parity, I came to believe, was the case *on empirical grounds*, but it was also incompatible with biblical teaching or its development by the teaching magisterium of the Roman Catholic Church. Moreover, Gilkey was clear that it was a mistake to understand rough parity as eviscerating the intuition of absoluteness on which every religious tradition stands. Conviction of its own truth was necessary, he knew, if a tradition is to articulate the ontology that grounds human obligations to act in accord "with the grain of the universe."[7] For Gilkey the quandary of the intellectual in every tradition today is knowing that his or her tradition needs to assert that absolute foundation while realizing that every other tradition was also asserting foundational claims. On philosophical grounds, Gilkey knew, these competing claims could not all be true, yet to rely on faith against evidence opened religion up to modern attacks that all religion was irrational.

In pondering Gilkey's thought I came to believe that Christian theology needed either to accept the demotion to "unreliable talk about mere opinion" necessitated by the relativism of the academy or had to find convincing grounds for maintaining the teaching of a biblical tradition that interprets Jesus as the Christ, uniquely the Son of God, heir of the promises of God in the covenant with Israel, the one pointed to in First Testament Scriptures and revelation. As I went more deeply into it, I realized that the gospel of and about Jesus is first and foremost a promise that *this* God alone saves the cosmos in a way both foreshadowed and realized in the history of Jesus. This promise entails hope and belief that the fate of the universe is revealed and foreshadowed in Jesus' death, resurrection, and conferral of the Spirit. In the end, what is at stake is whether Jesus *is* the Messiah, the unsurpassable revealer and definitive agent of the accomplishment of God's *mysterion* (Galatians 3:1–6), the divine plan to save humankind. In that frame of reference the "good news" of the Gospel is God's promise: (1) that Jesus, the Messiah/Christ, is the unique mediator of salvation; and (2) that in saying yes to him, one is embracing God's promise that the universe is saved in him and the Spirit.

These are also core elements in Pauline and Johannine theology that the progressive wing of scripture scholars had been attacking as mythological or later, less reliable biblical strands from the days of D. F.

6. See Gilkey, "Plurality," 41ff.

7. I take the pithy phrase, "with the grain of the universe," from Stanley Hauerwas's 2000-2001 Gifford lectures.

Strauss (1808–1875) and his *Life of Jesus* down through Rudolf Bultmann (1884–1976) and the contemporary Jesus Seminar and the new quest for the historical Jesus.

As I worked through the first two books of Dupuis, it became ever clearer to me that, if those who isolated the Jesus of history from the Christ of faith by trying to find a primitive "gospel" shorn of the elaborations of the Pauline and Johannine theological strata were right, then both the Bible and centuries-long Christian Tradition were making a big mistake. Jesus would then be—as most theologians of religious pluralism were saying—a teacher like Moses, Gautama, Confucius, or Mohammed. Instead of being *the* Redeemer, depending on the culture of the exegete doing the textual archeology, Jesus could be a wise teacher (like a nineteenth-century German professor), an Edwardian gentleman (modeling a healthy life, guarding children and the weaker sex, favoring a strong Royal Navy to maintain the Empire as a civilizing force), a political revolutionary (opposing Roman imperialism and counseling his followers to liberate the poor), or a gender-role path-breaker (the first to institute a truly egalitarian society of gender equality and malleable sexual identity). It helps, of course, that it is *not* a stretch to find each of these attributes in Jesus. The question, of course, is whether any or all such images captures *all* that Jesus is or the most important thing he is about.

Working as an editor on Dupuis's careful treatment of the biblical and subsequent conciliar and papal magisterial statements convinced me over time: (1) that the Synoptic materials were shaped by the Pauline proto-gospel and that reading Pauline theology out of the Synoptics or reading John as overly theologized fiction was to ignore the way in which the canon was formed; (2) that the primary Pauline letters (Romans, Galatians, Philippians, 1 and 2 Corinthians, 1 Thessalonians and Philemon) were thoroughly Hebrew in conception and written to show to a broader Mediterranean audience that Jesus was the fulfillment of the First Testament and was significant on a cosmic scale; (3) that the secondary or disputed Pauline letters (2 Thessalonians, Colossians, Ephesians, Titus, 1 and 2 Timothy) breathe the spirit of Paul and represent his or his close associates' attempts to translate Jewish theology into Greek; and finally (4) that the Gospel of John was similarly designed for the challenges of a later period.

Eventually the exegetical work of N. T. Wright and James D. G. Dunn gave me confidence that the judgments I had been making while I was absorbing the work of Dupuis and David Bosch were also founded in the scholarship of a new generation of scholars with far better credentials than my own. In other words, attempts to deal with Jesus as primarily a teacher or founder of a religious tradition were neglecting the primary categories in which both the Bible and Tradition portrayed him. A much deeper comparative theology was needed than religious pluralists were utilizing.

THE VISION OF DUPUIS AND ITS IMPLICATIONS

What I began to realize, as Dupuis led me to look at the biblical data in the light of the contemporary interreligious situation, was straight-forward: the New Testament *as-a-whole*, means to teach that Jesus is the one whose person, teaching, and history embody, reveal, foreshadow, and will accomplish God's promise for both the cosmos and humanity. *Either that or the New Testament is a fraud, since as-a-whole that's what the New Testament teaches.* That message, on Dupuis's reading of Tradition, was translated by church fathers such as Irenaeus, Justin Martyr, Origen, Athanasius, and Gregory of Nazianzus into language canonized in the third- to fifth-century ecumenical creeds. A piece of literary theory that I remember David Tracy or Paul Ricoeur expounding held that a literary work is composed with a purpose in mind. That purpose could be wrong, of course, and its adequacy had to be debated. Furthermore, authors lose control of the work when they publish it. The corollary to that is that the purpose with which the New Testament canon was put together was to advance the notions that the early Councils encapsulated in the creeds. Yes, there is much more in the first-order language of narrative and epistle that comprise the new Testament. Yes, complex texts like the First and New Testaments have many layers and a plethora of different meanings. But if the New Testament was not composed to advance the notion that Jesus was God's "Son" (God's "second-self," as it were) sent to accomplish God's universal salvific self-revelation and goals, it was and is a fraud. To be a Christian is to bet that it is not a fraud and to commit one's life to that message.

Dupuis may not have argued apologetically every step of the case he was making in the way I have outlined, but he was firmly rooted in the New Testament's teaching that Jesus is of universal and final significance, and that a *Christian* theological appraisal of Christianity's relations with other traditions must begin from that doctrine. To grasp that and his second major conviction—on "other" religious ways also being vehicles of God's purposes—Dupuis's work needs to be read carefully and not just cherry-picked for statements with which one agrees and disagrees. This, in my opinion is what *Dominus Iesus* and the CDF Notification do. Does he go further than the Roman magisterium? Yes. But the more important question is: Is he wrong in his proposals in ways that subvert the Christian message?

Where he goes further than *Dominus Iesus* is in at least three areas. First, he sees Christianity as an intrinsically *eschatological* faith. Its essential structure lies in trusting faith in God's promise that the final state of the cosmos, will be brought about through a process like the death and resurrection of Jesus. We live with the dangerous memory of the historical Jesus confounding attempts to make him a mere teacher or revolutionary, and we experience his presence in the life of the church. But his personhood is constituted by the union of humanity and the divine *Logos*. That *Logos* is present in the structure of world process and, on Dupuis's reading of the signs of the times, present in the religious traditions that help untold billions discern meaning in life. The structure of Christian existence is about the future, and Dupuis broadened that idea to include the notion that the history of the whole cosmos involved an eschatological convergence of religions in Jesus the Christ as its omega point.

Second, Dupuis is intensely Trinitarian, and in his Trinity, the Holy Spirit hovers over the entire process of cosmic history. Within human history, the Spirit leads all human beings toward the One who is both promised and revealed in the "Christ-event"—that is to say, to the God whom the New Testament calls "Father," Jesus' appellation for YHWH. But because human beings become aware of the deep, divine dimensions of life in concrete religious traditions, Dupuis also sees the Spirit active in leading human beings to this end *in and through their traditions*. Finding fault with this second element, it should be noted, is CDF's fundamental objection to his work.

Third, in his last two books (*Toward a Christian Theology of Religious Pluralism* and *Christianity and the Religions*), Dupuis increasingly draws attention to the fact that if the similarities and complementarities between the religions at the level of experience are such that words like "revelation," "teacher," "prophet," and "savior" are used to denote seemingly common aspects of the several traditions, then one must take care to understand them *analogically, not univocally*. He does not pretend to be a comparative historian of religion. Rather—committed to the truth of Christian revelation—he knows that the *genre* in which he writes is *Christian* theology, not something that is acceptable across traditions. His is a *Christian* theology aiming to explicate religious plurality and pluralism. He fully realizes that both individual terms within the various traditions and the traditions as a whole are *reciprocal, complementary*, and *asymmetrical* in an analogical but real relation to one another,

> in the sense that God has provided gifts to human beings in other religious traditions as well, which even though they find their fulfillment in the revelation of God in Jesus Christ, nonetheless represent authentic words of God and additional autonomous gifts from God. Such divine gifts to human beings do not in any way impede the transcendence and unsurpassability of God's gift in Jesus Christ, attested by the Christian sacred scriptures, is thus to be understood as *mutual, "asymmetrical" complementarity.* The term, "asymmetrical," as new as it might seem in this context, cannot be ignored [as the CDF seems intent on doing, ed.]; otherwise the complementarity might be understood in a way that is theologically incorrect. . . . Even while being reciprocal, their complementarity will have to be understood as "asymmetrical" for the very same reasons.[8]

In this citation, Dupuis goes further than CDF is willing to go. And I think that calling him a "conservative revisionist" is accurate. Certainly what he proposes is not thought to be irresponsible by a younger Jesuit confrere who has entered deeply in the comparative theology of religions. In a 1991 review Dupuis's fellow Jesuit, Frank Clooney, a leading representative of a generation of "comparative theologians," who take both difference and asymmetricality seriously, says the following about Dupuis's first book, *Jesus Christ at the Encounter of World Religions*:

> We have here a master theologian's mature reflections on Scripture, important moments in the Christian tradition, the documents of Vatican II, recent papal teaching, and the dynamics of the last twenty-five years of interreligious dialogue—all with an eye to ways attention to the traditional facilitates serious openness to the work of Christ in the world religions [including] a complementary uniqueness of the mystery of Jesus Christ vis-à-vis other salvific

8. Dupuis, *Christianity*, 136; see also 255–57.

figures and the founding experiences of other religious traditions [and the ways] terms such as "the word of God," "holy scripture," and "inspiration" may be used with reference to extra-Christian traditions.[9]

Clooney goes on to observe that Dupuis's years of teaching and scholarship in India help him "avoid most of the pitfalls of generalists, and so he is a model of how Christian theologians can speak sensitively and responsibly about the world religions." Still, Clooney (a Professor at Harvard, Indologist, historian of religions, and comparative theologian) wants to know how "this Christocentric theology will be articulated after 'specific situations' in different religious traditions have actually been examined from a Christocentric perspective." Clooney's own burgeoning body of work is of the greatest significance in answering this question. I cannot recommend it strongly enough. In addition, a series of books by recognized experts in the depths of both Christianity and other religious traditions that Catherine Cornille is editing will offer commentaries on the classic texts of other religions (for example the *Heart Sutra* and the *Bhagavad-Gita*); these will help us see the implications of Clooney's question and shed light on how it may be answered.

I brought up Clooney's question to Jacques on more than one occasion. At one point, with some exasperation, he answered that I had myself already answered that question in characterizing his lifework as one of "clearing space for serious dialogue" in my essay in the Orbis *Festschrift* in his honor.[10] His point is that he believes that without a recognition that there is real, important truth and wisdom in other traditions, Christians would not see the importance of dialogue. His own work, he realized, was no substitute for deeper dialogue and comparative theology. But he hoped he was providing theological warrants for Christians to engage in it.

At another level, although I do not know that he ever explicitly *wrote* about what I discuss next, in conversation with me he stated that his notion of convergence was inspired by the New Testament and brought into the world of contemporary thought by Teilhard de Chardin's vision of cosmic convergence and complexity-consciousness. In that Teilhardian vision, growing consciousness of the complexity and the dynamic, un-

---

9. Clooney, review of *Jesus Christ at the Encounter of World Religions.*

10. Burrows in Kendall and O'Collins.

derlying unity of the cosmos takes place as *human beings grasp it and implement its implications in science, religion, political economy, and art.* Science provides one level of global dialogue in that process. Politics another. Intercultural and history of religions studies another. Interreligious dialogue yet another. Christian faith, Dupuis believed, is not simply about the past, although it is rooted in historical events. It is about orienting humanity to the future and encouraging them to create new worlds as co-creators with God. One of Christianity's central insights—when integrated into a framework such as that envisioned in the work of Teilhard de Chardin or Thomas Berry's "new universe story"—is dramatic: *The way into the future is to undergo the law of the universe, submitting to death of one's self while putting one's trust in the gospel of God's promise to treat one's self and the universe as God had dealt with Jesus in the Resurrection.* That is Christianity's Christomorphic core, a core that has analogies in other traditions, but which, because of the realism of Christianity's belief in the glorification of Jesus, makes its belief in his uniqueness central. Being a Christian in its fullest sense is to enter into that paschal dynamic with Jesus as one's Lord as one embraces Jesus as the realization and personification of God's coming reign.

In essence, the Christian gospel is the promise of new life, not just for individuals but for the cosmos. As Christianity moved into the Western Mediterranean world, that promise was taken up into Platonic and Neo-Platonic conceptions of the separability of body and soul and the hyper-reality of spirit and soul. There is no such overarching metaphysic in today's global, multicultural, multireligious world. The world, of course, was always a multicultural, multireligious globe; and there never was a universal vision of the origin and destiny of the Whole; humanity—split into cultural-religious civilizations of various dimensions, however did not realize it. Instead, each tribe and people thought it was the center of the universe, its religion anchoring it as the *axis mundi.* The nearest we come to grasping "reality" as-a-Whole is in the conception of an ever-expanding universe in something like the manner explored cosmologically in *The New Universe* by Thomas Berry and Brian Swimme. What I was dealing with in my own STL *tesina* made me sensitive to this, since in the world of process thought, one cannot conceive of a final state of affairs, for, as the emblematic adage goes, "Process *is* the reality." Dupuis remained a cautious, intra-Christian, Catholic-doctrinal-sphere-of-discourse theologian, but the implications of his theology are clearly those that Berry and Swimme open and that Elizabeth Johnson exploits magnificently in the eighth and ninth chapters of her *capolavoro*, *Quest for the Living God*.

The central biblical affirmation of believing in the promises of God, however, does not depend on this or that metaphysics or scientific breakthrough. Religion and science, as John Haught's books show, offer insight into reality at different levels. It would take us far afield to enter into Haught's work.[11] What we can do is realize that Dupuis's proposal that religions complement one another as they converge on the future is rooted in the biblical vision of humanity and the cosmos taking their origin and heading toward their fulfillment in God. The concept of complementarity brings that convergence into relief. Qualifying complementarity by the adjective "asymmetrical" brings into relief the fact that, whatever similarities may exist at a phenomenal level, they do not ground an assertion that Jesus and, for example, Gautama (and the traditions taking their origin in them) are about the same thing.[12] Instead, Dupuis's years in India as a part of a small minority made him realize that the cultural and metaphysical worlds that founders of Christianity and Asian traditions lived in and that their traditions developed in were vastly different—conceptually, existentially, and culturally. He writes within the *genre* of Catholic doctrinal theology with full recognition of the wisdom contained in words I have heard David Tracy use often about the hermeneutics of events and texts coming from different places. We converse with the "other" by careful apprehension of metaphors, analogies, incongruities, and perhaps differences. In such a world, according to Tracy, one must attend to the differences and similarities in what we take note of, but we must also be aware that within differences unsuspected similarities can be found, just as chasms of difference may lie between the mountains of apparent similarities.[13]

11. See Haught, *Making Sense of Evolution* for a magisterial dissection of the different levels of reality referred to in common sense, scientific, and religious language.

12. For a masterful examination of how deep this plurality of religions goes and an interpretation of its meaning, see Heim, *Salvations*, a book whose erudition and careful reasoning fascinated Dupuis even though he could not bring himself to accept its conclusion that the various traditions were leading their followers to different ends. Though Dupuis was an inclusive pluralist, he believed the final state of salvation would be one for all humankind.

13. My formulation of Tracy here is taken from hearing him speak in classes at the University of Chicago and in conversations. For an overview of him on these issues see his *Plurality and Ambiguity*, 82–114 and *passim*.

As I was working through all this, I had the good fortune to encounter the person and thought of Raimon Panikkar (1918–2010). Orbis had published his *The Silence of the Buddha* at about the time I arrived there in March 1989. Soon thereafter one of Panikkar's students, David Krieger, did a book on Panikkar that took my breath away.[14] Over the next twenty years, always with Krieger's insights into the way in which Panikkar was attempting to break the distinction between philosophy and theology (a distinction that would have made no sense in the patristic era) and to break out of the academic captivity of both disciplines to render the wisdom of Christianity and Indian traditions, we did three more major books by Panikkar (for the titles, see the bibliography). Each merits at least a short commentary here. I will refrain from the temptation to write them, but I cannot refrain from telling a story. We were having difficulties with the translation of one of Raimon's books (*Christophany*), and it was much delayed. Taking advantage of the delay and feeling the need for a theologian of considerable *gravitas* to testify to *Christophany's* importance, I called to ask Jacques if he would give us a paragraph endorsing Panikkar's book. He had read it in Italian but there was a long silence. And then a quiet, "I don't think I should. I am enough trouble already without endorsing this book. I really don't know what to make of it."

"Raimon thinks highly of your work, Jacques," I replied, "and he would be pleased to have your endorsement." Dupuis demurred and again said he needed to think about it. An email came a few days later, saying he thought he ought not do it. By coincidence, I learned at about the same time that Raimon had received a hand-written note from one Joseph Ratzinger. Two women who read that note have verified its content. And before writing these pages I checked again with Milena Carrara (Panikkar's long-time associate and publisher of his *opera omnia*), who reconfirmed the story for me. According to them, in his note, Ratzinger praised *Christophany* (which he had read as *Cristofania* in the Italian edition), saying that he (Panikkar) was without peer as a cross-cultural and interreligious pilgrim, bringing together theological and philosophical wisdom of both the East and West, and transcending the relativism of the academy. I called Jacques to tell him what Ratzinger said. He was dumbfounded.

---

14. See Krieger, *New Universalism*.

Why? Because he was perplexed to think that his nemesis could blithely praise the work of Panikkar, who mixed literary genres and speculated about the homology of the Trinitarian structure of reality in Christian and Indian traditions, while he pounced on every ambiguity in Dupuis's own carefully constructed work. It was, I think, impossible for Dupuis to understand Panikkar.

It was my privilege to be friends with both of these octogenarians and to feel the authenticity and depth of their quite different spirits. I will not try to reconcile their differences. For that we need someone of the depth of David Krieger, Joseph Prabhu, or Scott Eastham, each a theologian and philosopher with a profound understanding of the many facets of Panikkar's *opus*. I will, however, suggest that only a sort of eschatological *Aufhebung*[15] can resolve the asymmetries of the complementarities of the great traditions. In using *Aufhebung*, I go against the advice of my distinguished theologian-friend, Peter Phan, who warns that I will be entering into much disputed terrain and involving myself in a high level of speculation on the nature of world process. He said that I run the risk of readers thinking I am invoking the conceptual world of Hegelian dialectics. I do not wish to do either. But if religious traditions exist in a state where they appear to be composed of conceptually incommensurable visions and ontologies, an eschatological transformation or *Aufhebung* raises the possibility of a deeper unity and a higher viewpoint that makes transparent complementarities now hidden.

The resurrection of Jesus itself is, I think, the paradigmatic example of the possibility of such a change. As Anthony Kelly says,

> Despite the differences and conflicts that have shaped the past of the various religious traditions, the future is what all have in common. At the point where all look forward to a hoped for future, Christian hope, centered on the resurrection of the crucified Jesus, has a vital mediating role . . . Dialogue may reach an impasse, and will certainly pose its problems, but the Christians involved must wait on the unfathomable freedom of the One "who by the power at work within us is able to accomplish abundantly far more than all we can ask or imagine" (Eph 3:20). The mission of dialogue must, in short, wait on its prayers to be answered and for the rev-

15. The German noun *Aufhebung* and the verb *aufheben* (past participle, *aufgehoben*) denote a state of affairs or process in which something now existent is superseded, lifted up, or abolished only to take life again as a transformation of the materials that give it birth.

elation that has occurred in the resurrection of Christ to keep on being revelation in ways still to be disclosed. If such an attitude is criticized for being too specifically Christian, then at least it will be criticized for the right reasons—namely, for having too much hope in the Other rather than too little—and for all others in our common longing for eternal life.[16]

Kelly's book as a whole is designed to drive home the "truth" that the resurrection is not just *a* doctrine in Christianity. It is, rather the primary *donum* of God and the single most important revelation of what Christianity is about, the key to the cipher of the way in which "embodied existence transcends the status of being simply a physical body in a material world," moving as it does against "excessively spiritual interpretations" of the universe both in its human and cosmic dimensions.[17]

Can an eschaton foreshadowed by the resurrection of a Jesus be the fulfillment of the cosmos? Such an eschaton would be a transformation in which there is both continuity and discontinuity. The new state will be radically new, to be sure, but seen to have been rooted all along in what went before. Similarly, in the post-resurrection narratives, the friends and disciples of the late Jesus of Nazareth encounter him. But something has to happen *within them* to let them realize that one whom they encounter outside the empty tomb, on the road to Emmaus, in the upper room, and (for all the exegetical problems the story presents) at the lakeside cooking fish is the one they knew before: changing water into wine, multiplying loaves, curing a centurion's servant, teaching from a boat, talking to a woman at a well.

The question cannot be avoided. Could the *eschaton* be the occasion of exactly such a radically new understanding of *this* Jesus? And could such an *Aufhebung* enable, for example, Buddhists to see him with new eyes, just as Christians might see the Buddha with new eyes? or for Hindus to see *advaita's* envisionment of the paradoxical unity of Absoluteness and finitude as an example of the *logos* of Reality? At the eschaton, in other words, could there occur the revelation of a complementarity between Christianity and Buddhism such that what is *aufgehoben* ("superseded," "lifted up," "abolished," "transformed" or "sublated") are aspects of the religious traditions that are conceptually irreconcilable under the conditions of history in this aeon . . . but which might be reconciled at the

16. Kelly, *Resurrection Effect*, 171–72.

17. Ibid., 35–38.

eschaton when God's relation to universal history and the *kosmos* will be fully revealed?

May we at least hope for that?

I think this is what Dupuis was invoking in his last book, where he asks the question about how we are

> to understand the relationship between the historical reality of the Reign of God and its eschatological fullness. Is the fullness of salvation to be understood in terms of the fulfillment of the Church at the end of time? Or will the Church in heaven be part of an eschatological Reign which extends beyond it? Or will the fulfillment of the eschatological Kingdom bring the time of the Church to a close, its sacramental role now having been completed?[18]

With all the risks entailed in using *Aufhebung* to characterize the sort of transformation entailed in his vision, I believe my way of framing the issue is both consonant with Dupuis's work and makes explicit what is implicit in it. How? By reason of the fact that the "Ultimate Reality" mediated by the various "revelations" and "enlightenments" of the worlds' religions, *as grasped in the present aeon*, may be revealed at the *eschaton* to have always enjoyed a complementarity hidden from us today because of their radical asymmetry. This is a way to understand an analogy between the way that the path of the Buddha leads to enlightenment and baptism in the Spirit leads to new eyes with which to know Jesus as the *Logos* of God become human. But as asymmetrical, we need not press the analogy to say they are ways of knowing the same reality. Only those who have received *both* baptism in the Spirit *and* enlightenment are fully qualified to speak of their complementarity. But in the present aeon, warned by Tracy, we must also realize that we also need to beware of retreats into special knowledge available only to believers.[19] For Tracy, dialogue needs to stay in the public realm even if the texts one is interpreting point beyond, as is the case, for example in 1 Corinthians 13:12, speaking of a transcendent "then" when ambiguity will end.

In this framework, the action of God at the eschaton might be imagined as a concrete, saving reconciliation of what today divides us, a transformation in which the divine *pleroma* ("fullness," Rom 11: 12) fulfills the promise of redemption and forgiveness realized in Jesus as Christ as good news *for all*, not just for Christians and Jews (as in Rom

18. Dupuis, *Toward*, 356–57.

19. Tracy, *Plurality and Ambiguity*, 110.

11:12)[20] but also for Muslims, Hindus, followers of African, Melanesian, and Native American Traditional Religions, secularists, and atheists. An important difference between what I am understanding in this admittedly speculative vision of God's final revelation at the *eschaton* and some contemporary pluralist conceptions of religious plurality is contained in the way Ephesians 1:17–23 portrays this *pleroma*.

> I pray that the God of our Lord Jesus Christ, the Father of glory, may give you a spirit of wisdom and revelation as you come to know him, so that, with the eyes of your heart enlightened, you may know what is the hope to which he has called you, what are the riches of his glorious inheritance among the saints, and what is the immeasurable greatness of his power for us who believe, according to the working of his great power. God put this power to work in Christ when he raised him from the dead and seated him at his right hand in the heavenly places, far above all rule and authority and power and dominion, and above every name that is named, not only in this age but also in the age to come. And he has put all things under his feet and has made him the head over all things for the church, which is his body, the fullness of him who fills all in all.

The Pauline letter envisages all the world recognizing the Christ who is being built up in his body, the church, which is the inclusive sacrament of a Christ who embodies the promise of God to be all in all in the final reconciliation spoken of in 2 Corinthians 5: 16–21. In that passage several elements merit attention: "If anyone is in Christ, there is a new creation" and "everything has become new" (v. 17) as Christians become a people whom God has reconciled to God through Christ and to whom God has given the ministry of reconciliation not counting their trespasses against them, and entrusting the message of reconciliation to them (vv. 19–20).

In a personal letter to me of 4 May 2011, my friend and teacher John Navone characterizes the final reconciliation of God's Kingdom at the eschaton as follows:

> The final revelation at the eschaton will simultaneously reveal who we are and who God/Jesus as the Christ is. In the divine light we shall finally discover our full identity in the universal creation, the particular sentence that we are in the universal story that the Divine Word has fully told, the particular note we are in the divine symphony, the part we are in the whole. The Last Judgment occurs

---

20. See also Eph 1:23, 3:19, 4:13; Col 1:19, 25, 2:9–10.

only when all the evidence of world history, the universal story, is in. Only then, shall we fully know ourselves in the context of all the past that has poured into our lives and the impact that our lives have effected in others, tingling down to the last moment/period of the universal story. We cannot truly understand anything taken out of context; likewise, we cannot truly understand ourselves outside our ultimate context: God and his universal story. Each human being is an irreplaceable element in story that the Creator Logos/Word is telling. Ephesians implies this in affirming that the mystery of each human life is hidden in Christ, to be revealed at the end of time. Revelations implies this in the mystery of the white stone at the heart of each human life, beautifully brought out in the BBC special on "The Monastery."

The first word of God to us in the Bible, in the form a question, "Where are you?" implies our lifelong quest to discover where/ who we are. The Question-Raising Mystery of God at the heart of every human life is also the Question-Answering Mystery. To hear the Question is to be already in touch with the Answer. The dynamic of the question is the dynamic of all human moral, intellectual, cultural and religious development/maturation. At the end of time, I believe all humans shall see what God has done for them in Jesus Christ.

Does Dupuis write with the concreteness of Navone's dramatic portrayal of the eschaton? Not that I recall. Nor does he use the language I suggest to delineate the sort of eschatological *Aufhebung* that could reveal that God has been becoming "all in all" (1 Cor 15:23), working from the beginning in Christ whom God "raised from the dead" establishing him "head over all things for the church, which is his body, the fullness of him who fills all in all" (Eph 1:20–23). Nor does he write at any great length about the church's *kerygma* or role in bearing witness to such a construal of Christ. Indeed, in a conversation with Karl Josef Becker, SJ, and Ilaria Morali, after Jacques' death, as we were planning their monumental *The Catholic Engagement with World Religions*, I once said that Dupuis had spoken in these terms. Both looked at me quizzically. Karl Josef said, "I don't think it's in his writings." When I returned to New York, I examined the record. It was not there the way I was putting it, and Karl Josef was right. But Jacques had commented favorably when I brought up this vision in conversation, and in his first book with Orbis, he said the following:

> . . . while the Holy Spirit is in a special way the soul of the church, it is also the soul of the universe, for Christ pours forth his fullness

upon the whole of creation and the universe is filled with his presence. (cf. Col 1:19)

Summarizing we may say: The Spirit poured forth on Pentecost causes the action of the Pascal event to be an action of today, as well. It is by the Spirit that the mystery of salvation, accomplished once for all in Jesus Christ, becomes concrete reality for human beings. As principle of the new creation, the Spirit makes the sovereignty of Christ actually present in history. The activity of the Spirit gives birth to the community of the church but transcends the boundaries of the Christian fold to give life to men and women and transform the cosmos.[21]

I had been so struck by our conversations and the role Dupuis accorded the Spirit in *Jesus Christ at the Encounter of World Religions* that, when Orbis's executive director Robert Gormley once asked me what was so radical in Dupuis that the Vatican might censor him, I replied immediately, "He has a real Trinity, and the Holy Spirit has really important work to do outside the boundaries of the church." Although it oversimplifies CDF's objections to Dupuis, it is not a bad summary of them.

It is clear that when the contemporary papal magisterium and CDF use the words "uniqueness" and "unicity," they are synonyms for maintaining that the person and both the redemptive and revelatory work of Jesus as the Christ are absolutely superior to that of any other religious tradition. As carefully as Dupuis attempted to use the teaching of Vatican II and Pope John Paul II to propose that, in principle, there was no contradiction between the uniqueness of Christ and proposing that the Spirit was active in other, his efforts were found deficient by CDF because they were alleged to diminish the uniqueness of Christ and the role of the church in mediating salvation.

I am sympathetic with CDF's concern and am on record as approving Pope Benedict XVI's strictures against a contemporary culture that breathes the dictatorship of relativism. Nevertheless, a question must be asked. Must uniqueness be understood as "absolutely superior"? In his monumental book *Uniqueness*, Gabriel Moran suggests that it does not. Moran articulates the idea that if uniqueness is important, the uniqueness of Christ must be explicated as good news for *all* persons, not just Christians. Unfortunately, he notes, the usual way uniqueness is defined heads Christians toward claims of privilege, exclusivity, and superiority.

21. Dupuis, *Christ at the Encounter*, 156.

The motivation for mission, accordingly, becomes the necessity of making everyone Christian lest they be condemned to hell, a fate Christians escape because in God's providence they have been chosen for salvation.

Moran suggests an alternative view of uniqueness that opens toward radical inclusiveness, such that a "unique" revelation (of God, as Christians claim for Jesus) might open "itself to Muslims and any other groups for whom the term revelation is sufficiently intelligible." Moran goes on to say, "As revelation has no historical endpoint, so also it is not geographically closed to any religious groups. Conversations that include eastern religions would probably need other terms as important as revelation is to Christians, Jews, and Muslims . . . [including] the word enlightenment, with different connotations from those of nineteenth century Europe."[22]

For Christians, Moran's words, "revelation has no historical endpoint," could make this citation a hard one to reconcile with the doctrine that Jesus as the Christ is God's full and final revelation. It would require volumes to give a full account of the doctrine of revelation or the rich texture of Moran's thought. For our purposes it may suffice, however, simply to note that the doctrine that the revelation of Christ is final has always been complemented with another important one. Namely, that we live in an "in-between age," a now in which what will come to be is real but not yet fully realized, something future yet already present, a reality that has not come to its consummation. In such a dialectic the process of coming to faith in the present age is analogous to a "revelation," but in this act, what is revealed in the inner consciousness of a person is what has already been revealed. Put another way, coming to faith is a participation at the deepest level of one's being in God's *mysterion* in Christ, recognition that, already now in becoming one with the risen Christ, one participates in the beginning of a reality that is promised as the fruition of *all* creation, one that human beings participate in by nature of being alive, but become conscious of only in faith. Or as Romans 8:19–27 puts it:

> [T]he creation waits with eager longing for the revealing of the children of God; for the creation was subjected to futility, not of its own will but by the will of the one who subjected it, in hope that the creation itself will be set free from its bondage to decay and will obtain the freedom of the glory of the children of God. We know that the whole creation has been groaning in labor pains until now; and not only the creation, but we ourselves, who have

22. Moran, *Uniqueness*, 56.

the first fruits of the Spirit, groan inwardly while we wait for adoption, the redemption of our bodies. For in hope we were saved. Now hope that is seen is not hope. For who hopes for what is seen? But if we hope for what we do not see, we wait for it with patience.

Likewise the Spirit helps us in our weakness; for we do not know how to pray as we ought, but that very Spirit intercedes with sighs too deep for words. And God, who searches the heart, knows what is the mind of the Spirit, because the Spirit intercedes for the saints according to the will of God.

This text can be interpreted restrictively to apply only to the salvation of an elect few. Can it not also be interpreted more expansively to apply to the role of those elected to be followers of Jesus as bearers of witness to the great *mysterion* at work in the groans of an incomplete universe struggling toward its fulfillment in an eschaton when its meaning will become apparent for all? A fulfillment that also might involve the reconciliation of elements that appear incommensurable among religions being reconciled in Christ, the *Logos* of God, who may be much grander than the church that is his body now?

Navone's vision of Jesus as the Christ and of the eschaton is Moran's alternative kind of uniqueness. It is a uniqueness whose final revelation will be good news for all, not unlike the vision that the contemporary author Rob Bell unfolds in his *Love Wins*. Bell begins his book with a story that illustrates well the gap between the uniqueness of Christ understood in an exclusive as opposed to an all-inclusive way. People at his church were invited to display paintings, poems, and sculptures that illustrated what they understood a peacemaker to be. One woman chose a quote from Gandhi for her work. Another parishioner, however, attached a piece of paper that read, "Reality check: He's in Hell." To which Bell responds:

Really?
Gandhi's in hell?
He is?
We have confirmation of this?
Somebody knows this?
Without a doubt?
And that somebody decided to take on the responsibility of letting the rest of us know?[23]

23. Bell, *Love Wins*, 1–2.

Theologians tend to be suspicious of preachers who write popular books, but I wager that anyone who reads Bell with an open mind will come away knowing that he's given us a set of eyes with which to envision a wideness in God's love that is incompatible with denying recognition that God works in "other" religious ways to open their followers to saving transcendence.

During the period I was working on this book, I was privileged to be on the doctoral committee of a Finnish Lutheran, Jukka Kaariainen, now on the staff of China Lutheran Seminary in Hsinschu, Taiwan, who was doing his dissertation at Fordham University on Lutheran missiology over against the background of Karl Rahner's and Jacques Dupuis's theologies of religion and religious pluralism.[24] By the time Kaariainen had finished his thesis, I was convinced that the Lutheran way of stating what occurred in Christ and how it related to people who had not come to explicit faith in him, had advantages over the way Catholics have typically framed these issues—Catholics falling back one way or another to a "grace perfects nature" paradigm. While Lutherans run the risk of over-emphasizing transactional and juridical images in St Paul's account of the forgiveness of sin and what occurs in Christ, their clarity on the *nature of the gospel as promise* is rooted in the interpersonal and historical narratives of both the First and Second Testaments much better than Catholicism's often recondite speculations. Ultimately, they are right, I believe, to maintain that in its semantic and historical roots *the gospel of Jesus is a promise, and faith is a trusting embrace of that promise, a trust rooted in the resurrection and the coming of the Spirit* (see, for example, Rom 5:5). More concretely, the gospel is essentially a promise that God will forgive our sins,[25] regenerate us in the Spirit, and bring the entire world through the Christic pattern of death-to-self to resurrection—if we turn to God and trust the promise. The question of theology of religions, accordingly is: How does God relate to those who do not know God in the Trinitarian revelation of the life, teaching, and paschal mystery of Jesus?

24. Kaariainen, "Missio Shaped by Promissio: Lutheran Missiology Confronts the Challenge of Religious Pluralism."

25. Lest the reader think I construe sin and forgiveness in narrow and juridical *ex opere operato* terms, I refer him or her to my presidential address for the American Society of Missiology (see Burrows, "Importance" in bibliography). There I develop the thought that the biblical teaching on sin is far deeper than typical Western understandings of that reality, and forgiveness is much more than merely saying that they don't matter to God.

That fundamental hermeneutic of gospel as promise makes sense of the New Testament as a whole and in the Lutheran emphasis on the ancient doctrine that—despite God's self-disclosure in Christ—God remains hidden in a cloud of unknowing and that our ground for hoping that the first half of a text such as John 3:16 ("For God so loved the world that he gave his one and only Son, that whoever believes in him shall not perish but have eternal life") is open to an interpretation like that of Dupuis. In Kaariainen's retrieval and interpretation of God's hiddenness and the ambiguity of our everyday world, moreover, Lutheran missiology can evoke the central text of both Dupuis and Vatican II without claiming to know more than we actually do. I refer, of course, to the Vatican II teaching revolving around *Gaudium et Spes* 22: "For, since Christ died for all, and since all are called to one and the same destiny, which is divine [the unity of the economy of salvation in a single history, a notion intrinsic to the revelation of God's intentions in Christ], we must hold that the Holy Spirit offers to all the possibility of being made partners *in a way known to God*, in the paschal mystery" (my italics). Luther's retrieval of Paul's teaching lets God be God while centering the Christian "mission" around making known God's promise revealed in Jesus.

The vision of Dupuis—which at root is complementary to that of Kaariainen, though complicated by his need to deal with the role of the church in the economy of salvation—seems mistaken to those who mount the ramparts of exclusivism (i.e., to maintain that only *explicit* faith in Christ suffices for salvation). On the whole, though, Catholics have had little difficulty accepting the formulation of *Lumen Gentium* 16 that "those who have not yet received the Gospel are related in various ways to the people of God." Further in *Lumen Gentium* 16, the Council says: "Nor does Divine Providence deny the helps necessary for salvation to those who, without blame on their part, have not yet arrived at an explicit knowledge of God and with His grace strive to live a good life. Whatever good or truth is found amongst them is looked upon by the Church as a preparation for the Gospel."

Dupuis's problems, as one sees in both the text of *Dominus Iesus* and the CDF Notification, began at another level. Are the positive elements in other religions *only* a preparation for membership in the church, as CDF seems to think? His answer to that question is nuanced, but the bedrock of his position rests in texts like John Paul II's encyclical *Dominum et Vivificantem* for support. There the pope links the Spirit's work of mak-

ing Christians adopted children of God to the Spirit who performs that
action *outside visible Christianity.* If the Spirit uses these elements to lead
people to Christ, does their value immediately become zero after they
are moved to accept the Spirit's testimony? Speaking in the context of
the Jubilee celebrations he had ordered for the year 2000 to observe the
second millennium since the birth of Christ John Paul II says in section
53 of that encyclical:

> We cannot limit ourselves to the two thousand years which have
> passed since the birth of Christ. We need to go further back, to
> embrace the whole of the action of the Holy Spirit even before
> Christ-from the beginning, throughout the world, and especially
> in the economy of the Old Covenant. For this action has been
> exercised, in every place and at every time, indeed in every in-
> dividual, according to the eternal plan of salvation, whereby this
> action was to be closely linked with the mystery of the Incarnation
> and Redemption, which in its turn exercised its influence on those
> who believed in the future coming of Christ. This is attested to
> especially in the Letter to the Ephesians (1:3–14). Grace, there-
> fore, bears within itself both a Christological aspect and a pneu-
> matological one, which becomes evident above all in those who
> expressly accept Christ: "In him [i.e., in Christ] you . . . were sealed
> with the promised Holy Spirit, which is the guarantee of our in-
> heritance, until we acquire possession of it (Eph 1:13f.).
>
> But, still within the perspective of the great Jubilee, we need to
> look further and go further afield, knowing that "the wind blows
> where it wills," according to the image used by Jesus in his conver-
> sation with Nicodemus Paschal Mystery" (Jn 3:8).

Given that quote, I think one can say that the Pope is on Dupuis's
side, so one wonders if CDF's real goal in mounting its case against
Dupuis was to walk back Pope John Paul's teaching. Certainly there are
those in Rome who feel John Paul had gone too far in this document and
in his 27 October 1986 meeting with world religious leaders in Assisi.
They raise the point that at Assisi and in *Dominum et Vivificantem* John
Paul seems to contradict what he says in *Redemptoris Missio.* In the later
text, the Spirit's role is presented in more traditional terms. Be that as it
may, Dupuis's goal is to help his fellow Christians understand the implications of the notion that the Spirit and *Logos* were active outside visible Christianity both before the incarnation and during the life of the
historical Jesus, and are still active since the resurrection and pentecost.

Following that logic, dialogue aimed at arriving at a deeper understanding of the other as an integral aspect of bearing witness to Christian faith in Christ, is not an optional aspect of Christian life and mission. *Prophetic Dialogue,* a recent book on theology of mission by Stephen Bevans and Roger Schroeder, is an excellent example of how Dupuis's insights can undergird contemporary theory of mission. Their second chapter, entitled "We Were Gentle Among You," is devoted to the idea that the core of the church's mission is respectful but prophetic dialogue. Their third chapter, "I Am Not Ashamed of the Gospel," explicates the idea that "Christians in mission prophesy the future—*God's* future revealed in Christ. Like Jesus, Christians in mission explain to one another and to the world—if asked (see 1 Peter 3:15)—what the future of the world will be under God's loving providence.[26] In the context of 1 Peter, of course, hope grounds one's ethical conduct in this age.

One of the complaints Vatican officials had about Dupuis's theology of religion was that it undercut the motivation for mission. No less than John Paul II, with the encouragement of the Congregation for Evangelization, wrote *Redemptoris Missio* (the subtitle of which is "On the Permanent Validity of the Missionary Mandate") to counter that idea. In December of 2000, a little more than ten years after its publication and during the middle of the period in which CDF was putting pressure on Dupuis to sign their Notification, the prefect of CEP, Cardinal Josef Tomko, was at the centennial observances of the Divine Word Missionaries in Techny, Illinois. He stayed for and took part in a two-day colloquium among twenty-five missiologists on the future of mission, including the superior general of the Divine Word Missionaries (Father Anthony Pernia, who had been directed by Dupuis in his doctoral dissertation at the Gregorian). Cardinal Tomko, whom I had met and had a long and productive conversation several years earlier, and I stayed back after a coffee break to chat. I asked him about the health of Archbishop Zago (who was suffering from cancer) and how things were proceeding in the Dupuis case. Tomko, who was a member of CDF, said that he recognized many solid aspects in Dupuis's work but also said it was being used in Asia as a justification for withdrawing from the effort to invite non-Christians into the church. *Dominus Iesus,* he conceded, had not

---

26. Bevans and Schroeder, *Prophetic Dialogue,* 44.

been well-received, but was no less necessary for being unpopular. We disagreed about both Dupuis and *Dominus Iesus,* but did so politely.

In February of 2004, Dupuis was in the United States for a week, invited by the New York Interfaith Center to give a major public lecture. We spent a great deal of time together that week, but it was in the friendly confines of Maryknoll that I realized how deeply Dupuis had thought about the question of mission, especially in Asia. He had agreed to spend an afternoon with a dozen invited Maryknollers. Over thirty responded! In that venue I asked a question based on Cardinal Tomko's criticism that his work undercut mission. A veteran missionary among missioners, he answered in a way that captured everyone's attention.

He began by outlining the five-element taxonomy of mission of the 1984 Secretariat for Non-Christians document, *Dialogue and Mission* (§ 13). In that document, mission is portrayed: (1) as the witness of Christian life; (2) as commitment to the service of humankind; (3) as liturgical life, prayer, and contemplation as testimony to "a living and liberating relationship with the active and true God"; (4) as the dialogue of life wherein "Christians meet the followers of other religious traditions in order to walk together toward truth and to work together in projects of common concern"; and (5) as proclamation and catechesis about the good news of the gospel and its "consequences for life and culture are analyzed."

Dupuis went on to show that this vision of mission was actually much more demanding than the classic notion of mission popular in the past several centuries. That understanding involved a group of specialists going to areas where non-Christians lived and attempting to make them members of whichever church sent the missionaries. It was undergirded by a sense both of the rise of the West and the superiority of its culture, becoming in some measure part of the self-imposed *mission civilisatrice* ("civilizing mission") of a sending national church, so much so that J. P. Daughton reports that it was said in Madagascar, "*Qui dit Français dit catholique; qui dit protestant dit Anglais*"[27] ("Who says French says Catholic; who says Protestant says English"). As a Belgian fully conscious that some of the worst colonial predation took place under King Leopold in Congo, Dupuis knew the importance of Christianity assuming a post-Western identity in Asia.

---

27. Naughton, *Empire Divided,* 167.

By contrast with older notions based in one sort of superiority or another, Dupuis observed, "Mission since Vatican II is more profoundly rooted in biblical categories and is understood as the task of the whole church. It is something much deeper than seeking to enlarge its membership. To carry it out demands a high level of authenticity on the part of the entire church as a body of genuine disciples, since the church is not just something one joins to get the keys to heaven. The church is part of God's mission to bring the world to its fulfillment." Everyone in that room felt the passion with which Dupuis spoke. On that February afternoon at Maryknoll, ten months before his death, he had been a missionary as a Jesuit for sixty-three years. He understood his vocation as a Jesuit-missionary-theologian to be his way of carrying out his call to mission.

I have been influenced heavily by Bernard Lonergan, SJ (1904–1984), a predecessor of Dupuis at the Gregorian University and whose work accentuates the way in which truth is much more than a correspondence between thought and reality. It is dynamic and involves attaining the sort of authenticity Dupuis spoke of as necessary for mission, an authenticity wherein the theologian is engaged not just in a process of reading, research, correlation, and correction, but more importantly responding to God's gift of God's self and appropriating in one's inmost being the wisdom imparted by the Holy Spirit. Lonergan's work is notoriously difficult to penetrate, but is perhaps most accessible in his book *Method in Theology*. There he speaks of religious communities requiring clear expressions of what they believe and notes the problem of doing so in the midst of changing times and situations. But most profoundly he notes that theology in its deepest *Christic* sense can only be written if one recognizes the following:

> The dynamic state of being in love [with God] has the character of a response. There is a personal entrance of God himself into history, a communication of God to his people, the advent of God's word into the world of religious expression. Such was the religion of Israel. Such has been Christianity.
>
> Then not only the inner word that is God's gift of his love, but also the outer word of the religious tradition comes from God. God's gift of his love is matched by his command to love unrestrictedly, with all one's heart and all one's soul and all one's mind and all one's strength. The narrative of religious origins is the narrative of God's encounter with his people. Religious effort towards authenticity through prayer and penance and religious love in

good deeds becomes an apostolate, for "you will recognize them by their fruits" (Mt 7:20).[28]

Lonergan goes on to distinguish the difference between faith and belief that is the basis "both for ecumenical encounter and for an encounter between all religions with a basis in religious experience." Dupuis's theological work was not mere scholarship. It was, in Lonergan's sense of the word, an "apostolate." He knew more deeply than Lonergan the problem of seemingly insurmountable differences between religions, but he sought a way to express in orthodox terminology a conviction that Lonergan expressed when he went on to say that behind such differences between religions, "there is a deeper unity. For beliefs result from judgments of value, and the judgments of value relevant for religious belief come from faith, the eye of religious love, an eye that can discern God's self-disclosures."[29]

Let us let Father Dupuis, who saw that clearly, have the last word. As he wrote his last book, his goal was, after all,

> to propose some guidelines for reflection which could lead to a "qualitative leap" by the Christian and Catholic theology of the religions towards a more positive theological assessment of them and a more open concrete stance toward their followers . . . [which] is required for the Christian message to retain its credibility in today's multicultural and multireligious worlds. . . . I am convinced that a broader approach and a more positive attitude, provided that they be theologically well grounded, will help us to discover, to our surprise, new breadths and new depths in the Christian message.[30]

28. Lonergan, *Method*, 119.
29. Ibid.
30. Dupuis, *Christianity*, 259.

Appendix 1

CONGREGATION FOR THE DOCTRINE OF THE FAITH DECLARATION *"DOMINUS IESUS"* ON THE UNICITY AND SALVIFIC UNIVERSALITY OF JESUS CHRIST AND THE CHURCH

INTRODUCTION

1. The *Lord Jesus,* before ascending into heaven, commanded his disciples to proclaim the Gospel to the whole world and to baptize all nations: "Go into the whole world and proclaim the Gospel to every creature. He who believes and is baptized will be saved; he who does not believe will be condemned" (Mk 16:15–16); "All power in heaven and on earth has been given to me. Go therefore and teach all nations, baptizing them in the name of the Father, and of the Son, and of the Holy Spirit, teaching them to observe all that I have commanded you. And behold, I am with you always, until the end of the world" (Mt 28:18–20; cf. Lk 24:46–48; Jn 17:18, 20, 21; Acts 1:8).

The Church's universal mission is born from the command of Jesus Christ and is fulfilled in the course of the centuries in the proclamation of the mystery of God, Father, Son, and Holy Spirit, and the mystery of the incarnation of the Son, as saving event for all humanity. The fundamental contents of the profession of the Christian faith are expressed thus: "I believe in one God, the Father, Almighty, maker of heaven and earth, of all that is, seen and unseen. I believe in one Lord, Jesus Christ, the only Son of God, eternally begotten of the Father, God from God, Light from Light, true God from true God, begotten, not made, of one being with the Father. Through him all things were made. For us men and for our salvation, he came down from heaven: by the power of the Holy Spirit he became incarnate of the Virgin Mary, and became man. For our sake he was crucified under Pontius Pilate; he suffered death and was buried. On the third day he rose again in accordance with the Scriptures; he ascended into heaven and is seated at the right hand of the Father. He will come again in glory to judge the living and the dead, and his kingdom will have no end. I believe in the Holy Spirit, the Lord, the giver of life, who proceeds from the Father. With the Father and the Son he is worshipped and glorified. He has spoken through the prophets. I believe in one holy catholic and apostolic Church. I acknowledge one baptism for the forgiveness of sins. I look for the resurrection of the dead, and the life of the world to come."[1]

2. In the course of the centuries, the Church has proclaimed and witnessed with fidelity to the Gospel of Jesus. At the close of the second millennium, however, this mission is still far from complete.[2] For that reason, Saint Paul's words are now more relevant than ever: "Preaching the Gospel is not a reason for me to boast; it is a necessity laid on me: woe to me if I do not preach the Gospel!" (1 Cor 9:16). This explains the Magisterium's particular attention to giving reasons for and supporting the evangelizing mission of the Church, above all in connection with the religious traditions of the world.[3]

In considering the values which these religions witness to and offer humanity, with an open and positive approach, the Second Vatican Council's Declaration on the relation of the Church to non-Christian religions states: "The Catholic Church rejects nothing of what is true and holy in these religions. She has a high regard for the manner of life and conduct, the precepts and teachings, which, although differing in many ways from her own teaching, nonetheless often reflect a ray of that truth which enlightens all men."[4] Continuing in this line of thought, the Church's proclamation of Jesus Christ, "the way, the truth, and the life" (Jn 14:6), today also makes use of the practice of inter-religious dialogue. Such dialogue certainly does not replace, but rather accompanies the *missio ad gentes*, directed toward that "mystery of unity," from which "it follows that all men and women who are saved share, though differently, in the same mystery of salvation in Jesus Christ through his Spirit."[5] Inter-religious dialogue, which is part of the Church's evangelizing mission,[6] requires an attitude of understanding and a relationship of mutual knowledge and reciprocal enrichment, in obedience to the truth and with respect for freedom.[7]

3. In the practice of dialogue between the Christian faith and other religious traditions, as well as in seeking to understand its theoretical basis more deeply, new questions arise that need to be addressed through pursuing

new paths of research, advancing proposals, and suggesting ways of acting that call for attentive discernment. In this task, the present Declaration seeks to recall to Bishops, theologians, and all the Catholic faithful, certain indispensable elements of Christian doctrine, which may help theological reflection in developing solutions consistent with the contents of the faith and responsive to the pressing needs of contemporary culture.

The expository language of the Declaration corresponds to its purpose, which is not to treat in a systematic manner the question of the unicity and salvific universality of the mystery of Jesus Christ and the Church, nor to propose solutions to questions that are matters of free theological debate, but rather to set forth again the doctrine of the Catholic faith in these areas, pointing out some fundamental questions that remain open to further development, and refuting specific positions that are erroneous or ambiguous. For this reason, the Declaration takes up what has been taught in previous Magisterial documents, in order to reiterate certain truths that are part of the Church's faith.

4. The Church's constant missionary proclamation is endangered today by relativistic theories which seek to justify religious pluralism, not only *de facto* but also *de iure (or in principle)*. As a consequence, it is held that certain truths have been superseded; for example, the definitive and complete character of the revelation of Jesus Christ, the nature of Christian faith as compared with that of belief in other religions, the inspired nature of the books of Sacred Scripture, the personal unity between the Eternal Word and Jesus of Nazareth, the unity of the economy of the Incarnate Word and the Holy Spirit, the unicity and salvific universality of the mystery of Jesus Christ, the universal salvific mediation of the Church, the inseparability— while recognizing the distinction—of the kingdom of God, the kingdom of Christ, and the Church, and the subsistence of the one Church of Christ in the Catholic Church.

The roots of these problems are to be found in certain presuppositions of both a philosophical and theological nature, which hinder the understanding and acceptance of the revealed truth. Some of these can be mentioned: the conviction of the elusiveness and inexpressibility of divine truth, even by Christian revelation; relativistic attitudes toward truth itself, according to which what is true for some would not be true for others; the radical opposition posited between the logical mentality of the West and the symbolic mentality of the East; the subjectivism which, by regarding reason as the only source of knowledge, becomes incapable of raising its "gaze to the heights, not daring to rise to the truth of being;"[8] the difficulty in understanding and accepting the presence of definitive and eschatological events in history; the metaphysical emptying of the historical incarnation of the Eternal Logos, reduced to a mere appearing of God in history; the eclecticism of those who, in theological research, uncritically absorb ideas from a variety of philosophical and theological contexts without regard for consistency, systematic connection, or compatibility with Christian truth; finally, the tendency to read and to interpret Sacred Scripture outside the Tradition and Magisterium of the Church.

On the basis of such presuppositions, which may evince different nuances, certain theological proposals are developed—at times presented as assertions, and at times as hypotheses—in which Christian revelation and the mystery of Jesus Christ and the Church lose their character of absolute truth and salvific universality, or at least shadows of doubt and uncertainty are cast upon them.

I.

THE FULLNESS AND DEFINITIVENESS
OF THE REVELATION OF JESUS CHRIST

5. As a remedy for this relativistic mentality, which is becoming ever more common, it is necessary above all to reassert the definitive and complete character of the revelation of Jesus Christ. In fact, it must be *firmly believed* that, in the mystery of Jesus Christ, the Incarnate Son of God, who is "the way, the truth, and the life" (Jn 14:6), the full revelation of divine truth is given: "No one knows the Son except the Father, and no one knows the Father except the Son and anyone to whom the Son wishes to reveal him" (Mt 11:27); "No one has ever seen God; God the only Son, who is in the bosom of the Father, has revealed him" (Jn 1:18); "For in Christ the whole fullness of divinity dwells in bodily form" (Col 2:9–10).

Faithful to God's word, the Second Vatican Council teaches: "By this revelation then, the deepest truth about God and the salvation of man shines forth in Christ, who is at the same time the mediator and the fullness of all revelation."[9] Furthermore, "Jesus Christ, therefore, the Word made flesh, sent 'as a man to men,' 'speaks the words of God' (Jn 3:34), and completes the work of salvation which his Father gave him to do (cf. Jn 5:36; 17:4). To see Jesus is to see his Father (cf. Jn 14:9). For this reason, Jesus perfected revelation by fulfilling it through his whole work of making himself present and manifesting himself: through his words and deeds, his signs and wonders, but especially through his death and glorious resurrection from the dead and finally with the sending of the Spirit of truth, he completed and perfected revelation and confirmed it with divine testimony . . . The Christian dispensation, therefore, as the new and definitive covenant, will never pass away, and we now await no further new public revelation before the glorious manifestation of our Lord Jesus Christ (cf. 1 Tim 6:14 and Tit 2:13)."[10]

Thus, the Encyclical *Redemptoris Missio* calls the Church once again to the task of announcing the Gospel as the fullness of truth: "In this definitive Word of his revelation, God has made himself known in the fullest possible way. He has revealed to mankind who he is. This definitive self-revelation of God is the fundamental reason why the Church is missionary by her very nature. She cannot do other than proclaim the Gospel, that is, the fullness of the truth which God has enabled us to know about himself."[11] Only the revelation of Jesus Christ, therefore, "introduces into our history a universal and ultimate truth which stirs the human mind to ceaseless effort."[12]

6. Therefore, the theory of the limited, incomplete, or imperfect character of the revelation of Jesus Christ, which would be complementary to that found in other religions, is contrary to the Church's faith. Such a position would claim to be based on the notion that the truth about God cannot be grasped and manifested in its globality and completeness by any historical religion, neither by Christianity nor by Jesus Christ.

Such a position is in radical contradiction with the foregoing statements of Catholic faith according to which the full and complete revelation of the salvific mystery of God is given in Jesus Christ. Therefore, the words, deeds, and entire historical event of Jesus, though limited as human realities, have nevertheless the divine Person of the Incarnate Word, "true God and true man"[13] as their subject. For this reason, they possess in themselves the definitiveness and completeness of the revelation of God's salvific ways, even if the depth of the divine mystery in itself remains transcendent and inexhaustible. The truth about God is not abolished or reduced because it is spoken in human language; rather, it is unique, full, and complete, because he who speaks and acts is the Incarnate Son of God. Thus, faith requires us to profess that the Word made flesh, in his entire mystery, who moves from incarnation to glorification, is the source, participated but real, as well as the fulfillment of every salvific revelation of God to humanity,[14] and that the Holy Spirit, who is Christ's Spirit, will teach this "entire truth" (Jn 16:13) to the Apostles and, through them, to the whole Church.

7. The proper response to God's revelation is *"the obedience of faith* (Rom 16:26; cf. Rom 1:5; 2 Cor 10:5–6) by which man freely entrusts his entire self to God, offering 'the full submission of intellect and will to God who reveals' and freely assenting to the revelation given by him."[15] Faith is a gift of grace: "in order to have faith, the grace of God must come first and give assistance; there must also be the interior helps of the Holy Spirit, who moves the heart and converts it to God, who opens the eyes of the mind and gives 'to everyone joy and ease in assenting to and believing in the truth.'"[16]

The obedience of faith implies acceptance of the truth of Christ's revelation, guaranteed by God, who is Truth itself:[17] "Faith is first of all a personal adherence of man to God. At the same time, and inseparably, it is a *free assent to the whole truth that God has revealed."*[18] Faith, therefore, as *"a gift of God"* and as *"a supernatural virtue infused by him."*[19] involves a dual adherence: to God who reveals and to the truth which he reveals, out of the trust which one has in him who speaks. Thus, "we must believe in no one but God: the Father, the Son and the Holy Spirit."[20]

For this reason, the distinction between *theological faith* and *belief* in the other religions, must be *firmly held.* If faith is the acceptance in grace of revealed truth, which "makes it possible to penetrate the mystery in a way that allows us to understand it coherently,"[21] then belief, in the other religions, is that sum of experience and thought that constitutes the human treasury of wisdom and religious aspiration, which man in his search for truth has conceived and acted upon in his relationship to God and the Absolute.[22]

This distinction is not always borne in mind in current theological reflection. Thus, theological faith (the acceptance of the truth revealed by the One and Triune God) is often identified with belief in other religions, which is religious experience still in search of the absolute truth and still lacking assent to God who reveals himself. This is one of the reasons why the differences between Christianity and the other religions tend to be reduced at times to the point of disappearance.

8. The hypothesis of the inspired value of the sacred writings of other religions is also put forward. Certainly, it must be recognized that there are some elements in these texts which may be *de facto* instruments by which countless people throughout the centuries have been and still are able today to nourish and maintain their life-relationship with God. Thus, as noted above, the Second Vatican Council, in considering the customs, precepts, and teachings of the other religions, teaches that "although differing in many ways from her own teaching, these nevertheless often reflect a ray of that truth which enlightens all men."[23]

The Church's tradition, however, reserves the designation of *inspired texts* to the canonical books of the Old and New Testaments, since these are inspired by the Holy Spirit.[24] Taking up this tradition, the Dogmatic Constitution on Divine Revelation of the Second Vatican Council states: "For Holy Mother Church, relying on the faith of the apostolic age, accepts as sacred and canonical the books of the Old and New Testaments, whole and entire, with all their parts, on the grounds that, written under the inspiration of the Holy Spirit (cf. Jn 20:31; 2 Tim 3:16; 2 Pet 1:19–21; 3:15–16), they have God as their author, and have been handed on as such to the Church herself."[25] These books "firmly, faithfully, and without error, teach that truth which God, for the sake of our salvation, wished to see confided to the Sacred Scriptures."[26]

Nevertheless, God, who desires to call all peoples to himself in Christ and to communicate to them the fullness of his revelation and love, "does not fail to make himself present in many ways, not only to individuals, but also to entire peoples through their spiritual riches, of which their religions are the main and essential expression even when they contain 'gaps, insufficiencies and errors."[27] Therefore, the sacred books of other religions, which in actual fact direct and nourish the existence of their followers, receive from the mystery of Christ the elements of goodness and grace which they contain.

II.

THE INCARNATE LOGOS
AND THE HOLY SPIRIT IN THE WORK OF SALVATION

9. In contemporary theological reflection there often emerges an approach to Jesus of Nazareth that considers him a particular, finite, historical figure, who reveals the divine not in an exclusive way, but in a way complementary with other revelatory and salvific figures. The Infinite, the Absolute, the Ultimate Mystery of God would thus manifest itself to humanity in many ways and in many historical figures: Jesus of Nazareth would be one of these. More concretely, for some, Jesus would be one of the many faces which the Logos has assumed in the course of time to communicate with humanity in a salvific way.

Furthermore, to justify the universality of Christian salvation as well as the fact of religious pluralism, it has been proposed that there is an economy of the eternal Word that is valid also outside the Church and is unrelated to her, in addition to an economy of the incarnate Word. The first would have a greater universal value than the second, which is limited to Christians, though God's presence would be more full in the second.

10. These theses are in profound conflict with the Christian faith. The doctrine of faith must be *firmly believed* which proclaims that Jesus of Nazareth, son of Mary, and he alone, is the Son and the Word of the Father. The Word, which "was in the beginning with God" (Jn 1:2) is the same as he who "became flesh" (Jn 1:14). In Jesus, "the Christ, the Son of the living God" (Mt 16:16), "the whole fullness of divinity dwells in bodily form" (Col 2:9). He is the "only begotten Son of the Father, who is in the bosom of the Father" (Jn 1:18), his "beloved Son, in whom we have redemption . . . In him the fullness of God was pleased to dwell, and through him, God was pleased to reconcile all things to himself, on earth and in the heavens, making peace by the blood of his Cross" (Col 1:13–14; 19–20).

Faithful to Sacred Scripture and refuting erroneous and reductive interpretations, the First Council of Nicaea solemnly defined its faith in: "Jesus Christ, the Son of God, the only begotten generated from the Father, that is, from the being of the Father, God from God, Light from Light, true God from true God, begotten, not made, one in being with the Father, through whom all things were made, those in heaven and those on earth. For us men and for our salvation, he came down and became incarnate, was made man, suffered, and rose again on the third day. He ascended to the heavens and shall come again to judge the living and the dead."[28] Following the teachings of the Fathers of the Church, the Council of Chalcedon also professed: "the one and the same Son, our Lord Jesus Christ, the same perfect in divinity and perfect in humanity, the same truly God and truly man . . . , one in being with the Father according to the divinity and one in being with us according to the humanity . . . , begotten of the Father before the ages according to the divinity and, in these last days, for us and our salvation, of Mary, the Virgin Mother of God, according to the humanity."[29]

For this reason, the Second Vatican Council states that Christ "the new Adam . . . 'image of the invisible God' (Col 1:15) is himself the perfect man who has restored that likeness to God in the children of Adam which had been disfigured since the first sin . . . As an innocent lamb he merited life for us by his blood which he freely shed. In him God reconciled us to himself and to one another, freeing us from the bondage of the devil and of sin, so that each one of us could say with the apostle: the Son of God 'loved me and gave himself up for me' (Gal 2:20)."[30]

In this regard, John Paul II has explicitly declared: "To introduce any sort of separation between the Word and Jesus Christ is contrary to the Christian faith . . . Jesus is the Incarnate Word—a single and indivisible person . . . Christ is none other than Jesus of Nazareth; he is the Word of God made man for the salvation of all . . . In the process of discovering and appreciating the manifold gifts—especially the spiritual treasures—that God has bestowed on every people, we cannot separate those gifts from Jesus Christ, who is at the center of God's plan of salvation."[31]

It is likewise contrary to the Catholic faith to introduce a separation between the salvific action of the Word as such and that of the Word made man. With the incarnation, all the salvific actions of the Word of God are always done in unity with the human nature that he has assumed for the salvation of all people. The one subject which operates in the two natures, human and divine, is the single person of the Word.[32]

Therefore, the theory which would attribute, after the incarnation as well, a salvific activity to the Logos as such in his divinity, exercised "in addition to" or "beyond" the humanity of Christ, is not compatible with the Catholic faith.[33]

11. Similarly, the doctrine of faith regarding the unicity of the salvific economy willed by the One and Triune God must be *firmly believed,* at the source and centre of which is the mystery of the incarnation of the Word, mediator of divine grace on the level of creation and redemption (cf. Col 1:15-20), he who recapitulates all things (cf. Eph 1:10), he "whom God has made our wisdom, our righteousness, and sanctification and redemption" (1 Cor 1:30). In fact, the mystery of Christ has its own intrinsic unity, which extends from the eternal choice in God to the parousia: "he [the Father] chose us in Christ before the foundation of the world to be holy and blameless before him in love" (Eph 1:4); "In Christ we are heirs, having been destined according to the purpose of him who accomplishes all things according to his counsel and will" (Eph 1:11); "For those whom he foreknew he also predestined to be conformed to the image of his Son, in order that he might be the firstborn among many brothers; those whom he predestined he also called; and those whom he called he also justified; and those whom he justified he also glorified" (Rom 8:29–30).

The Church's Magisterium, faithful to divine revelation, reasserts that Jesus Christ is the mediator and the universal redeemer: "The Word of God, through whom all things were made, was made flesh, so that as perfect man he could save all men and sum up all things in himself. The Lord . . . is he whom the Father raised from the dead, exalted and placed at his right hand, constituting him judge of the living and the dead."[34] This salvific mediation implies also the unicity of the redemptive sacrifice of Christ, eternal high priest (cf. Heb 6:20; 9:11; 10:12–14).

12. There are also those who propose the hypothesis of an economy of the Holy Spirit with a more universal breadth than that of the Incarnate Word, crucified and risen. This position also is contrary to the Catholic faith, which, on the contrary, considers the salvific incarnation of the Word as a trinitarian event. In the New Testament, the mystery of Jesus, the Incarnate Word, constitutes the place of the Holy Spirit's presence as well as the principle of the Spirit's effusion on humanity, not only in messianic times (cf. Acts 2:32–36; Jn 7:39, 20:22; 1 Cor 15:45), but also prior to his coming in history (cf. 1 Cor 10:4; 1 Pet 1:10–12).

The Second Vatican Council has recalled to the consciousness of the Church's faith this fundamental truth. In presenting the Father's salvific plan for all humanity, the Council closely links the mystery of Christ from its very beginnings with that of the Spirit.[35] The entire work of building the Church by Jesus Christ the Head, in the course of the centuries, is seen as an action which he does in communion with his Spirit.[36]

Furthermore, the salvific action of Jesus Christ, with and through his Spirit, extends beyond the visible boundaries of the Church to all humanity. Speaking of the paschal mystery, in which Christ even now associates the believer to himself in a living manner in the Spirit and gives him the hope of resurrection, the Council states: "All this holds true not only for Christians but also for all men of good will in whose hearts grace is active invisibly. For since Christ died for all, and since all men are in fact called to one and the same destiny, which is divine, we must hold that the Holy Spirit offers to all the possibility of being made partners, in a way known to God, in the paschal mystery."[37]

Hence, the connection is clear between the salvific mystery of the Incarnate Word and that of the Spirit, who actualizes the salvific efficacy of the Son made man in the lives of all people, called by God to a single goal, both those who historically preceded the Word made man, and those who live after his coming in history: the Spirit of the Father, bestowed abundantly by the Son, is the animator of all (cf. Jn 3:34).

Thus, the recent Magisterium of the Church has firmly and clearly recalled the truth of a single divine economy: "The Spirit's presence and activity affect not only individuals but also society and history, peoples, cultures and religions . . . The Risen Christ 'is now at work in human hearts through the strength of his Spirit' . . . Again, it is the Spirit who sows the 'seeds of the word' present in various customs and cultures, preparing them for full maturity in Christ."[38] While recognizing the historical-salvific function of the Spirit in the whole universe and in the entire history of humanity,[39] the Magisterium states: "This is the same Spirit who was at work in the incarnation and in the life, death, and resurrection of Jesus and who is at work in the Church. He is therefore not an alternative to Christ nor does he fill a sort of void which is sometimes suggested as existing between Christ and the Logos. Whatever the Spirit brings about in human hearts and in the history of peoples, in cultures and religions, serves as a preparation for the Gospel and can only be understood in reference to Christ, the Word who took flesh by the power of the Spirit 'so that as perfectly human he would save all human beings and sum up all things."[40]

In conclusion, the action of the Spirit is not outside or parallel to the action of Christ. There is only one salvific economy of the One and Triune God, realized in the mystery of the incarnation, death, and resurrection of the Son of God, actualized with the cooperation of the Holy Spirit, and extended in its salvific value to all humanity and to the entire universe: "No one, therefore, can enter into communion with God except through Christ, by the working of the Holy Spirit."[41]

III.

UNICITY AND UNIVERSALITY
OF THE SALVIFIC MYSTERY OF JESUS CHRIST

13. The thesis which denies the unicity and salvific universality of the mystery of Jesus Christ is also put forward. Such a position has no biblical foundation. In fact, the truth of Jesus Christ, Son of God, Lord and only Saviour, who through the event of his incarnation, death and resurrection has brought the history of salvation to fulfillment, and which has in him its fullness and centre, must be *firmly believed* as a constant element of the Church's faith.

The New Testament attests to this fact with clarity: "The Father has sent his Son as the Saviour of the world" (1 Jn 4:14); "Behold the Lamb of God who takes away the sin of the world" (Jn 1:29). In his discourse before the Sanhedrin, Peter, in order to justify the healing of a man who was crippled from birth, which was done in the name of Jesus (cf. Acts 3:1–8), proclaims: "There is salvation in no one else, for there is no other name under heaven given among men by which we must be saved" (Acts 4:12). St. Paul adds, moreover, that Jesus Christ "is Lord of all," "judge of the living and the dead", and thus "whoever believes in him receives forgiveness of sins through his name" (Acts 10:36, 42, 43).

Paul, addressing himself to the community of Corinth, writes: "Indeed, even though there may be so-called gods in heaven or on earth—as in fact there are many gods and many lords—yet for us there is one God, the Father, from whom are all things and for whom we exist, and one Lord,

Jesus Christ, through whom are all things and through whom we exist" (1 Cor 8:5–6). Furthermore, John the Apostle states: "For God so loved the world that he gave his only Son, so that everyone who believes in him may not perish but may have eternal life. God did not send his Son into the world to condemn the world, but in order that the world might be saved through him" (Jn 3:16–17). In the New Testament, the universal salvific will of God is closely connected to the sole mediation of Christ: "[God] desires all men to be saved and to come to the knowledge of the truth. For there is one God; there is also one mediator between God and men, the man Jesus Christ, who gave himself as a ransom for all" (1 Tim 2:4–6).

It was in the awareness of the one universal gift of salvation offered by the Father through Jesus Christ in the Spirit (cf. Eph 1:3–14), that the first Christians encountered the Jewish people, showing them the fulfillment of salvation that went beyond the Law and, in the same awareness, they confronted the pagan world of their time, which aspired to salvation through a plurality of saviors. This inheritance of faith has been recalled recently by the Church's Magisterium: "The Church believes that Christ, who died and was raised for the sake of all (cf. 2 Cor 5:15) can, through his Spirit, give man the light and the strength to be able to respond to his highest calling, nor is there any other name under heaven given among men by which they can be saved (cf. Acts 4:12). The Church likewise believes that the key, the center, and the purpose of the whole of man's history is to be found in its Lord and Master."[42]

14. It must therefore be *firmly believed* as a truth of Catholic faith that the universal salvific will of the One and Triune God is offered and accomplished once for all in the mystery of the incarnation, death, and resurrection of the Son of God.

Bearing in mind this article of faith, theology today, in its reflection on the existence of other religious experiences and on their meaning in God's salvific plan, is invited to explore if and in what way the historical figures and positive elements of these religions may fall within the divine plan of salvation. In this undertaking, theological research has a vast field of work under the guidance of the Church's Magisterium. The Second Vatican Council, in fact, has stated that: "the unique mediation of the Redeemer does not exclude, but rather gives rise to a manifold cooperation which is but a participation in this one source."[43] The content of this participated mediation should be explored more deeply, but must remain always consistent with the principle of Christ's unique mediation: "Although participated forms of mediation of different kinds and degrees are not excluded, they acquire meaning and value *only* from Christ's own mediation, and they cannot be understood as parallel or complementary to his."[44] Hence, those solutions that propose a salvific action of God beyond the unique mediation of Christ would be contrary to Christian and Catholic faith.

15. Not infrequently it is proposed that theology should avoid the use of terms like "unicity," "universality," and "absoluteness," which give the impression of excessive emphasis on the significance and value of the salvific event of Jesus Christ in relation to other religions. In reality, however, such language is simply being faithful to revelation, since it represents a development of the sources of the faith themselves. From the beginning, the community of believers has recognized in Jesus a salvific value such that he alone, as Son of God made man, crucified and risen, by the mission received from the Father and in the power of the Holy Spirit, bestows revelation (cf. Mt 11:27) and divine life (cf. Jn 1:12; 5:25–26; 17:2) to all humanity and to every person.

In this sense, one can and must say that Jesus Christ has a significance and a value for the human race and its history, which are unique and singular, proper to him alone, exclusive, universal, and absolute. Jesus is, in fact, the Word of God made man for the salvation of all. In expressing this consciousness of faith, the Second Vatican Council teaches: "The Word of God, through whom all things were made, was made flesh, so that as perfect man he could save all men and sum up all things in himself. The Lord is the goal of human history, the focal point of the desires of history and civilization, the center of mankind, the joy of all hearts, and the fulfillment of all aspirations. It is he whom the Father raised from the dead, exalted and placed at his right hand, constituting him judge of the living and the dead."[45] "It is precisely this uniqueness of Christ which gives him an absolute and universal significance whereby, while belonging to history, he remains history's center and goal: 'I am the Alpha and the Omega, the first and the last, the beginning and the end' (*Rev* 22:13)."[46]

IV.

UNICITY AND UNITY OF THE CHURCH

16. The Lord Jesus, the only Saviour, did not only establish a simple community of disciples, but constituted the Church as a *salvific mystery:* he himself is in the Church and the Church is in him (cf. Jn 15:1ff.; Gal 3:28; Eph 4:15–16; Acts 9:5). Therefore, the fullness of Christ's salvific mystery belongs also to the Church, inseparably united to her Lord. Indeed, Jesus Christ continues his presence and his work of salvation in the Church and by means of the Church (cf. Col 1:24–27),[47] which is his body (cf. 1 Cor 12:12–13, 27; Col 1:18).[48] And thus, just as the head and members of a living body, though not identical, are inseparable, so too Christ and the Church can neither be confused nor separated, and constitute a single "whole Christ."[49] This same inseparability is also expressed in the New Testament by the analogy of the Church as the *Bride* of Christ (cf. 2 Cor 11:2; Eph 5:25–29; *Rev* 21:2, 9).[50]

Therefore, in connection with the unicity and universality of the salvific mediation of Jesus Christ, the unicity of the Church founded by him must be *firmly believed* as a truth of Catholic faith. Just as there is one Christ, so there exists a single body of Christ, a single Bride of Christ: "a single Catholic and apostolic Church."[51] Furthermore, the promises of the Lord that he would not abandon his Church (cf. Mt 16:18; 28:20) and that he would guide her by his Spirit (cf. Jn 16:13) mean, according to Catholic faith, that the unicity and the unity of the Church—like everything that belongs to the Church's integrity—will never be lacking.[52]

The Catholic faithful *are required to profess* that there is an historical continuity—rooted in the apostolic succession[53]—between the Church founded by Christ and the Catholic Church: "This is the single Church of Christ . . . which our Saviour, after his resurrection, entrusted to Peter's pastoral care (cf. Jn 21:17), commissioning him and the other Apostles to extend and rule her (cf. Mt 28:18ff.), erected for all ages as 'the pillar and mainstay of the truth' (1 Tim 3:15). This Church, constituted and organized as a society in the present world, subsists in [*subsistit in*] the Catholic Church, governed by the Successor of Peter and by the Bishops in communion with him."[54] With the expression *subsistit in,* the Second Vatican Council sought to harmonize two doctrinal statements: on the one hand, that the Church of Christ, despite the divisions which exist among Christians, continues to exist fully only in the Catholic Church, and on the other hand, that "outside of her structure, many elements can be found of sanctification and truth,"[55] that is, in those Churches and ecclesial communities which are not yet in full communion with the Catholic Church.[56] But with respect to these, it needs to be stated that "they derive their efficacy from the very fullness of grace and truth entrusted to the Catholic Church."[57]

17. Therefore, there exists a single Church of Christ, which subsists in the Catholic Church, governed by the Successor of Peter and by the Bishops in communion with him.[58] The Churches which, while not existing in perfect communion with the Catholic Church, remain united to her by means of the closest bonds, that is, by apostolic succession and a valid Eucharist, are true particular Churches.[59] Therefore, the Church of Christ is present and operative also in these Churches, even though they lack full communion with the Catholic Church, since they do not accept the Catholic doctrine of the Primacy, which, according to the will of God, the Bishop of Rome objectively has and exercises over the entire Church.[60]

On the other hand, the ecclesial communities which have not preserved the valid Episcopate and the genuine and integral substance of the Eucharistic mystery,[61] are not Churches in the proper sense; however, those who are baptized in these communities are, by Baptism, incorporated in Christ and thus are in a certain communion, albeit imperfect, with the Church.[62] Baptism in fact tends per se toward the full development of life in Christ, through the integral profession of faith, the Eucharist, and full communion in the Church.[63]

"The Christian faithful are therefore not permitted to imagine that the Church of Christ is nothing more than a collection—divided, yet in some way one—of Churches and ecclesial communities; nor are they free to hold that today the Church of Christ nowhere really exists, and must be considered only as a goal which all Churches and ecclesial communities must strive to reach."[64] In fact, "the elements of this already-given Church exist, joined together in their fullness in the Catholic Church and, without this fullness, in the other communities."[65] "Therefore, these separated Churches and communities as such, though we believe they suffer from defects, have by no means been deprived of significance and importance in the mystery of salvation. For the spirit of Christ has not refrained from using them as means of salvation which derive their efficacy from the very fullness of grace and truth entrusted to the Catholic Church."[66]

The lack of unity among Christians is certainly a *wound* for the Church; not in the sense that she is deprived of her unity, but "in that it hinders the complete fulfillment of her universality in history."[67]

V.

THE CHURCH: KINGDOM OF GOD
AND KINGDOM OF CHRIST

18. The mission of the Church is "to proclaim and establish among all peoples the kingdom of Christ and of God, and she is on earth, the seed and the beginning of that kingdom."[68] On the one hand, the Church is "a sacrament—that is, sign and instrument of intimate union with God and of unity of the entire human race."[69] She is therefore the sign and instrument of the kingdom; she is called to announce and to establish the kingdom. On the other hand, the Church is the "people gathered by the unity of the Father, the Son and the Holy Spirit."[70] she is therefore "the kingdom of Christ already present in mystery"[71] and constitutes its *seed* and *beginning*. The kingdom of God, in fact, has an eschatological dimension: it is a reality present in time, but its full realization will arrive only with the completion or fulfillment of history.[72]

The meaning of the expressions *kingdom of heaven, kingdom of God*, and *kingdom of Christ* in Sacred Scripture and the Fathers of the Church, as well as in the documents of the Magisterium, is not always exactly the same, nor is their relationship to the Church, which is a mystery that cannot be totally contained by a human concept. Therefore, there can be various theological explanations of these terms. However, none of these possible explanations can deny or empty in any way the intimate connection between Christ, the kingdom, and the Church. In fact, the kingdom of God which we know from revelation, "cannot be detached either from Christ or from the Church . . . If the kingdom is separated from Jesus, it is no longer the kingdom of God which he revealed. The result is a distortion of the meaning of the kingdom, which runs the risk of being transformed into a purely human or ideological goal and a distortion of the identity of Christ, who no longer appears as the Lord to whom everything must one day be subjected (cf. 1 Cor 15:27). Likewise, one may not separate the kingdom from the Church. It is true that the Church is not an end unto herself, since she is ordered toward the kingdom of God, of which she is the seed, sign and instrument.

Yet, while remaining distinct from Christ and the kingdom, the Church is indissolubly united to both."[73]

19. To state the inseparable relationship between Christ and the kingdom is not to overlook the fact that the kingdom of God—even if considered in its historical phase—is not identified with the Church in her visible and social reality. In fact, "the action of Christ and the Spirit outside the Church's visible boundaries" must not be excluded.[74] Therefore, one must also bear in mind that "the kingdom is the concern of everyone: individuals, society and the world. Working for the kingdom means acknowledging and promoting God's activity, which is present in human history and transforms it. Building the kingdom means working for liberation from evil in all its forms. In a word, the kingdom of God is the manifestation and the realization of God's plan of salvation in all its fullness."[75]

In considering the relationship between the kingdom of God, the kingdom of Christ, and the Church, it is necessary to avoid one-sided accentuations, as is the case with those "conceptions which deliberately emphasize the kingdom and which describe themselves as 'kingdom centered.' They stress the image of a Church which is not concerned about herself, but which is totally concerned with bearing witness to and serving the kingdom. It is a 'Church for others,' just as Christ is the 'man for others' . . . Together with positive aspects, these conceptions often reveal negative aspects as well. First, they are silent about Christ: the kingdom of which they speak is 'theocentrically' based, since, according to them, Christ cannot be understood by those who lack Christian faith, whereas different peoples, cultures, and religions are capable of finding common ground in the one divine reality, by whatever name it is called. For the same reason, they put great stress on the mystery of creation, which is reflected in the diversity of cultures and beliefs, but they keep silent about the mystery of redemption. Furthermore, the kingdom, as they understand it, ends up either leaving very little room for the Church or undervaluing the Church in reaction to a presumed 'ecclesiocentrism' of the past and because they consider the Church herself only a sign, for that matter a sign not without ambiguity."[76] These theses are contrary to Catholic faith because they deny the unicity of the relationship which Christ and the Church have with the kingdom of God.

VI.

THE CHURCH AND THE OTHER RELIGIONS
IN RELATION TO SALVATION

20. From what has been stated above, some points follow that are necessary for theological reflection as it explores the relationship of the Church and the other religions to salvation.

Above all else, it must be *firmly believed* that "the Church, a pilgrim now on earth, is necessary for salvation: the one Christ is the mediator and the way of salvation; he is present to us in his body which is the Church. He himself explicitly asserted the necessity of faith and baptism (cf. Mk 16:16; Jn 3:5), and thereby affirmed at the same time the necessity of the Church which men enter through baptism as through a door."[77] This doctrine must not be set against the universal salvific will of God (cf. 1 Tim 2:4); "it is necessary to keep these two truths together, namely, the real possibility of salvation in Christ for all mankind and the necessity of the Church for this salvation."[78]

The Church is the "universal sacrament of salvation,"[79] since, united always in a mysterious way to the Saviour Jesus Christ, her Head, and subordinated to him, she has, in God's plan, an indispensable relationship with the salvation of every human being.[80] For those who are not formally and visibly members of the Church, "salvation in Christ is accessible by virtue of a grace which, while having a mysterious relationship to the Church, does not make them formally part of the Church, but enlightens them in a way which is accommodated to their spiritual and material situation. This grace comes from Christ; it is the result of his sacrifice and is communicated by the Holy Spirit,"[81] it has a relationship with the Church, which "according to the plan of the Father, has her origin in the mission of the Son and the Holy Spirit."[82]

21. With respect to the *way* in which the salvific grace of God—which is always given by means of Christ in the Spirit and has a mysterious relationship to the Church—comes to individual non-Christians, the Second Vatican Council limited itself to the statement that God bestows it "in ways known to himself."[83] Theologians are seeking to understand this question more fully. Their work is to be encouraged, since it is certainly useful for understanding better God's salvific plan and the ways in which it is accomplished. However, from what has been stated above about the mediation of Jesus Christ and the "unique and special relationship"[84] which the Church

has with the kingdom of God among men—which in substance is the universal kingdom of Christ the Saviour—it is clear that it would be contrary to the faith to consider the Church as *one way* of salvation alongside those constituted by the other religions, seen as complementary to the Church or substantially equivalent to her, even if these are said to be converging with the Church toward the eschatological kingdom of God.

Certainly, the various religious traditions contain and offer religious elements which come from God,[85] and which are part of what "the Spirit brings about in human hearts and in the history of peoples, in cultures, and religions."[86] Indeed, some prayers and rituals of the other religions may assume a role of preparation for the Gospel, in that they are occasions or pedagogical helps in which the human heart is prompted to be open to the action of God.[87] One cannot attribute to these, however, a divine origin or an *ex opere operato* salvific efficacy, which is proper to the Christian sacraments.[88] Furthermore, it cannot be overlooked that other rituals, insofar as they depend on superstitions or other errors (cf. 1 Cor 10:20–21), constitute an obstacle to salvation.[89]

22. With the coming of the Saviour Jesus Christ, God has willed that the Church founded by him be the instrument for the salvation of *all* humanity (cf. Acts 17:30–31).[90] This truth of faith does not lessen the sincere respect which the Church has for the religions of the world, but at the same time, it rules out, in a radical way, that mentality of indifferentism "characterized by a religious relativism which leads to the belief that 'one religion is as good as another.'"[91] If it is true that the followers of other religions can receive divine grace, it is also certain that *objectively speaking* they are in a gravely deficient situation in comparison with those who, in the Church, have the fullness of the means of salvation.[92] However, "all the children of the Church should nevertheless remember that their exalted condition results, not from their own merits, but from the grace of Christ. If they fail to respond in thought, word, and deed to that grace, not only shall they not be saved, but they shall be more severely judged."[93] One understands then that, following the Lord's command (cf. Mt 28:19–20) and as a requirement of her love for all people, the Church "proclaims and is in duty bound to proclaim without fail, Christ who is the way, the truth, and the life (Jn 14:6). In him, in whom God reconciled all things to himself (cf. 2 Cor 5:18–19), men find the fullness of their religious life."[94]

In interreligious dialogue as well, the mission *ad gentes* "today as always retains its full force and necessity."[95] "Indeed, God 'desires all men to be saved and come to the knowledge of the truth' (1 Tim 2:4); that is, God wills the salvation of everyone through the knowledge of the truth. Salvation is found in the truth. Those who obey the promptings of the Spirit of truth are already on the way of salvation. But the Church, to whom this truth has been entrusted, must go out to meet their desire, so as to bring them the truth. Because she believes in God's universal plan of salvation, the Church must be missionary."[96] Interreligious dialogue, therefore, as part of her evangelizing mission, is just one of the actions of the Church in her mission *ad gentes*.[97] *Equality,* which is a presupposition of inter-religious dialogue, refers to the equal personal dignity of the parties in dialogue, not to doctrinal content, nor even less to the position of Jesus Christ—who is God himself made man—in relation to the founders of the other religions. Indeed, the Church, guided by charity and respect for freedom,[98] must be primarily committed to proclaiming to all people the truth definitively revealed by the Lord, and to announcing the necessity of conversion to Jesus Christ and of adherence to the Church through Baptism and the other sacraments, in order to participate fully in communion with God, the Father, Son and Holy Spirit. Thus, the certainty of the universal salvific will of God does not diminish, but rather increases the duty and urgency of the proclamation of salvation and of conversion to the Lord Jesus Christ.

CONCLUSION

23. The intention of the present *Declaration,* in reiterating and clarifying certain truths of the faith, has been to follow the example of the Apostle Paul, who wrote to the faithful of Corinth: "I handed on to you as of first importance what I myself received" (1 Cor 15:3). Faced with certain problematic and even erroneous propositions, theological reflection is called to reconfirm the Church's faith and to give reasons for her hope in a way that is convincing and effective.

In treating the question of the true religion, the Fathers of the Second Vatican Council taught: "We believe that this one true religion continues to exist in the Catholic and Apostolic Church, to which the Lord Jesus entrusted the task of spreading it among all people. Thus, he said to the Apostles: 'Go therefore and make disciples of all nations baptizing them in the name of the Father and of the Son and of the Holy Spirit, teaching them to observe all that I have commanded you' (Mt 28:19–20). Especially in those things that concern God and his Church, all persons are required to seek the truth, and when they come to know it, to embrace it and hold fast to it."[99]

The revelation of Christ will continue to be "the true lodestar"[100] in history for all humanity: "The truth, which is Christ, imposes itself as an all-embracing authority."[101] The Christian mystery, in fact, overcomes all barriers of time and space, and accomplishes the unity of the human family: "From their different locations and traditions all are called in Christ to share in the unity of the family of God's children . . . Jesus destroys the walls of division and creates unity in a new and unsurpassed way through our sharing in his mystery. This unity is so deep that the Church can say with Saint Paul: 'You are no longer strangers and sojourners, but you are saints and members of the household of God'(Eph 2:19)."[102]

The Sovereign Pontiff John Paul II, at the Audience of June 16, 2000, granted to the undersigned Cardinal Prefect of the Congregation for the Doctrine of the Faith, with sure knowledge and by his apostolic authority, ratified and confirmed this Declaration, adopted in Plenary Session and ordered its publication.

Rome, from the Offices of the Congregation for the Doctrine of the Faith, August 6, 2000, the Feast of the Transfiguration of the Lord.

JOSEPH Card. RATZINGER
Prefect

TARCISIO BERTONE, S.D.B.
Archbishop Emeritus of Vercelli
Secretary

End Notes

1   First Council of Constantinople, *Symbolum Constantinopolitanum: DS* 150.

2   Cf. John Paul II, Encyclical Letter *Redemptoris Missio*, 1: *AAS* 83 (1991), 249–340.

3   Cf. Second Vatican Council, Decree *Ad Gentes* and Declaration *Nostra Aetate*; cf. also Paul VI Apostolic Exhortation *Evangelii Nuntiandi: AAS* 68 (1976), 5–76; *Redemptoris Missio.*

4   Second Vatican Council, Declaration *Nostra Aetate*, 2.

5   Pontifical Council for Inter-religious Dialogue and the Congregation for the Evangelization of Peoples, Instruction *Dialogue and Proclamation*, 29; cf. Second Vatican Council, Pastoral Constitution *Gaudium et Spes*, 22.

6   Cf. *Redemptoris Missio*, 55.

7   Cf. *Dialogue and Proclamation*, 9.

8   John Paul II, Encyclical Letter *Fides et Ratio*, 5.

9   *Dei Verbum*, 2.

10   *Dei Verbum*, 4.

11   John Paul II, Encyclical Letter *Redemptoris Missio*, 5.

12   *Fides et Ratio*, 14.

13   Council of Chalcedon, *Symbolum Chalcedonense: DS* 301; cf. St. Athanasius, *De Incarnatione*, 54, 3: *Sources Chrétiennes* 199, 458.

14   *Dei Verbum*, 4.

15   *Dei Verbum*, 5.

16   *Dei Verbum*, 5.

17   Cf. *Catechism of the Catholic Church*, 144.

18   *Catechism of the Catholic Church*, 150.

19   *Catechism of the Catholic Church*, 153.

20   *Catechism of the Catholic Church*, 178.

21   *Fides et Ratio*, 13.

22   *Fides et Ratio*, 31–32.

23   *Nostra Aetate*, 2; cf. *Ad Gentes*, 9, where it speaks of the elements of good present "in the particular customs and cultures of peoples"; *Lumen Gentium*, 16, where it mentions the elements of good and of truth present among non-Christians, which can be considered a preparation for the reception of the Gospel.

24   Cf. Council of Trent, *Decretum de libris sacris et de traditionibus recipiendis*: *DS* 1501; First Vatican Council, Dogmatic Constitution *Dei Filius*, chapter. 2: *DS* 3006.

25   *Dei Verbum*, 11.

26   *Dei Verbum*, 11.

27   *Redemptoris Missio*, 55; cf. 56 and Pope Paul VI, *Evangelii Nuntiandi*, 53.

28   First Council of Nicaea, *Symbolum Nicaenum*: *DS* 125.

29   Council of Chalcedon, *Symbolum Chalcedonense*: *DS* 301.

30   *Gaudium et Spes*, 22.

31   *Redemptoris Missio*, 6.

32   Cf. St. Leo the Great, *Tomus ad Flavianum*: *DS* 294.

33   Cf. St. Leo the Great, Letter to the Emperor Leo I *Promisisse me memini*: *DS* 318: "... *in tantam unitatem ab ipso conceptu Virginis deitate et humanitate conserta, ut nec sine homine divina, nec sine Deo agerentur humana.*" Cf. also *ibid. DS* 317.

34   *Gaudium et Spes*, 45; cf. also Council of Trent, *Decretum de Peccato Originali*, 3: *DS* 1513.

35   *Lumen Gentium*, 3–5.

36   *Gaudium et Spes*, 7; cf. St. Irenaeus, who wrote that it is in the Church "that communion with Christ has been deposited, that is to say: the Holy Spirit" (*Adversus haereses* III, 24, 1: *Sources Chrétiennes* 211, 472).

37   *Gaudium et Spes*, 22.

38   *Redemptoris Missio*, 28. For the "seeds of the Word" cf. also St. Justin Martyr, *Second Apology* 8, 1–2; 10, 1–3; 13, 3–6: ed. E.J. Goodspeed, 84; 85; 88–89.

39   *Redemptoris Missio*, 28-29.

40   *Redemptoris Missio*, 29.

41   *Redemptoris Missio*, 5.

42   *Gaudium et Spes*, 10. Cf. St. Augustine, who wrote that Christ is the way, which "has never been lacking to mankind . . . and apart from this way no one has been set free, no one is being set free, no one will be set free" *De Civitate Dei* 10, 32, 2.

43   *Lumen Gentium*, 62

44   *Redemptoris Missio*, 5.

45   *Gaudium et Spes*, 45. The necessary and absolute singularity of Christ in human history is well expressed by St. Irenaeus in contemplating the

preeminence of Jesus as firstborn Son: "In the heavens, as firstborn of the Father's counsel, the perfect Word governs and legislates all things; on the earth, as firstborn of the Virgin, a man just and holy, reverencing God and pleasing to God, good and perfect in every way, he saves from hell all those who follow him since he is the firstborn from the dead and Author of the life of God" (*Demonstratio Apostolica*, 39: *Sources Chrétiennes*, 406, 138).

46   *Redemptoris Missio*, 6.

47   *Lumen Gentium*, 14

48   *Lumen Gentium*, 7.

49   Cf. St. Augustine, *Enarratio in Psalmos*, Ps. 90, *Sermo* 2,1: *Corpus Christianorum Series Latina* 39, 1266; St. Gregory the Great, *Moralia in Iob*, Praefatio, 6, 14: *Patrologia Latina* 75, 525; St. Thomas Aquinas, *Summa Theologiae*, III, q. 48, a. 2 ad 1.

50   *Lumen Gentium*, 6.

51   *Symbolum maius Ecclesiae Armeniacae: DS* 48. Cf. Boniface VIII, *Unam Sanctam: DS* 870–72; *Lumen Gentium*, 8.

52   Cf. Second Vatican Council, Decree *Unitatis Redintegratio*, 4; John Paul II, Encyclical Letter *Ut Unum Sint*, 11: *AAS* 87 (1995), 927.

53   *Lumen gentium*, 20; cf. also St. Irenaeus, *Adversus haereses*, III, 3, 1–3: *Sources Chrétiennes* 211, 20–44; St. Cyprian, *Epist*. 33, 1: *Corpus Christianorum Series Latina* 3B, 164–65; St. Augustine, *Contra adver. legis et prophet.*, 1, 20, 39: *Corpus Christianorum Series Latina* 49, 70.

54   *Lumen Gentium*, 8.

55   *Lumen Gentium*, 8; cf. *Ut Unum Sint*, 13. Cf. also *Lumen Gentium*, 15 and the Vatican II Decree *Unitatis Redintegratio*, 3.

56   The interpretation of those who would derive from the formula *subsistit in* the thesis that the one Church of Christ could subsist also in non-Catholic Churches and ecclesial communities is therefore contrary to the authentic meaning of *Lumen Gentium*. "The Council instead chose the word *subsistit* precisely to clarify that there exists only one 'subsistence' of the true Church, while outside her visible structure there only exist *elementa Ecclesiae*, which—being elements of that same Church—tend and lead toward the Catholic Church" (Congregation for the Doctrine of the Faith, *Notification on the Book "Church: Charism and Power" by Father Leonardo Boff: AAS* 77 [1985], 756–62).

57   *Unitatis Redintegratio*, 3.

58   Cf. Congregation for the Doctrine of the Faith, Declaration *Mysterium Ecclesiae*, 1: *AAS* 65 (1973), 396–98.

59   *Unitatis Redintegratio*, 14 and 15; Congregation for the Doctrine of the Faith, Letter *Communionis notio*, 17: *AAS* 85 (1993), 848.

60   Cf. First Vatican Council, Constitution *Pastor Aeternus*: *DS* 3053–64; *Lumen Gentium*, 22.

61   *Unitatis Redintegratio*, 22.

62   *Unitatis Redintegratio*, 3.

63   *Unitatis Redintegratio*, 22

64   Congregation for the Doctrine of the Faith, Declaration *Mysterium Ecclesiae*, 1.

65   *Ut Unum Sint*, 14.

66   *Unitatis Redintegratio*, 3.

67   Congregation for the Doctrine of the Faith, Letter *Communionis notio*, 17; cf. *Unitatis Redintegratio*, 4.

68   *Lumen Gentium*, 5.

69   *Lumen Gentium*, 1.

70   *Lumen Gentium*, Cf. St. Cyprian, *De Dominica Oratione* 23: *Corpus Christianorum Series Latina*, 3A, 105.

71   *Lumen Gentium*, 3.

72   [72]Cf. *Lumen Gentium*, 9; cf. also the prayer addressed to God found in the *Didache* 9,4: *Sources Chrétiennes* 248, 176: "May the Church be gathered from the ends of the earth into your kingdom" and *ibid.* 10, 5: *Sources Chrétiennes* 248, 180: "Remember, Lord, your Church . . . and, made holy, gather her together from the four winds into your kingdom which you have prepared for her".

73   *Redemptoris Missio*, 18; cf. Apostolic Exhortation *Ecclesia in Asia*, 17: *L'Osservatore Romano* (November 7, 1999). The kingdom is so inseparable from Christ that, in a certain sense, it is identified with him (cf. Origen, *In Mt. Hom.*, 14, 7: *Patrologia Graeca* 13, 1197; Tertullian, *Adversus Marcionem*, IV, 33,8: *Corpus Christianorum Series Latina* 1, 634.

74   *Redemptoris Missio*, 18.

75   *Redemptoris Missio*, 15.

76   *Redemptoris Missio*, 17.

77   *Lumen Gentium*, 14; cf. *Ad Gentes*, 7; *Unitatis Redintegratio*, 3.

78   *Redemptoris Missio*, 9; cf. *Catechism of the Catholic Church*, 846–47.

79   *Lumen Gentium,* 48.

80   Cf. St. Cyprian, *De Catholicae Ccclesiae Unitate,* 6: *Corpus Christianorum Series Latina* 3, 253–54; St. Irenaeus, *Adversus haereses,* III, 24, 1: *Sources Chrétiennes* 211, 472–74.

81   *Redemptoris Missio,* 10.

82   *Ad Gentes,* 2. The famous formula *extra Ecclesiam nullus omnino salvatur* is to be interpreted in this sense (cf. Fourth Lateran Council, Cap. 1. *De fide catholica: DS* 802). Cf. also the *Letter of the Holy Office to the Archbishop of Boston: DS* 3866–72.

83   *Ad Gentes,* 7.

84   *Redemptoris Missio,* 18.

85   These are the seeds of the divine Word (*semina Verbi*), which the Church recognizes with joy and respect (cf. *Ad Gentes,* 11; *Nostra Aetate,* 2).

86   *Redemptoris Missio,* 29.

87   Cf. *Redemptoris Missio,* 29; *Catechism of the Catholic Church,* 843.

88   Cf. Council of Trent, *Decretum de s\Sacramentis,* can. 8, *De Sacramentis in Genere: DS* 1608.

89   *Redemptoris Missio,* 55.

90   *Lumen Gentium,* 17; Encyclical Letter *Redemptoris Missio,* 11.

91   *Redemptoris Missio,* 36.

92   Cf. Pius XII, Encyclical Letter *Mystici corporis: DS* 3821.

93   *Lumen Gentium,* 14.

94   *Nostra Aetate,* 2.

95   *Ad Gentes,* 7.

96   *Catechism of the Catholic Church,* 851; cf. also 849–56.

97   *Redemptoris Missio,* 55; Apostolic Exhortation *Ecclesia in Asia,* 31.

98   Cf. Second Vatican Council, *Declaration, Dignitatis Humanae,* 1.

99   *Dignitatis Humanae,* 1.

100   *Fides et Ratio,* 15

101   *Fides et Ratio,* 92.

102   *Fides et Ratio,* 70.

Appendix 2

NOTIFICATION
on the book
Toward a Christian Theology of Religious Pluralism
(Orbis Books: Maryknoll, New York 1997)
by Father
JACQUES DUPUIS, S.J.

Preface

After a preliminary study of the book *Toward a Christian Theology of Religious Pluralism* by Father Jacques Dupuis, S.J., the Congregation for the Doctrine of the Faith decided to proceed to a comprehensive examination of the text by means of its ordinary procedure, in accordance with Chapter 3 of the *Regulations for Doctrinal Examination.*

It must be emphasized that this text is an introductory reflection on a Christian theology of religious pluralism. It is not simply a theology of religions, but a theology of religious pluralism, which seeks to investigate, in the light of Christian faith, the significance of the plurality of religious traditions in God's plan for humanity. Aware of the potential problems in this approach, the author does not conceal the possibility that his hypothesis may raise as many questions as it seeks to answer.

Following the doctrinal examination of the book and the outcome of the dialogue with the author, the Bishop and Cardinal Members of the Congregation, in the Ordinary Session of June 30, 1999, evaluated the analysis and the opinions of the Congregation's Consultors regarding the author's *Responses.* The Members of the Congregation recognized the author's attempt to remain within the limits of orthodoxy in his study of questions hitherto largely unexplored. At the same time, while noting the author's willingness to provide the necessary clarifications, as evident in his *Responses,* as well as his desire to remain faithful to the doctrine of the Church and the teaching of the Magisterium, they found that his book contained notable ambiguities and difficulties on important doctrinal points, which could lead a reader to erroneous or harmful opinions. These points concerned the interpretation of the sole and universal salvific mediation of Christ, the unicity and completeness of Christ's revelation, the universal salvific action of the Holy Spirit, the orientation of all people to the Church, and the value and significance of the salvific function of other religions.

At the conclusion of the ordinary procedure of examination, the Congregation for the Doctrine of the Faith decided to draft a *Notification,*[1] intended to safeguard the doctrine of the Catholic faith from errors, ambiguities or harmful interpretations. This *Notification,* approved by the Holy Father in the Audience of November 24, 2000, was presented to Father Jacques Dupuis and was accepted by him. By signing the text, the author committed himself to assent to the stated theses and, in his future theological activity and publications, to hold the doctrinal contents indicated in the *Notification,* the text of which must be included in any reprinting or further editions of his book, as well as in all translations.

The present *Notification* is not meant as a judgment on the author's subjective thought, but rather as a statement of the Church's teaching on certain aspects of the above-mentioned doctrinal truths, and as a refutation of erroneous or harmful opinions, which, prescinding from the author's intentions, could be derived from reading the ambiguous statements and insufficient explanations found in certain sections of the text. In this way, Catholic readers will be given solid criteria for judgment, consistent with the doctrine of the Church, in order to avoid the serious confusion and misunderstanding which could result from reading this book.

I.

· On the Sole and Universal Salvific Mediation of Jesus Christ

1. It must be firmly believed that Jesus Christ, the Son of God made man, crucified and risen, is the sole and universal mediator of salvation for all humanity.[2]

2. It must also be firmly believed that Jesus of Nazareth, Son of Mary and only Saviour of the world, is the Son and Word of the Father.[3] For the unity of the divine plan of salvation centred in Jesus Christ, it must also be held that the salvific action of the Word is accomplished in and through Jesus Christ, the Incarnate Son of the Father, as mediator of salvation for all humanity.[4] It is therefore contrary to the Catholic faith not only to posit a separation between the Word and Jesus, or between the Word's salvific activity and that of Jesus, but also to maintain that there is a salvific activity of the Word as such in his divinity, independent of the humanity of the Incarnate Word.[5]

II.

On the Unicity and Completeness of Revelation of Jesus Christ

3. It must be firmly believed that Jesus Christ is the mediator, the fulfilment and the completeness of revelation.[6] It is therefore contrary to the Catholic faith to maintain that revelation in Jesus Christ (or the revelation of Jesus Christ) is limited, incomplete or imperfect. Moreover, although full knowledge of divine revelation will be had only on the day of the Lord's coming in glory, the historical revelation of Jesus Christ offers everything necessary for man's salvation and has no need of completion by other religions.[7]

4. It is consistent with Catholic doctrine to hold that the seeds of truth and goodness that exist in other religions are a certain participation in truths contained in the revelation of or in Jesus Christ.[8] However, it is erroneous to hold that such elements of truth and goodness, or some of them, do not derive ultimately from the source-mediation of Jesus Christ.[9]

III.

On the Universal Salvific Action of the Holy Spirit

5. The Church's faith teaches that the Holy Spirit, working after the resurrection of Jesus Christ, is always the Spirit of Christ sent by the Father, who works in a salvific way in Christians as well as non-Christians.[10] It is therefore contrary to the Catholic faith to hold that the salvific action of the Holy Spirit extends beyond the one universal salvific economy of the Incarnate Word.[11]

IV.

On the Orientation of All human Beings to the Church

6. It must be firmly believed that the Church is sign and instrument of salvation for all people.[12] It is contrary to the Catholic faith to consider the different religions of the world as ways of salvation complementary to the Church.[13]

7. According to Catholic doctrine, the followers of other religions are oriented to the Church and are all called to become part of her.[14]

V.

On the Value and Salvific Function of the Religious Traditions

8. In accordance with Catholic doctrine, it must be held that "whatever the Spirit brings about in human hearts and in the history of peoples, in cultures and religions, serves as a preparation for the Gospel (cf. Dogmatic Constitution *Lumen Gentium,* 16).[15] It is therefore legitimate to maintain that the Holy Spirit accomplishes salvation in non-Christians also through those elements of truth and goodness present in the various religions; however, to hold that these religions, considered as such, are ways of salvation, has no foundation in Catholic theology, also because they contain omissions, insufficiencies and errors[16] regarding fundamental truths about God, man and the world.

Furthermore, the fact that the elements of truth and goodness present in the various world religions may prepare peoples and cultures to receive the salvific event of Jesus Christ does not imply that the sacred texts of these religions can be considered as complementary to the Old Testament, which is the immediate preparation for the Christ event.[17]

The Sovereign Pontiff John Paul II, at the Audience of January 19, 2001, in the light of the further developments, confirmed the present Notification, which had been adopted in Ordinary Session of the Congregation, and ordered its publication.[18]

Rome, from the Offices of the Congregation for the Doctrine of the Faith, January 24, 2001, the Memorial of Saint Francis de Sales.

+ JOSEPH Card. RATZINGER
Prefect

+ Tarcisio BERTONE, S.D.B.
Archbishop Emeritus of Vercelli
Secretary

End Notes

1   Because of tendencies in some circles, which have become increasingly evident in the thinking of the Christian faithful, the Congregation for the Doctrine of the Faith published the Declaration *"Dominus Iesus"* on *the Unicity and Salvific Universality of Jesus Christ and the Church* (*AAS* 92 [2000], 742-765) in order to protect essential truths of the Catholic faith. The *Notification* draws from the principles expressed in *Dominus Iesus* in its evaluation of Father Dupuis's book.

2   Cf. Council of Trent, Decree *De Peccato originali*: DS 1513; Decree *De Iustificatione*: DS 1522, 1523, 1529, 1530; Second Vatican Council, Pastoral Constitution *Gaudium et Spes*, 10; Dogmatic Constitution *Lumen Gentium*, 8, 14, 28,49,60; John Paul II, Encyclical Letter *Redemptoris missio*, 5: *AAS* 83 (1991), 249–340; Apostolic Exhortation *Ecclesia in Asia*, 14: *AAS* 92 (2000), 449–528; Congregation for the Doctrine of the Faith, Declaration *Dominus Iesus*, 13–15.

3   Cf. First Council of Nicea: DS 125; Council of Chalcedon: DS 301

4   Cf. Council of Trent, Decree *De Iustificatione*: DS 1529, 1530; Second Vatican Council, Constitution on the Liturgy *Sacrosanctum Concilium*, 5; Pastoral Constitution *Gaudium et Spes*, 22

5   Cf. John Paul II, Encyclical Letter *Redemptoris Missio*, 6; Congregation for the Doctrine of the Faith, Declaration *Dominus Iesus*, 10.

6   Cf. Second Vatican Council, Dogmatic Constitution *Dei Verbum*, 2, 4; John Paul II, Encyclical Letter *Fides et ratio*, 14–15, 92: *AAS* 91 (1999), 5–88; *Dominus Iesus*, 5.

7   *Dominus Iesus*, 6; *Catechism of the Catholic Church*, 65–66.

8   Second Vatican Council, Dogmatic Constitution *Lumen Gentium*, 17; Decree *Ad Gentes*, 11; Declaration *Nostra Aetate*, 2.

9   *Lumen Gentium*, 16; *Redemptoris Missio*, 10.

10   *Gaudium et Spes*, 22; Letter *Redemptoris Missio*, 28–29.

11   *Redemptoris missio*, 5; Apostolic Exhortation *Ecclesia in Asia*, 15–16; *Dominus Iesus*, 12.

12   *Lumen Gentium*, 9, 14, 17, 48; *Redemptoris Missio*, 11; *Dominus Iesus*, 16.

13   *Redemptoris missio*, 36; *Dominus Iesus*, 21–22.

14   Cf. *Lumen Gentium*, 16; *Nostra Aetate*, 2; *Ad Gentes*, 9; Paul VI, Apostolic Exhortation *Evangelii Nuntiandi*, 53; *Redemptoris Missio*, 55; *Dominus Iesus*, 8.

15   *Redemptoris Missio*, 29.

16   *Lumen Gentium,* 16; *Nostra Aetate,* 2; *Ad Gentes,* 9; *Evangelii Nuntiandi,* 53; *Redemptoris Missio,* 55; *Dominus Iesus,* 8.

17   Cf. Council of Trent, Decree *De Libris Sacris et de Traditionibus Recipiendis:* DS 1501; First Vatican Council, Dogmatic Constitution *Dei Filius,* 2: DS 3006; Declaration *Dominus Iesus,* 8.

18   Editor's Note: The Notification was actually published on 26 February 2001.

Bibliography

Batlogg, Andreas R. "Interreligiöser Dialog als Dauerauftrag. Das Erbe von Jacques Dupuis." *Stimmen der Zeit* (December 2010) 849–52.

Bediako, Kwame. *Theology and Identity: The Impact of Culture Upon Christian Thought in the Second Century and in Modern Africa*. Oxford: Regnum, 1992.

Becker, Karl Josef. "The Church and Vatican II's 'Subsistit in' Terminology." *Origins* 35 (2006) 514–22.

Becker, Karl J., and Ilaria Morali, editors. *Catholic Engagement with World Religions: A Comprehensive Study*. Maryknoll, NY: Orbis, 2010.

Bell, Rob. *Love Wins: A Book About Heaven, Hell, and the Fate of Every Person Who Has Ever Lived*. New York: HarperCollins, 2011.

Berry, Thomas, and Brian Swimme. *The Dream of the Earth*. San Francisco: Sierra Club, 1988.

Bevans, Stephen B., and Roger P. Schroeder. *Prophetic Dialogue: Reflections on Christian Mission Today*. Maryknoll, NY: Orbis, 2011.

Burrows, William R. "Catholics, Carey's 'Means,' and Twenty-First Century Mission." *International Bulletin of Missionary Research* 34 (2010) 131–38.

———. "Creating Space to Rethink the Mission of Christians." In *In Many and Diverse Ways: In Honor of Jacques Dupuis*, edited by Daniel Kendall and Gerald O'Collins, 211–21. Maryknoll, NY: Orbis, 2003.

———. "The Importance of Liturgy in Ecclesial Mission Animation." *Missiology* 38 (January 2010) 37–49.

———, editor. *Redemption and Dialogue: Reading Redemptoris Missio and Dialogue and Proclamation*. Maryknoll, NY: Orbis, 1993.

Capéran, Louis. *Le Problème Du Salut Des Infidèles*. 2 vols. Vol. 1, *Essai Historique*; vol. 2, *Essai Théologique*. Toulouse: Grand Séminaire, 1934.

Carpenter, David. *Revelation, History, and the Dialogue of Religions: A Study of Bhartrhari and Bonaventure*. Maryknoll, NY: Orbis, 1995.

Cheruvally, Santosh Sebastian. *Jesus Christ: Quest and Context in Abhishiktananda (Henri LeSaux OSB)*. New Delhi: ISPCK, 2009.

Clooney, Francis Xavier. *Comparative Theology: Deep Learning across Religious Borders* Malden, MA: Wiley-Blackwell, 2010.

———. "Review of *Jesus Christ at the Encounter of World Religions*." *Theological Studies* 1 (1992) 178–79.

———. *Theology after Vedanta: An Experiment in Comparative Theology*. Albany: State University of New York Press, 1993.

Congregation for the Doctrine of the Faith. *Dominus Iesus* ("The Lord Jesus"), "Declaration on the Unicity and Salvific Universality of Jesus Christ and the Church" (6 August 2000). www.vatican.va/roman_curia/congregations/cfaith/documents/rc_con_cfaith_doc_20000806_dominus-iesus_en.html.

———. "Instruction *Donum Veritatis* on the Ecclesial Vocation of the Theologian" (24 May 1990). http://www.vatican.va/roman_curia/congregations/cfaith/documents/rc_con_cfaith_doc_19900524_theologian-vocation_en.html.

———. "Notification on the Book *Toward a Christian Theology of Religious Pluralism* by Father Jacques Dupuis, S.J." Rome, 2001 (24 January). www.vatican.va/roman_curia/congregations/cfaith/documents/rc_con_cfaith_doc_20010124_dupuis_en.html.

Cornille, Catherine, *The Im-Possibility of Interreligious Dialogue*. New York: Crossroad, 2008.

———, editor. *Many Mansions? Multiple Religious Belonging and Christian Identity*. Maryknoll, NY: Orbis, 2002.

———. *Song Divine: Christian Commentaries on the Bhagavad Gita*. Christian Commentaries on Non-Christian Sacred Texts. Leuven Peeters, 2006.

Damboriena, Prudencio. *La Salvación En Las Religiones No Cristianas*. Madrid: Biblioteca de Autores Cristianos, 1973.

Daughton, J. P. *An Empire Divided: Religion, Republicanism, and the Making of French Colonialism*. New York: Oxford, 2006.

Delicata, Nadia. "The Trinitarian Theology of Jacques Dupuis." *Didaskalia* 19.1 (2008) 23–49.

De Rosa, Giuseppe. "Review of *Gesu Cristo Incontro Alle Religioni*." *Civiltà Cattolica* (1992) 364–75.

Denzinger, Henricus, and Adolfus Schönmetzer, editors. *Enchiridion Symbolorum Definitionum Et Declarationum De Rebus Fidei Et Morum*. 36th ed. Freiburg: Herder, 1976.

Dhavamony, Mariasusai. *Jesus Christ in the Understanding of World Religions*. Rome: Gregorian University Press, 2004.

DiNoia, J. A. *The Diversity of Religions: A Christian Perspective*. Washington, DC: Catholic University of America Press, 1992.

Dunn, James D. G. *Jesus and the Spirit: A Study of the Religious and Charismatic Experience of Jesus and the First Christians as Reflected in the New Testament*. London: SCM, 1975.

Dupuis, Jacques. "Christianity and Religions: Convergence and Complementarity." In *Many Mansions: Multiple Religious Belonging and Christian Identity*, edited by Catherine Cornille, 61–75. Maryknoll, NY: Orbis, 2002.

———. *Christianity and the Religions: From Confrontation to Dialogue*. Translated by Phillip Berryman. Maryknoll, NY: Orbis, 2002.

———. *Jesus Christ at the Encounter of World Religions*. Translated by Robert R. Barr. Maryknoll, NY: Orbis, 1991.

———. "My Pilgrimage in Mission." *International Bulletin of Missionary Research* 27.4 (2003) 168–71.

———. "La teologia del pluralism religioso revisitata." *Rassegna di Teologia* 40 (1999) 669–93.

———. "Review of Hans Küng, *Incarnation of God*." *Gregorianum* 69.4 (1988): 728–31.

———. *Toward a Christian Theology of Religious Pluralism*. Maryknoll, NY: Orbis, 1997.

———. "The Truth Will Make You Free: The Theology of Religious Pluralism Revisited." *Louvain Studies* 24.3 (1999) 211–63.

———. *Who Do You Say I Am? Introduction to Christology*. Maryknoll, NY: Orbis, 1994.

Dupuis, Jacques, and Josef Neuner, editors. *The Christian Faith in the Doctrinal Documents of the Catholic Church*. 7th ed. Staten Island, NY: Alba House, 2001

Flannery, Austin, editor. *Vatican Council II: The Conciliar and Postconciliar Documents.* 2 vols. Northport, NY: Costello, 1975–1998.

Fletcher, Richard. *The Barbarian Conversion: From Paganism to Christianity.* New York: Henry Holt, 1997.

Geffré, Claude. "From the Theology of Religious Pluralism to an Interreligious Theology." In *In Many and Diverse Ways: In Honor of Jacques Dupuis,* edited by Daniel Kendall and Gerald O'Collins, 45–59. Maryknoll, NY: Orbis, 2003.

———. *La prétension du christianisme à l'universel: implications missiologiques,* In *Cristologia e Missione Oggi.* Edited by Gianni Colzani, Paolo Giglione and Sebastian Karotemprel, 47–65. Rome: Urbaniana University Press, 2001. Available also at www .sedos.org/french/geffre.htm.

Gilkey, Langdon. "Plurality and Its Theological Implications." In *The Myth of Christian Uniqueness: Toward a Pluralistic Theology of Religions,* edited by Paul F. Knitter, and John Hick, 37–50. Maryknoll, NY: Orbis, 1987.

Gioia, Francesco, editor. *Interreligious Dialogue: The Official Teaching of the Catholic Church (1963–1995).* Boston: Pauline Books and Media, 1997.

Hauerwas, Stanley. *With the Grain of the Universe: The Church's Witness and Natural Theology.* Grand Rapids: Brazos, 2001.

Haught, John F. *Christianity and Science: Toward a Theology of Nature.* Maryknoll, NY: Orbis, 2007.

———. *Making Sense of Evolution: Darwin, God, and the Drama of Life.* Louisville, KY: Westminster John Knox, 2010.

Heim, S. Mark. *Salvations: Truth and Difference in Religion.* Maryknoll, NY: Orbis, 1995.

Jacobsen, Douglas. *The World's Christians: Who They Are, Where They Are, and How They Got There.* Malden, MA: Wiley-Blackwell, 2011.

Johnson, Elizabeth A. *Quest for the Living God: Mapping the Frontiers of the Theology of God.* New York: Continuum, 2007.

Kaariainen, Jukka. "Missio Shaped by Promissio: Lutheran Missiology Confronts the Challenge of Religious Pluralism." PhD diss., Fordham University, 2010.

Kelly, Anthony. *The Resurrection Effect: Transforming Christian Life and Thought.* Maryknoll, NY: Orbis, 2008.

Kasper, Walter. "The Unicity and Universality of Jesus Christ." In *Cristologia e Missione Oggi,* edited by Gianni Colzani, Paolo Giglione and Sebastian Karotemprel, 35–45. Rome: Urbaniana University Press, 2001.

Kendall, Daniel, and Gerald O'Collins, eds. *In Many and Diverse Ways: In Honor of Jacques Dupuis.* Maryknoll, NY: Orbis, 2003.

Knitter, Paul F. *No Other Name? A Critical Survey of Christian Attitudes toward the World Religions.* Maryknoll, NY: Orbis, 1985.

———. *Jesus and the Other Names: Christian Mission and Global Responsibility.* Maryknoll, NY: Orbis, 1996.

Krieger, David J. *The New Universalism: Foundations for a Global Theology.* Maryknoll, NY: Orbis, 1991. (Now available from Wipf & Stock)

Küng, Hans. *The Incarnation of God: An Introduction to Hegel's Theological Thought as Prologomena to a Future Christology.* Translated by J. R. Stephenson. New York: Crossroad, 1987.

Lonergan, Bernard J. F. *Collection: Papers by Bernard Lonergan.* New York: Herder & Herder, 1967.

———. *Insight: A Study of Human Understanding.* New York: Philosophical Library, 1957.

————. *Method in Theology.* New York: Herder & Herder, 1972.

Moran, Gabriel. *Uniqueness: Problem or Paradox in Jewish and Christian Traditions.* Maryknoll, NY: Orbis, 1992.

Navone, John. *Enjoying God's Beauty.* Collegeville, MN: Liturgical, 1999.

————. *The Jesus Story: Our Life as Story in Christ.* Collegeville, MN: Liturgical, 1979.

————. *Towards a Theology of Story.* Slough, UK: St Paul's, 1977.

Odasso, Giovanni. *Bibbia e Religioni: Prospettive Bibliche per la Teologia Delle Religioni.* Rome: Urbaniana University Press, 1998.

O'Collins, Gerald. "Christ and the Religions," *Gregorianum* 84 (2003) 347–62.

————. "Jacques Dupuis: His Person and Work." In *In Many and Diverse Ways: In Honor of Jacques Dupuis,* edited by Daniel Kendall and Gerald O'Collins, 18–29. Maryknoll, NY: Orbis, 2003.

————. "Jacques Dupuis's Contributions to Interreligious Dialogue." *Theological Studies* 64.2 (2003) 388–97.

————. *Living Vatican II: The 21st Council for the 21st Century.* Mahwah, NJ: Paulist, 2006. Includes a significant text by Dupuis written after the 1974 bishops synod (173–201).

————. *Salvation for All God's Peoples.* Oxford: Oxford University Press, 2008.

Panikkar, Raimon. *Christophany: The Fullness of Man.* Maryknoll, NY: Orbis, 2004.

————. *The Cosmotheandric Experience: Emerging Religious Consciousness.* Maryknoll, NY: Orbis, 1993.

————. *The Intra-Religious Dialogue.* 2nd ed. Mahwah, NJ: Paulist, 1999.

————. *The Rhythm of Being,* Gifford Lectures 1989/1990. Maryknoll, NY: Orbis, 2010.

————. *The Silence of God: And the Answer of the Buddha.* Maryknoll, NY: Orbis, 1989.

Pataskar, Bhagyalata, Shubhash Anand, and Christopher Shelke. "Hinduism and Christianity." In *Catholic Engagement with World Religions: A Comprehensive Study,* edited by Karl J. Becker and Ilaria Morali, 459–86. Maryknoll, NY: Orbis, 2010.

Pew Charitable Trusts. "Many Americans Mix Multiple Faiths." 9 December 2009.

————. "U.S. Religious Landscape Survey," 2008.

Phan, Peter C. *Being Religious Interreligiously: Asian Perspectives on Interreligious Dialogue.* Maryknoll, NY: Orbis, 2004.

Pontifical Council for Interreligious Dialogue (known as the Secretariat for Non-Christians when this document was issued in 1984). *The Attitude of the Church Towards the Followers of Other Religions: Reflections and Orientations on Dialogue and Mission AAS* 75 (1984) 816–28; also *Bulletin Secretariatus pro non Christianis* 56:13 (1984/2); and in Gioia, 567–78.

————. "Dialogue and Proclamation" (1991). In Burrows, ed., *Redemption and Dialogue,* 1993; and Gioia, ed., *Interreligious Dialogue,* 1997.

Rahner, Karl. "Basic Theological Interpretation of the Second Vatican Council." In *Theological Investigations* 20, 1986. New York: Crossroads, 1986.

Ratzinger, Joseph. *Jesus of Nazareth: From the Baptism in the Jordan to the Transfiguration.* New York: Doubleday, 2007.

————. *Jesus of Nazareth, Part Two: Holy Week, from the Entrance into Jerusalem to the Resurrection.* San Francisco: Ignatius, 2011.

Russell, James C. *The Germanization of Early Medieval Christianity: A Sociohistorical Approach to Religious Transformation.* New York: Oxford University Press, 1994.

Sanneh, Lamin. *Disciples of All Nations: Pillars of World Christianity,* Oxford Studies in World Christianity. Oxford; New York: Oxford University Press, 2008.

———. *Translating the Message: The Missionary Impact on Culture.* Maryknoll, NY: Orbis, 1989.

———. *Whose Religion Is Christianity? The Gospel Beyond West.* Grand Rapids: Eerdmans, 2003.

Secretariat for Non-Christians. "The Attitude of the Church toward Followers of Other Religions: Reflections and Orientations on Dialogue and Mission." In *Interreligious Dialogue: The Official Teaching of the Catholic Church (1963–1995),* edited by Francesco Gioia, 566–78. Boston: Pauline Books and Media, 1997.

Sidey, Ken. "Church Growth Fine Tunes Its Formulas." *Christianity Today,* June 24, 1991.

Sullivan, Francis A. "*Quaestio Disputata:* A Response to Karl Becker, SJ, on the Meaning of Subsistit In." *Theological Studies* 67 (2006) 395–409.

———. "Ways of Salvation? On the Investigation of Jacques Dupuis." *America* (April 9, 2001) 28–31.

Sydnor, Jon Paul. "Beyond the Text: Revisiting Jacques Dupuis' Theology of Religions." *International Review of Mission* 96.380/381 (2007) 56–71.

Tanner, Norman, editor. *Decrees of the Ecumenical Councils.* 2 vols. Washington, DC: Georgetown University Press, 1990.

Tilley, Terrence W. "'Christianity and the World Religions,' a Recent Vatican Document." *Theological Studies* 60.2 (1999) 318–37.

———. "Christian Orthodoxy and Religious Pluralism." *Modern Theology* 22.1 (2006) 51–63.

Tracy, David. *Blessed Rage for Order: The New Pluralism in Theology.* New York: Seabury, 1975.

———. *Plurality and Ambiguity: Hermeneutics, Religion, Hope.* San Francisco: Harper & Row, 1987.

United States Conference of Catholic Bishops, Committee on Doctrine. "Clarifications Required by the Book *Being Religious Interreligiously* by Peter C. Phan." Washington, DC, 7 December 2007

———. "Statement on *Quest for the Living God* by Elizabeth A. Johnson." Washington, DC, 24 March 2011.

Walls, Andrew F. *The Cross-Cultural Process in Christian History.* Maryknoll, NY: Orbis, 2002.

———. *The Missionary Movement in Christian History: Studies in the Transmission of Faith.* Maryknoll, NY: Orbis, 1996.

Wright, N. T. *The Challenge of Jesus: Rediscovering Who Jesus Was and Is.* Downers Grove, IL: InterVarsity Academic, 1999.

———. *Paul in Fresh Perspective.* Minneapolis: Fortress, 2005.

Name Index

Abhishiktananda, xviii. *See also*
LeSaux, Henri, OSB
Alberigo, Giuseppe, 105
Alfaro, Juan, SJ, xviii, xviin6, 107–8
Alfonso, Herbie, SJ, 4
Alszeghy, Zoltan, 107
Amalodoss, Michael, xx
Amato, Angelo, Cardinal, xxi–xxii,
24, 28
Anderson, Allan, 106
Anselm, 32
Arrupe, Pedro, xiv, 7
Athanasius, 83, 114
Augustine, 160n42

Basil of Caesarea, 91
Becker, Karl Josef, SJ, 125
Bell, Rob, 128–29
Bernard of Clairvaux, 14
Berry, Thomas, 118
Berryman, Phillip, 3
Bertone, Tarcisio, Cardinal, xxi–xxii,
24, 28, 158, 168
Bevans, Stephen, SVD, 3, 4, 22, 106,
132
Bhartrhari (Vedic commentator),
111n5
Bonaventure, 111n5
Bonhoeffer, Dietrich, xix
Bosch, David, 105
Bosco, John, xxi
Bultmann, Rudolf, 113
Burrows, Linda, 3, 4, 22, 111
Burrows, William
as missionary, 109
Protestant influences on, 105–6

Society of the Divine Word and,
109
theological autobiography of,
104–9
theological education of, 18,
107–8

Carpenter, David, 111n5
Carr, Anne, 110
Clooney, Frank, 116–17
Cobb, John B., 108–9
Congar, Yves, 6, 106
Cornille, Catherine, 117
Cyprian (saint), 60

Danielou, Jean, 6
Daughton, J. P., 133
de Lubac, Henri, 107
de Mattei, Roberto, 105
De Rosa, Giuseppe, SJ, 10, 12, 13
Denzinger, Heinrich, 41–42n12
Dhavamony, Mariasusai, 13, 13n20
DiNoia, J. Augustine, OP, xxii,
xxiin8
Doniger, Wendy, 19
Dunn, James D. G., 113–14
Dupuis, Jacques
1984 return to Rome by, 7, 8–9
2004 Maryknoll speech by,
133–34
apostolate of, 135
carefulness of as author, 126
CDF interrogatories and, xx
Christology course of, 2–3
as clearing space for serious
dialogue, 117

Subject Index